It's Time to #LevelTheWealth!
Amanda Campbell

D1194456

Michelle Riley

"Strengthen, Empower, Inspire...
Train to be Fierce & Fit"

XOXO

Amanda Campbell and Michelle Riley

THE
HEALTH & WEALTH SISTERS'
360°
Action Plan

Total Self-Care
for the Modern Woman's Fiscal, Physical,
and Emotional Well-Being

H&W
BOOKS

H&W
BOOKS

ISBN-13: 978-1-7363071-2-0
Library of Congress Control Number: 2021901119

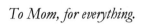

To Mom, for everything.

CONTENTS

INTRODUCTION

I t all started with a phone call.

As busy adult sisters and best friends, we got into the habit of talking to each other on the phone each night as Amanda drove home from work—even more so after her Jeep's radio broke and she just didn't care enough to get it fixed. During those calls, we'd talk about our days, swapping tales of success and frustration.

Born two years apart, we shared a childhood that ultimately led to two completely different career paths. Amanda, the eldest, became a Certified Financial Planner™. Her life's mission, through extreme passion, is to empower the modern woman and guide her to her own financial independence. We live in a world in which almost 60 percent of women today are solely responsible for making wealth decisions, whether that be by personal choice, widowhood, or divorce. It can't be ignored that approximately 40 percent of American women now out-earn their husbands, and that in the next decade the vast majority of new income growth will come from women.

If this is true, then why do so many women feel misunderstood by financial advisors? Why is it that only 20 percent of female breadwinners say they feel "very well prepared" to make wise financial decisions?

As a Certified Financial Planner™, Amanda has sat through her fair share of continuing education seminars in a sea of middle-aged white men wearing blue and black suits sharing inside jokes about their time at the country club. She's endured conversation after conversation with male financial advisors who say things like: "Mitch is the only one that comes to our meetings anyway. His wife, Peggy, is always out getting her nails done or at a book club during our meetings." Or the one that really drives her insane: "Matt understands what I'm talking about during our meetings. Janet always looks bored and uninterested. It takes up

1

too much of my mental space when she's there because then I don't feel like I'm having a good meeting." Wait, what? *Seriously? Have you invited her to your meetings? Are you making eye contact with her while you speak about her family's wealth? Are you actively engaging her to make her feel like a valuable part of the conversation?* So many times, Amanda already knew the disappointing answers to those questions.

Too often we hear how women are overwhelmed by, and tired of, the jargon-y type financial self-help books that are already out there that say things like: "Stocks, bonds, mutual funds, diversification, allocation, alpha, standard deviation, blah, blah, blah." We need to reach our fellow sisters differently. We know you need to be able to read words that don't seem like they're written in Latin or for a man on the trading floor of the New York Stock Exchange. Whether you are single or married, you are the lead of your wealth management team. You call the shots. And, statistically speaking, if you're married, you will be the one left holding the bag as women tend to outlive their husbands.

As a certified physical trainer and nutrition coach, Michelle's lifelong goal is to fix the equally broken system of women's health, and to empower women to achieve their optimal health through their own physical and mental awareness. As a society, we have taken the word "fit" and misconstrued it to belong only to women with washboard abs and zero stretch marks, who flaunt around in a bikini while posing on beachfront vacations. It is Michelle's heartfelt mission to change those health standards and transform them into something even deeper that stems from the soul.

We can't sugarcoat this. The need is urgent. According to the CDC (Center for Disease Control), cardiovascular disease is still the number one cause of death in the U.S.A. One-third of all female deaths are due to cardiovascular disease and stroke, of which 80 percent are preventable.[1] We repeat, *80 percent of these cardiovascular diseases can be prevented!* This is not a drill. Picture you and two of your closest girlfriends sitting in a room, perhaps drinking your usual wine on a Friday night. From the statistics, one of you is going to die from heart disease. As blunt as that may sound, how does this make you feel? More personally, what if *you* were the one woman in the room of three? We can no longer feel the burden of this by and large preventable disease in our rising female population.

As driven sisters, we've often wished to find a way to work together, as we serve the same type of client: busy, badass women who are ready to make a change in their lives. The women who reach out to Michelle, ready to make the changes needed to live a healthier and more fulfilling lifestyle, are the same women who would sit in training sessions with her and complain about spending too much on fast food, or wonder if paying for her services was the right thing to do. Or better yet, had to check in with their husbands to make sure there was enough money in the budget to fit a training session into their household plan.

Amanda was constantly saying, "Just give them my name. I'll see what's going on with her finances and then she won't have to worry about that stuff. She'll understand what the heck is going on with her life."

And we found the opposite to be just as true. Those who reach out to Amanda after becoming suddenly single through divorce or widowhood, who are at a point in their lives when they finally had no choice but to understand their Wealth Empowerment Plans, would confess that because of their current situations, they've taken to watching way too much TV, eating all the wrong things, and lacking self-confidence.

We would be on the phone each night, wondering how we could make women understand that they needed to be empowered both from a health perspective *and* a wealth perspective if they were truly on the path to becoming their best selves. We intuitively knew that women needed to understand that neither health nor wealth, on their own, make a whole woman. Instead, it is the complete and absolute entanglement of these two things that make a confident, beautiful, strong, and empowered woman feel whole and complete.

A total 360° action plan was needed.

And then it *clicked*.

Peace of mind around your money *and* your wealth is self-care at its finest. If you're constantly stressed about money or your wealth, do you really think your body is performing at its optimal health? Stress, fear of the unknown, anxiety, *whatever you want to call it*, around wealth is just one more stressor on your plate that will keep you from living the life of freedom and empowerment that you so desperately deserve. It clouds your mind and takes focus away from the things in life that deserve your utmost attention. Wealth shouldn't be a source of stress in your life. Instead, it is a *tool* to help you live your best life.

Health and wealth encompasses, well, everything about our lives.

Are you tired of wondering if you're healthy enough or wealthy enough? Maybe you've found yourself canceling yet another unused gym membership because you just don't seem to be able to find the time to put yourself first. Or you're tired of looking at your bank statements month after month wondering where all the money is going.

Your path to true health and wealth and its limitless opportunities, is blocked by only one thing: YOU—your habits, your guilt, your negative self-talk, and having no real plan or understanding in place. Listen, we get it. We know too well that there are only twenty-four hours in a day and thirty-six hours' worth of to-dos to magically fit into that time frame. We know you already have a full plate with work, and kids, and being a wife, best friend, and everything that comes in between. But

4

what if we could prove to you that taking just one hour a day to put yourself first and truly start to understand your health and wealth could optimize your efficiency and help you to regain control of your life?

We are here to show you exactly how to create a life in which you can have the best of both worlds in your financially stable career and quality of life. The time of running yourself to exhaustion and creating a life of chronic stress and anxiety is over. You were not meant to live this constant life of burnout and hustle as if you were going to earn some sort of badge of honor for being the "Busiest Woman Alive." As a modern woman, you are meant to be financially, professionally, and personally healthy in order to be that happy, vibrant, energetic bombshell elite woman who means business.

So ask yourself, right now, before you continue reading this book: Are you going to stay on autopilot and continue making excuses, or are you ready to make a change and put yourself first in a real and meaningful way?

Good. You're still here so that means you're ready to take charge of your health and wealth. We believe these topics go so hand-in-hand for the female population that we instinctively knew we had to unite our expertise and write a game-changing guide as a way to get women, just like you, to see that you truly can't have one without the other. Our minds, lives, and journeys as women are tangled balls of wire—everything's connected, nothing's independent of the other. The book in your hands speaks to wealth and how a powerful woman just like you can achieve it, understand it, and feel empowered by it, no matter what your current financial situation looks like. But just as importantly, it embraces all aspects of physical and mental health and how you owe it to yourself to live a nourishing life full of joy, confidence, and the ability to perform in all aspects of your day-to-day life.

First, we must acknowledge, and meaningfully understand these truths:

1. You must be healthy to be wealthy.

To be the best version of yourself, you must be healthy. You must take time every single day to check in on your physical, spiritual, and emotional health. When you do this, and make it a regular habit, you are putting your best self into the universe. When you truly feel strong, confident, beautiful, and amazing deep within your bones and soul, you are the best version of yourself as a person, mother, wife, friend, employee, business owner, etc.

When you're happy and healthy, you're able to work more efficiently. Your mind is sharp and focused and you have the energy to perform. The best version of yourself is going to be hard to overlook for that promotion. The best version of yourself is going to finally take that chance on starting that business you've been thinking about starting forever. The best version of yourself can support all the people in your life, all while knowing you must put yourself first and make yourself a priority. The best version of yourself knows you owe it to yourself, and those you love, to be as healthy as you can possibly be. Your health has to come first.

2. Wealth is nothing if you don't have your health.

You've heard this time and time again, but think about it literally. If you don't take care of yourself today, you will be spending all your hard-earned dollars taking care of yourself in the future. Reflect on the cautionary story of the woman who finally made it to her retirement, and right before her celebratory cruise died suddenly of a heart attack. Or of the woman who waited her entire life to buy that beach home in retirement, but now that she's made it, her knees are so bad she can't bear to walk on the sand. Or of the woman whose health deteriorated so much that retirement came by force, rather than voluntarily.

Ladies, we must keep ourselves healthy so that instead of spending the wealth we've worked so hard to accumulate during our lifetime on reactive health measures (i.e., doctor visits, medicines, hospital stays, etc.), we're spending that wealth on the unique and special dreams we worked so hard to fulfill.

Consider *The Health and Wealth Sisters' 360° Action Plan* the start of your journey to living the life of health and wealth that you deserve. Rest assured, this is not a book full of empty motivation, but rather actionable plans that will make you think, make you work, and take you on your own journey of self-discovery and self-efficacy. We won't ask you to write negative self-talk on note cards and then burn them while chanting some weird voodoo around a bonfire.

Nope, sorry to disappoint, girlfriend. *This* book is for the modern woman who needs a swift kick in the pants in order to stop taking the back seat to her own life. It's time to turn the autopilot mode off and to confidently and unabashedly start showing the heck up for yourself.

It's time for us to take charge of our wealth. It's time to understand what the heck is going on with our wealth as it relates so intimately and deeply with our physical health, spiritual health, emotional health, and social health.

Don't be the woman who works herself into the ground, forgets to put her health first, and wakes up sixty-five years old ready to retire, but too unhealthy to enjoy it. Don't be the woman who spends her retirement at the doctor's office with a drawer full of medications. And listen, we get that there are genetic exceptions to all this and there are things that are truly out of our control, but being proactive with your health and truly living a healthy lifestyle can help you to avoid so many issues in the future.

Be the woman who reaches retirement vibrantly, vivaciously, and ready to take on the next chapter of her life. Be the woman who fulfills all the value-backed goals she has set forth for herself in her Wealth Empowerment Plan. Be the woman who takes charge of her health and wealth and feels empowered in every stage of her life.

You are worthy and deserving of being that woman. Together, via our 360° Action Plan, we're going to show you *how* to bring health and wealth in sync.

PART ONE

AMANDA TALKS WEALTH

CHAPTER ONE

MY WHY

For you to truly understand my passion for empowering women through their own financial independence, I should first share the story of how I got there. And to be honest, my story doesn't start with me. It starts with my mom, Ines Riley, a barely five-foot tall, petite, Puerto Rican woman with thick, black shoulder-length hair that most days she tries to beat into submission with a straightener. My girls call her "Aba," which they've deemed short for *Abuela* ("grandmother" in Spanish). She is the most Aba-iest Aba. She *loves* being a grandma and can be found crocheting little booties, clothes, and blankets for anyone having a baby.

However, before Ines Riley was Aba, she was Ines Rosario, a small girl who grew up very poor in the tiny town of San Lorenzo, Puerto Rico. As the middle child of three girls with an absent and abusive father, the most memorable story she told me was about her eighth birthday. My abuela, her mother, was one of the most hard-working women in the world. She worked at the lottery, paying people out for their winning tickets. For my mom's eighth birthday, my abuela had saved enough money to buy her daughter a small change purse. My mom still remembers how excited she was to receive the gift, knowing how hard her mother worked, all by herself, to put food on the table.

By learning from her mom the value of hard work, my mom was the first in her family to go to college, and ended up working for the Social Security Administration in Puerto Rico. Several years into her career, a project led her to speaking with a linguist in Virginia, John Riley, who knew perfect Spanish, even though he was of Irish and German descent. They went from talking on the phone about work to learning more about each other—laughing, writing each other letters, and exchanging pictures.

Mom sent him a picture of her sitting on her desk: petite; island tan; with short, curly, black hair; brown eyes; and wearing a fitted yellow-and-blue knee-length dress and pumps. John sent back a picture of himself standing outside: pale-skinned with strawberry-blond hair that hung over his ears, wearing a blue button-down shirt that fit nicely over his stocky body and played up the blue of his eyes. The rest, as they say, is history. They fell in love, my mom left Puerto Rico, and her entire family, behind, and embarked on a brand-new life in Baltimore, Maryland with her new husband.

A few years later, they moved to rural Maryland and decided to start a family. That's where I come into the story and my sister, Michelle, joined us two years later. We grew up in Sykesville, Maryland in an upper-middle-class neighborhood with two parents who worked for the government. My mom spoke Spanish to Michelle and me, and it was my first language. Dad spoke English to Michelle and me. And Mom and Dad spoke Spanish to each other.

Overall, I had a great childhood. Since both our parents worked out of the house, we were daycare kids. Michelle and I spent most of our days at Mrs. Lynn's house, who to this day we call our Daycare Mom. She had four kids of her own who became our best friends—and family. Summers were spent in Puerto Rico visiting my mom's family and playing in the crystal-clear waters of the island. We had an awesome dad who encouraged me to pursue playing the clarinet because I loved it, even though it was painfully obvious that "master clarinetist" was never something I would be able to put on my resume. In our basement was a custom-built playhouse our dad made for us out of plywood and two-by-fours. There was vinyl tile on the floor, and the walls were painted my favorite color, bubble-gum pink. He had set up a small table and a pretend kitchen inside, and Michelle and I would spend hours playing house and making pretend meals for each other.

Looking back, we had the most typical, average, two-parent, two-kid household. It was perfect and I was happy.

But it didn't last.

I remember the exact night I realized things had taken a turn. It was early in the fall of 2000, and Dad had been put on an extended assignment in Washington, D.C. This meant he was up and out before Mom would get us ready for the sitter's house, and was back home after we had eaten dinner as a family of three and night had already settled in. This was also the first time since they were married that my mom and dad didn't drive to work together. Dad had thought that taking the year-long assignment in D.C. would be just what he needed to do to get that next promotion in his career.

But that weeknight, Dad didn't walk through the front door and continue to the kitchen, which was connected to the living room where we'd usually be watching TV or doing homework. Instead, he remained in the hallway and was silent. I remember him quietly asking for my mom to "Come here." She got up from the couch to meet him and for the first time I heard my dad cry.

In Spanish, I overheard him tell my mom that after his year-long assignment, the one that he had worked so hard on, the promotion was given to the boss's nephew who had been in the department for only two years. Dad would go on to say that he couldn't believe he'd given up a year of their commutes together, a year of their cafeteria lunches together (every single day they met for lunch at the giant cafeteria in the Social Security Administration Building, even though they were on opposite sides of the campus), a year of dinners as a family (coming from a divorced home, Dad was always so insistent that we ate dinner as a family at the dinner table), but most of all, that he had given up a year of his family and all the moments that made up that year, for a promotion that had been promised to someone else by way of nepotism a year ago.

Even though I was only eleven, I remember thinking to myself how unfair that sounded. Weren't adults the ones in charge of all the rules? How could they not be following the same rules of kindness and fairness they were so diligently bestowing upon us since the beginning of time? Were adults really that messed up? Boy was I naive.

Depression runs on my dad's side of the family. His mother suffered from it; her mother suffered from it. And now, depression had finally made its way to my dad. It took a bit of time for the effects to really set in, but when depression made itself at home in its newest host, it was clear that it had no intention of leaving.

Dad would spend entire days in the master bedroom, never coming out. On weekends, Mom would often be upstairs comforting him most of the day, so Michelle and I grew both very independent and dependent on each other. At the ages of eleven and nine, we obviously couldn't drive, and this was before cell phones, so we learned to rely on each other. We would watch TV together in the living room and microwave frozen meals or make sandwiches for lunch. We'd entertain ourselves with games, eating snacks, or fighting over who got to use the desktop computer in the office. We became self-sufficient, but we always kept one ear open, waiting for the master bedroom door to open, which meant our mom was finally coming downstairs. It would usually be around late afternoon that she'd resurface for a while—to talk to us, watch TV, make dinner, and most likely to clear her own head.

With depression comes insomnia. I vividly remember waking up in the middle of the night, watching through my open door as Dad paced the dark hallway, his restless form faintly lit by the night-light in my room. He never slept. My mom would later tell me, in my adult life, that she would frequently ask him what he was thinking of while he paced all night. His reply was always the same: how to kill himself, or how he would kill us and then himself. While I suspect some of you just shuddered, he was still my Dad, who loved all his girls. Whenever he'd tell my mom about how he wanted us all to die, it was because he didn't want to leave a mess in his wake. His depression would tell him that it would be better if we were all gone together. To this day, I have no idea how my mom wasn't more of a mess. I would've been! She was strong and would always talk him off his ledge when he arrived at these conclusions. She'd tell him that we all, including him, will be fine and encouraged him to continue getting the help he needed.

When his depression truly set in, he was no longer going to work. He couldn't. He was a shell of the man that he used to be and couldn't even get out of bed in the morning. Thankfully, he had more than a year of time built up in his leave bank with the federal government, so he was able to take a sabbatical. Mom continued to drop us off at the sitter's house in the morning and drive herself to work—all while still making sure Dad was getting the care he needed, Michelle and I were cared for, and ensuring the house was running as smoothly as possible.

By this point, Dad was seeing psychiatrists and psychologists regularly. He took cocktails of antidepression medication, waiting to see which combination would do the trick. I remember him crying when he realized "the combination of the month" wasn't going to work and he'd have to be put on to a new dosage, a new medication, or a different cocktail entirely. My poor dad. As an adult, I can't imagine the ultimate pit of despair he must've been in and the fervent prayer for something, just anything, to work so he could stop feeling "this way."

With every failed medication, came a new and inventive way to kill himself. And again, my mom shielded us from all of it. Later, she told us of the time that she came home from a long day of work, got us settled in for the evening, and then found Dad in the master bathroom's jacuzzi tub. With the tub filled all the way to the top, he had been mustering the courage to fight his survival instinct that kept bringing him to the surface every time he slipped his face under the water. Another time, Mom caught him trying to electrocute himself by sticking a fork in the toaster while it was on.

On one particularly scary weekday evening, Dad drove himself to an undisclosed location and called Mom to say his goodbyes. We were at Mrs. Sharon's house, a friend of Mom's from church who agreed to watch Michelle and me before and after school. Mrs. Lynn, our original Daycare Mom, had gotten out of the daycare game. This was fine with us since Mrs. Sharon and her husband had two daughters, Ashley and Heather, close to our same ages. After Mom hung up with our dad, she called the town police and pleaded with them to go look for him, as she was scared this would be the time he actually succeeded in his plan. The police told her that there wasn't much they could do since it hadn't been twenty-four hours and he was an adult. After some negotiation and Mom telling them a little bit of Dad's history, they finally conceded—one of the benefits of growing up in a small, sleepy town with nothing ever going on, I suppose.

They found him at the shooting range. He had been firing some rounds, and from what he told Mom later, was just waiting until he felt brave enough to shoot himself instead of the target. Knowing that he was armed and battling with depression, the police handled him with kid gloves, under the assumption that he would do something to hurt himself or them. However, Dad was always a gentleman to company, and obliged as they asked him to put his hands behind his back to handcuff him. He was taken away in the back of a police car to the mental institution forty-five minutes away from home. Mom quickly left to go meet the police and my dad at the hospital, and Mrs. Sharon assured her that it was fine if Michelle and I stayed the night.

I remember trying to fall asleep that night in Ashley's room. She was in her bed and I was in the daybed off to the side that I tried to make myself comfortable in. She was used to falling asleep to the radio, so the local pop station played quietly as a backdrop to my racing mind. *When was Mom going to be home? How long would Dad have to stay at the hospital? What were they doing to him there?* I eventually fell asleep after what felt like hours of listening to the soft radio playing and staring at the wall, alone with my thoughts in the pitch black.

That next day, after school, Mom picked us up from Mrs. Sharon's and drove us to the hospital to see our dad. We walked through the labyrinth of sterile corridors and eventually, at the end of a long white hallway, reached a heavy, guarded door with a small square window in it and an open stairwell off to the side. Mom and the guard exchanged words. After he found out we were visiting a family member, he used his key to let us in.

We walked into an expansive, open-floor plan with blue officelike carpet, sofas, and fake potted plants. In the distance, I could see meeting rooms, recreation rooms, and more hallways. Nurses and security guards walked around leisurely. To the right was a long, half-circular receptionist desk. The seated receptionist took one look at Michelle and me and informed Mom that today was not a day they were letting minor children onto the unit.

Mom tried to explain to her that our father, and her husband, had just been admitted twenty-four hours prior, and we were all here to visit him. But the receptionist wouldn't budge on the policy and reiterated that Mom was welcome to stay, but that Michelle and I would have to wait outside the unit. My mom obliged and walked Michelle and me back out the heavy, guarded door. We had brought our bookbags and homework, so we wouldn't be completely bored to sit and wait in the stairwell. The now-friendly guard assured Mom that he would keep an eye on us and that we'd be just fine. Michelle and I watched as she slipped back through the big white door.

I remember sitting and waiting on those white hospital steps with Michelle, dutifully completing our assignments for school the next day, when we heard a knock on glass. The guard, who had his back to the door, turned around and both Michelle and I looked up. What I saw still haunts me to this day as the saddest thing I have ever seen. It's the image that I see most when I remember him—and I hate that fact. Dad's face—his glasses over his blue eyes—was looking back at us through the small square of a window. He had a smile on his face, but not the bright, toothy smiles we had seen during our childhood. It was close enough that you could trick yourself into seeing the real deal, but I knew better. Michelle and I both smiled and waved excitedly back at Dad's smiling face. Slowly, his hand came into the frame and he offered a small wave back. The three of us stared at one another for what felt like minutes.

We knew he couldn't hear us and he knew we couldn't hear him. I felt an ache in my heart. My dad was in insane jail. But, why? He wasn't insane. Dad was sane and safe . . . just really sad right now. Why couldn't we talk to him? Why couldn't I ask him what he had for lunch and if he was getting to eat Utz potato chips—his favorite snack besides mini powdered doughnuts—while he watched TV at night. Did they have mini powdered doughnuts for him? And what were they giving him for breakfast? He didn't like to eat breakfast, preferring only a Diet Coke and an unwrapped slice of yellow Kraft Singles American cheese in the morning. Were they being nice to him? Did he have friends?

I NEED TO TALK TO MY DAD!

As quickly as he had appeared in the window, he disappeared. And then I heard the sound of a key unlocking the door. The doorknob turned, the guard took a step back, and

Mom slipped back through the door to help Michelle and I grab our things off the steps so we could leave. She thanked the guard for keeping an eye on us and we left. As we walked down the hallway, I turned one more time to see if Dad's face would again be looking back at mine through the tiny window. It wasn't.

The next day after school, Mom took us once again to see Dad. This time we were allowed onto the unit as long as a guard was within a safe distance. Again, we walked through the heavy door, but weren't stopped by the receptionist. In fact she had been expecting us. She handed us visitor badges, then picked up the phone to make a call.

About two minutes later, Dad emerged from one of the hallways in the distance and greeted us. He was wearing his normal clothes and seemed "fine." I hugged him around his waist and he hugged me back, patting the top of my head like he usually did. Then it was Michelle's turn. After some superficial small talk ("How was school?" "Were we being good?"), a man my father's height with dark brown hair, who looked to be about twenty-five and was visibly mentally challenged, approached and stood very closely to us, his mouth open and eyes glazed over. Dad, forever a gentleman with others, turned and smiled at the young man, then looked back at Mom, Michelle, and me. With a gentle, calm voice, Dad said, "This is my friend Arthur."

Until the day I die, I'll be able to replay that sentence in his voice, verbatim.

It haunts me. I remember glancing at Arthur, then looking at my dad and thinking, *Friend? This is your* friend? Clearly the relationship they had built over the last forty-eight hours had been one in which Arthur would simply follow my dad around, as Arthur could barely speak. How was that a friend for my dad? Dad, a professional writer for the U.S. federal government. Dad, who could speak five languages with no trace of an accent. Dad, who enjoyed intelligent conversation and was a habitual reader of all genres . . . was now friends with Arthur. And please, know that this had nothing to do with Arthur, but everything to do with my dad. My father couldn't be fulfilled having Arthur as his only friend. He could care for Arthur in a brotherly way, and they could watch TV together, but who was Dad actually talking to and bonding with? My heart shattered.

Before long, a nurse came and walked Arthur away, reassuring him that "John is visiting with his family so we're going to find you another activity for a little while." Arthur waved goodbye. Dad showed us to one of the more private meeting rooms which had a couple of sofas and a big table in it. We sat down and Mom immediately started asking him questions in Spanish: "What have you eaten today?" "What activities did you do today?" "Who did you speak with?" "What medications are you taking?" Mom and Dad talked for a while between themselves as Michelle and I helped ourselves to some of the therapeutic art supplies on the table.

We were there for a while until Mom announced it was time that we leave since we had school the next day and the drive was forty-five minutes. I remember being sad to leave—thinking that we were his only foothold to the normal world "out there." "In here," Dad was one of "them"—the people who hear voices, or see clowns in the corner of the room, or think the government is out to get them. It didn't seem right that he was being lumped in with everyone else. Dad wasn't clinically insane. He was struggling with depression. And even at the age of eleven, I thought to myself, *Being the only* not *insane person in an insane unit, can't be helping him to start feeling happy.*

And it didn't. After that hospital stay, things never got better, even after he got home. It was a slow and steady descent into his own personal hell on Earth.

A couple weeks later, another incident took place. Michelle and I were upstairs at our desks in the extra bedroom. I was drawing a point-of-view picture of my best friend's house with colored pencils and a ruler, to ensure that the lines were just right. Michelle was probably drawing one of her cartoon people. Both of us were startled out of our focus when we heard the master bedroom door slam open and heavy footsteps rush down the hall and stairs. We jumped up and hurried to the doorway in time to see our mom now running down the stairs at full speed, chasing after our father. By the time Mom had reached the bottom step, Dad was already running out the front door.

We, too, ran down the stairs, witnessing Dad rush to the family car and turn on the engine. Mom made it to the front passenger door just in time to hop in as the car started rolling backward out of the driveway. In disbelief, Michelle and I ran out the front door, still wide open, and just stood in the front yard next to each other as we watched the car drive away.

In the flurry of our parents leaving so fast, Michelle and I didn't even have time to think. Also, if you know anything about my mom, she is as overprotective and overbearing as they come (I say that with all the love in the world), so I knew for her to leave without even saying a word, there was a good reason. Luckily for my parents, Michelle and I were good kids. I'm pretty sure we spent the next several hours playing and watching TV while waiting for them to return, despite being in limbo of not knowing if they'd be home the next minute, the next hour, or if we'd be alone the rest of the night.

Finally, after what felt like an eternity, we heard the front door open. It was late afternoon and the sun had already started to set. Michelle and I got up from the living room couch, hurriedly walked through the kitchen to the hallway, and watched as Dad walked up the steps to his room without saying a word, shutting the door behind him. Next, Mom, looking exhausted, stepped inside the house. "Everything is fine," she said, but didn't go into any further detail. I caught her quickly glance upstairs before she went to the kitchen to make us dinner.

On November 8, 2000, my twelfth birthday came and went. It was nothing special, as Mom was too busy caring for Dad. Then came her own birthday, five days after mine. Again, no fuss. Their anniversary went uncelebrated on November 17, followed by Thanksgiving. I wouldn't say these events were lackluster; they simply ceased to exist that year. There wasn't time to focus on anything else, but my dad.

December 25, 2000, was exceptionally lonely. Anyone who knows me knows how much I LOVE Christmas—the magic, the family, the decorations, the love, the joy that overflows everywhere you go. Christmastime is my favorite drug. I remember waking Michelle up that Christmas morning and running down the steps to see what Santa (which by this time we knew was our parents) had left under the tree. Mom would always decorate our formal living room so beautifully for Christmas. I remember Dad getting a tree out of obligation that year. He was very clearly not in the Christmas spirit, but went to the tree lot, strapped our tree of choice to the top of the Buick, brought it into the house, and put it up in its stand before withdrawing back to his room.

What Michelle and I rushed down to was a dark tree. The string lights hadn't even been turned on yet. And beneath the tree, it was empty—not a single present in sight. Michelle and I just looked at each other, stunned, wondering what to do next. We eventually went back upstairs to her room and watched TV.

About an hour or two later, Michelle and I had decided to go back downstairs to eat breakfast and watch TV in the living room. Mom came in with two large shopping bags—one for each of us. Inside were a couple of unwrapped gifts. I don't remember what they were and I don't recall our mom being proud of the haul. I would later learn that Dad was always the shopper and gift giver extraordinaire. Normally he enjoyed picking out toys for us and would do anything he could—use lunch breaks, get up early in the mornings, go out to the stores after we went to bed—to get his hands on the toys that his beloved daughters most desired. Gift giving had always been Dad's love language. Although he wasn't good at saying "I love you" or offering a big hug, or expressing his feelings in general, he was amazing at picking out the perfect gift.

This year, Mom had been left to her own devices—along with dealing with Dad.

By late afternoon, Dad made his way down to the living room. His eyes were sunken in. He wished us a quiet "Merry Christmas." Clearly, the greeting came from a sense of obligation, not because he truly felt "merry" this Christmas. Mom made dinner, and Dad retreated back to his room right after the subdued meal was finished.

Depression stole my Father away from us. New Year's Eve and Day came and went and we were officially in 2001. We didn't go anywhere to celebrate, and Dad didn't partake in his usual tradition of serving everyone twelve grapes that you had to scarf down before the clock struck 12:01 a.m.—a Mexican tradition he had picked up during his college study abroad, where he learned to speak impeccable Spanish. Michelle's tenth birthday on January 5, came and went with no fanfare, as did Three Kings Day on January 6.

Our mom tried her hardest in January to get Dad out of the house. I remember her physically putting his big Baltimore Ravens coat on him after forcing him to get dressed. Mom, who NEVER drinks due to being raised by an alcoholic father, had gone to the liquor store and was now putting a six-pack of Budweiser in his hand and all but shoving him out the door to go watch a game with his fishing buddies. She told him she would be calling Mr. Gary's house (the host for the night) to ensure that he got there. Dad was quietly crying that he didn't want to go. Mom told him to just try to have fun and that all he had to do was show up, to just see if visiting his friends would help a little. It was his first time out of the house in weeks other than doctors and psychiatry appointments.

Little did we know that January would be the last full month we had with Dad, the darkness of despair was swallowing him more with each passing day. The efforts of those close to us, family and friends, from visiting and just sitting with Dad, to praying with him, to trying to talk to him—none of it was enough to make him hold on for any longer. The toll the depression took on him began to prove itself as too much for one man to bear. The infinite cocktails of medications that wouldn't work, the failed attempts at suicides—he just couldn't take it anymore. So, he decided not to.

FEBRUARY 5, 2001

I was twelve years old and in sixth grade at Oklahoma Road Middle School. Such an awkward age. I wasn't part of the popular crowd, and in fact, my closest friends were the ones I'd had my entire life from daycare and a couple of girls from the church youth group. Mom had always made sure we were involved in church. We went faithfully every Sunday morning, Sunday night, and Wednesday night.

On the night of February 4, 2001, I went to bed desperately wishing for a snow day. All the news outlets were calling for it and the entire school had been abuzz with excited squealing and hushed whispers that we were going to have the next day off. I remember looking outside and thinking that the sky was giving away its game plan. You know how the sky looks before it's going to snow—like, really snow? It's just one gray, cold blanket, but at the same time, it's so warm and reassuring and still. And I swear, you can even smell when it's going to happen. The outside smelled so crisp. It smelled like snow.

I sleepily opened my eyes the morning of February 5, 2001, to the sound of Mom waking me up, as she always did, for school. Immediately, after getting my wits about me, I opened the blinds of the window right next to my bed, and pressed my nose against the cold glass and squinted in the dark abyss. Snow. Perfect, virgin, not-yet-even-been-touched-by-the-plow snow covered our street. Quickly I turned to my mom and asked, "Do we have school?"

Back then, you had to wait for the TV news station to run through the list of school closings before you knew if you had school or not for the day. I was praying she already knew the answer and would be able to save me the agony of desperately waiting for CARROLL COUNTY SCHOOLS—CLOSED to pop up on the banner under the talking head of the local meteorologist's weather report. Sure enough, Mom already knew the answer, and in a lackluster fashion in Spanish replied, "No, no school today, but I have work, so I'm still taking you to Mrs. Sharon's."

That was totally fine with me. I remember being so excited! This snow day off from school in which my mom still had to take us to our sitter's house was the perfect excuse to snuggle up with our great friends, watch movies, drink hot cocoa, play outside, and eat ramen noodles for lunch. What. Could. Be. Better?

I got up, brushed my teeth, got dressed, packed some snow stuff for playing outside, ate a quick breakfast, and was ready to go. Michelle, too. My parents' house has a double story foyer with a staircase leading up to a little landing, almost like a Juliette balcony, outside my parents' room. I remember waiting in the foyer in the hallway under that landing overhearing Mom talk to Dad, saying things in Spanish like: "Are you sure it's okay that I go to work? What are you going to do while I'm gone? I'm going to call you once an hour. Are you going to pick up? Maybe I should stay home. I'm running out of PTO, though." Now, my mom is loud by default. It's part of being Puerto Rican, I'm sure.

Whenever we visit her family in Puerto Rico, it's like everyone is sitting in a room yelling at one another, when, in reality, it's a lovely conversation about how good the food was last night. But all that is to say, while I could clearly hear my mom, I couldn't overhear what my dad was saying at all. Partly because he always had a balanced tone to his voice—only yelling when he was mad or getting loud with his boisterous laughter (which I've been told I inherited)—and partly because the depression had taken his voice along with everything else I loved about him.

Mom came downstairs to Michelle and I waiting in the little foyer. "Let's go," she said in Spanish. And out the front door we went. My dad, no doubt, was still in bed, fighting as hard as he could to find the will to face another day. I didn't say goodbye. This had become life. I'd see him when I got home in his same blue and green striped shirt, the only shirt he could ever seem to find comfortable, and his navy-blue pants. He'd be sitting on the couch when we got home blankly staring at the TV screen.

The actual day, and what I did at Mrs. Sharon's, isn't part of my memory. Where my memory picks up again is realizing it was well past five o'clock. There were certainly days in the months of my father's depression where we didn't get picked up at all, but our mom would always call Mrs. Sharon before five p.m. to work out the details. But never was Mom late to come pick us up. In fact, she was almost always painfully early.

The clock kept creeping, and I remember thinking how slow a minute really was. Sixty full seconds. Every minute past five fifteen p.m. was now an eternity. Even though all us girls were in the living room watching TV, I kept turning around and checking the visible stove clock, only to see that it was exactly two minutes since the last time I had checked. I remember Michelle, my oblivious little sister, not even seeming to notice that Mom was late.

Finally, around 5:50 p.m., Mrs. Sharon came into the living room and asked her girls to go play in the basement for a little while. She had clearly been crying and wouldn't look Michelle or me directly in the eyes. That's when I knew. I could sense it deep in my soul—a place you don't know exists until something like this happens to you.

There we were, Michelle and I sitting in the living room of a friend's house, "watching TV" by ourselves. It's funny how unaware Michelle was as she kept staring at the TV screen. For the life of me, I have no idea what was on. But everything else in the room made its presence known. The blue couches that we always sat on now felt hard and uncomfortable. Why was the entertainment center so "oak-y"? Was it always that color? It seemed bland. Was the room getting smaller? Why was the dining room table so close to the coffee table? Whose idea was the floral-patterned wallpaper in the kitchen? The view from the couch straight to the outside slider and beyond gave way to the saddest, gray sky you had ever seen. The deck now seemed rotted to me. Had so many planks always been pulling up at the edges?

The entire house and world around me seemed to lack life—every single thing a shell of what it once used to be. Nothing was overly welcoming, nothing seemed "nice." This house that had been a safe haven, now became a dark, deserted island as I waited for our mom to arrive.

Then I saw Mom's white Buick pull up in front of the house. From my spot on the couch, all I had to do was turn around and I had a perfect view out the front window. To my surprise, another car pulled up right behind hers. My mom got out of her car and then, of all people, our church pastor got out of the other car. They talked to each other for a brief second and then started to walk cautiously up the snow-covered driveway. I watched, in what felt like slow motion, as they reached the front steps and opened the front door. I swiveled my head to the left, and now I was staring at both Mom, in her work attire, and our pastor, as they shuffled their feet on the doormat so as to not track snow into the house.

No one said a word.

My mom came over and sat in between Michelle and me on the couch.

Ines Riley has never been, and still isn't, an overly affectionate woman—unless it comes to her *nietas* (granddaughters). However, I remember how tightly she held us close to her small frame. She started crying—another thing she never did. Ever. The pastor pulled an armchair from five feet away to a suffocating foot from us and said some jumble to the effect of: "Your dad has gone to be with the Lord." I genuinely cannot tell you how it was told to me that my father had passed. Words that forever changed my life. I remember the words sounding far away, like I was underwater and in a cocoon.

I didn't need to hear the words because I already knew the outcome of the sentence. Dad was dead. The end. No need to sugarcoat it. I remember thinking, *I know. Why does he feel the need to deliver this message? And why is* he *the one delivering it? Wasn't there anyone else on the planet that was closer to our family that would've been more appropriate to have this sit-down with?* It's amazing what thoughts the mind will busy itself with in an attempt to protect you.

Michelle started hysterically crying and my mom held her with her right arm as tightly as she could. Mom's face contorted into that of a woman I had never seen before—immensely shattered, full of despair and uncertainty. Hot tears streamed down both of their faces and the sound of their crying pulled me out of my thoughts.

I can "see" myself in that moment as if through a camera—like I'm watching some sort of horrible reality TV show. My face is blank. No tears. Nothing. I watch as I turn my head slowly to the right and look at my mom's face, then Michelle's, then the pastor's. He had an incredible look of pity all over his face as he watched Michelle cry. I just sat there. I get this from my mom. I rarely cry, much less in front of other people. Michelle has always been so much more open with her emotions. I remember thinking, *I'll deal with this later when I'm alone.* And to be fair, I did. I dealt with it in the days that followed from behind my bedroom door, a place where I could cry with reckless abandon and not worry or think about a single other living creature around me.

Over the hour that followed, we worked through all the logistics of Dad no longer being with us. How, why, when, what now . . . The questions a twelve- and ten-year-old brain need to work themselves through. We learned that he had hung himself in the attic of our house. He had taken the yellow rope that he kept in the trunk of his beautiful black vintage fifties Buick, the ladder we kept in the garage, a two-by-four, a hammer, and some nails, and carried them all to my mom's closet, where he pulled down the attic door and climbed with the intent to end his life. He succeeded.

My mom said she had spent the day calling him on the hour, every hour. When he hadn't picked up for two hours, she called the church pastor and our next-door neighbor, Mr. Jeff, to see if they could go check on him. Our church was less than a five-minute drive from home, and Mr. Jeff, a house painter, was working at a residence in the neighborhood over from ours, so he had no trouble getting back home quickly. Thank God the pastor and Mr. Jeff were able to check the house and make the discovery before Mom.

The rest of that night is a blur. I remember a lot of people coming over that evening and all our house lights being on and people occupying every room. If I'm being honest, it almost plays out like a party in my head. I don't remember people crying. I remember a lot of laughter. Small groups sharing stories of Dad—the time he and his buddies went fishing, a very regular weekend occurrence, and him catching a huge rockfish and how they all couldn't believe how big this thing was. They'd joke about how loud and contagious his laugh was—again, unfortunately/fortunately something I inherited from him. They reminisced about his favorite food—hot dogs and Diet Coke—and how for being such a traveled man, he had the simplest palate. The laughter and light of the house felt good. It felt like he was with us again. He was more with us that evening than he had been in the past year. The house was warm despite the cold outside, and I was comforted despite my world changing at such a rapid pace.

I remember heading up to bed that evening later than usual. A family friend stayed with us overnight and she had already retreated to the living room couch that had been set up for her. Together, Mom, Michelle, and I all walked up the stairs. We grazed past Dad's favorite navy-blue coat, the one that always resided on the bottom banister of the stairs. It was still there, just like it had been for years. When we reached the top, we all stood there, staring at one another, not quite sure of what to do next. Mom turned and walked into her room. Michelle and I followed.

The queen-size bed in their room always looked big to me, but it looked especially large in the dark of this night. Mom got into Dad's side of the bed and pulled the covers up to her shoulders. Michelle followed suit and laid in the middle, and I took Mom's usual side of the bed. The room still showed evidence that Dad would be coming back any minute. His books were stacked on the nightstand. He never went to bed without reading. His gold wristwatch rested on his tall oak dresser.

In the dark, we held one another, and Mom prayed. Afterward, the three of us lay in silence. Even though the house had been so full of people, it now felt so incredibly empty. A thought slammed into me like a brick wall: *It's just us three now, the Riley girls; that's it.* I can't even begin to imagine the thoughts that were going through Mom's head.

Tomorrow, a new day would start. The first day in our new chapter.

I landed on one final thought before drifting off . . . *I didn't say goodbye to him this morning. I didn't say "I love you" one last time.*

THE JOURNEY SINCE

It's so interesting to look back now, in my early thirties, and try to recall the days that followed such a defining juncture in my life. It's crazy to me that at this point in my life, I've lived longer without a dad than with a dad. I know that many of you reading this share this truth with me. It's hard. There are so many moments that I wish he could've been there. Moments I longed to see his bearded face with his joyful smile and big glasses. So many times people have looked at me and said, "You look so much like your father." And honestly, now I have to look at an old picture and search his face to find the resemblance. My memory of him isn't serving me as well as it did in those first days after his death, and I suppose I have the protection of the fantastic, fascinating, mysterious hardwiring of our brains to thank for that.

The days that immediately followed my dad's death were another blur. There were food trains and people stopping by day in and day out. There was the viewing and funeral, in which friends, family, and even strangers would walk up to me and start sobbing uncontrollably, almost falling into my small, twelve-year-old frame for support, or enveloping me in a suffocating hug. So many times, people cried not for the loss of my father, but out of pity for Michelle and me because we were "too young to have to go through something like this."

I remember Dad's best friend, and my godfather, Eddie, a giant, six-foot-three black man whose body resembled that of a linebacker, absolutely crumbling in front of the casket. It was like his soul had left his body and his bones had turned to mush. My mom, being all of five feet, went over to try to help him stand up, but it wasn't long before three of Dad's male cousins came

31

to Eddie's rescue and struggled to get him to his feet and over to a pew. I've never seen a man cry that hard in my life and I felt so sorry for Eddie in that moment. He had lost his best friend in the entire world and wasn't sure how he could go on.

I remember being excused from school for a week and feeling unsure of how people would treat me when I went back. I had never been popular by any stretch of the imagination, as I mostly kept to myself in seventh grade and had a few good friends. I wasn't disliked at all, just mostly liked and ignored, which was fine with me. But then, after coming back from "my dad's death hiatus," it seemed that classmates were quicker to offer a smile, or say hi. One of the popular girls even offered me a cheese curl during band practice the week I came back. However, the new niceness hadn't shielded me from the rumor mill that was circulating at one hundred miles per hour since my return.

I heard through the grapevine that my father had hung himself from the chandelier in my house, which was ridiculous, as there is no chandelier, just a hanging pendant light in the foyer. I remember thinking, *How would that have even worked logistically?* That was an easy rumor to ignore, though, and honestly, one that I found a sick sense of humor in. Then there were the more realistic rumors—that he had shot himself in the head or hung himself out in the woods behind our house. Those hurt a little more and I wondered how my peers had even found out that Dad had killed himself.

As an adult, I now know how fast the rumor mill works in a small town.

One of my classmates, Clare, asked me what happened to my dad as we were getting ready for band class to start. We both played clarinet and sat in the third and fourth to last chairs (I told you I was bad at playing the clarinet) and it was noisy as we all tuned our instruments, talked, and waited for the teacher to assume her position at the podium. I suppose during all the commotion she thought we could have a private conversation. Even at the young age of twelve, I remember thinking that Clare had never taken a particular interest in me before, as she was part of the popular crowd, and that she clearly just wanted to know for her own curiosity's sake. Or to share with her group of friends over lunch period that day.

This is the exact moment I came up with the story I told people about my father's death, well, until this book came out anyway.

"He had a heart attack," I said.

She looked at me a little surprised, probably trying to reconcile all the suicide rumors with hearing straight from the source that my dad's death had actually been from a natural cause. "Oh. I'm really sorry," she replied. And I genuinely think she was really sorry.

Just as quickly as we had started having our hushed conversation, we ended it as our band teacher took her spot at the head of the classroom, picked up her baton and clinked it against her metal music stand in an effort to calm the class and start us on our warm-ups.

As expected, it wasn't long before my peers started treating me like just another classmate again, no special treatment, and the rumors about how Dad had stopped. Both of which I was thankful for.

I remember when Mom finally moved Dad's coat from the bottom banister of our steps. For as long as we lived in our house, the one that my parents had built from the ground up when I was four, the one that kept our entire lives and memories within its walls, Dad had always walked through the front door, removed his jacket or coat, and hung it on the banister knob. It's funny looking back now as a wife and mother. We had a coat closet next to the kitchen. Why didn't it go there where it belonged? However, my mom always had the wisdom to pick her battles with him, which is one of the reasons I think their marriage was so strong. She was never a neat freak by any means, but the moment his navy-blue coat was put away in the coat closet for good, probably two weeks after his death . . . wow, that moment hurt. It was the first time we, the Riley girls, really acknowledged that he wasn't coming back.

Slowly, I got used to our new normal. We were now a family of three girls. We had to learn how to get by as just the three of us, no "man of the house." The biggest shift was Mom had to learn to speak for herself. She and Dad had always spoken Spanish to each other and my dad would take care of speaking for her in public so Mom wouldn't have to feel embarrassed or shy by her thick accent when she spoke English. I'm not talking about with friends or family—my mom spoke for herself plenty—but when it came to ordering food at a restaurant, or talking with teachers at school, or classmates' parents at a party, it was usually Dad navigating those conversations for the both of them.

Looking back, I see how Dad was showing protection and love in those situations by making sure Mom never had to feel uncomfortable. But after Dad died, she had to learn to get around with her thick accent. To this day, Mom's accent when she speaks in Spanish is so incredibly thick, even though she's been here for more than thirty years. Michelle and I regularly poke fun at her mispronunciation of everyday words. Our favorite is when she asks for a "sheet of paper" or says "bed sheet," it always comes out "*shit*." My mom is such a good sport and always laughs and says, "Well, why don't you guys try speaking in Spanish then?"

After our dad died, my sister and I quickly became the people that would speak for Mom if we saw someone she was speaking with really struggling to understand what she was saying. We got very used to repeating her orders at restaurants, or repeating what she was saying to a friend, or just asking her to tell us in Spanish what she wanted to say and then simply translating it for her. Michelle and I still do this for our mom to this day, out of habit, but it's clear that she needs it so much less than she did in those first years after Dad had passed.

I can't imagine what it was like for Mom raising a twelve- and ten-year-old all by herself with no family around to help. Dad's parents were divorced and lived in Virginia. Neither were up for the challenge of hanging out with us to give my mom a break. Mom's mom and sisters lived in Puerto Rico, so there definitely wasn't anything Abuela could do to help her. So, there she was, completely on her own to figure out how to raise two girls to become adult, productive members of society.

It certainly wasn't always pretty. The three of us fought a lot. My mom still jokes that sometimes Michelle and I would be fighting and she'd try to get involved to break it up and then we'd both team up and turn on her. With the exception of a typical teenage bad attitude, I was for the most part, a good kid. I liked to have good grades, I was generally respectful of others, and I didn't drink until I got to college. I hung out with the same group of girls most weekends and our idea of trouble was wandering around the reservoir and the old boarded up insane asylum after dark. Mostly though, we'd end up at the mall or the movie theater.

My biggest fault was that I was mouthy as all hell with my mom and I couldn't stand my sister. Michelle and I fought all the time. It was truly nonstop. We had nothing in common, and I found her to be a true annoyance.

Michelle's daddy issues manifested themselves by getting her first tattoo at the age of sixteen, trying multiple piercings on different parts of her body, and partying by the time she was in high school. She wasn't bad by any means, just a little out of control as Mom would say. She still got good grades and ended up graduating a year early from high school, but definitely enjoyed living life on the wilder side. I can't emphasize enough how completely different we were from each other at the time.

My mom had an incredible task on her hands: raising a hormonal teenage bitch with an attitude problem and the mouth of a sailor, and raising a wild child who wasn't afraid of anything and wanted to grow up as fast as she could.

I eventually went off to college at McDaniel College in Westminster, Maryland, which was only a twenty-five-minute drive from my house. I commuted to and from school until my junior year, when I told my mom I wanted to live in an off-campus duplex with some of the girls I had met through a January study abroad program in Italy. Mom was anything but happy about this decision, as she couldn't understand why I needed to move away from home to go to a school that had only a twenty-five-minute commute.

Even at that age, I knew I needed to begin spreading my own wings. I am incredibly blessed in that my mom paid for my college tuition, but when I told her I was moving into an off-campus house, she made it very clear that I would have to fund that adventure on my own. And that's when I ended up being the crazy housemate that was either studying for one of my three majors, or working at one of my three jobs. The three girls I lived with all had wealthy parents and none of them had a job while in college, but we had an amazing experience nonetheless and I wouldn't trade those two years for the world.

It wasn't until I was away at college that Michelle and I became friends. Now that we weren't forced housemates, we were able to see the human who had been shrouded as an annoying sister for so many years. She would come visit me and we'd hang out with my friends and housemates. We'd get dinner together at the local pub and drink cheap liquor. Those years marked some of the best times of my life, and it was truly when Michelle and I learned the value of the person that God had put on this planet for us to walk with as a lifelong companion.

I met my husband, Alex, at the beginning of my junior year in college. I knew the night we met that he was the person I was supposed to spend the rest of my life with. He took a little longer to realize that, but that's another story for another time. I remember bringing him home to my mom for the first time about six months after we had met. He drove us from McDaniel to my house in his green Jeep Cherokee. I tried my best to prepare him for meeting my mom, which was hard because how do you set expectations for a white dude meeting a super Puerto Rican, loud, overbearing mother?

We walked through the small front lawn up to the front door of the house and I proceeded to let myself in, as I had done thousands of times before. However, this time was different. I was about to make a declaration to my mom that this was my boyfriend, and a declaration to myself that this was the real deal. As I watched them talk—Mom in her broken English and Alex with his shaggy hair, leaning into the conversation more than usual, because if he leaned in he could concentrate better and realize that she was saying "dog" and not "Doug"—I wondered what it would've been like if Dad had been there. Would he warmly welcome Alex into the living room and offer him a Budweiser? My dad always had a stash of Budweiser cans in the bottom left drawer of the fridge, although he rarely drank. Would they talk about football or what Alex was majoring in in college? Would they laugh at the same jokes and would we all finally decide to go into downtown Sykesville to grab some dinner together because we were all having such a great time? It's a story that I've written in my head a thousand times.

I remember my mixed emotions when I graduated from college. The absolute pride I felt in myself was undeniable. As I donned my cap and gown and got ready to walk into the college gymnasium, I felt the sting of longingness mix in with the excitement and elation that was already coursing through me. Growing up, Dad always stressed the importance of a college education to Michelle and me with such an understated fervor. I remember conversations just like these all throughout my childhood:

DAD:	Amanda, what do you want to be when you grow up?
ME:	A race car driver!

DAD:	Amanda, what do you want to be when you grow up?
ME:	An actress!

And he always had the same response.

DAD:	You can be anything you want *as long as you go to college.*

As I walked into the gymnasium, I wanted so badly to see Dad's face in the crowd, right next to Mom's. I wanted to see him smile so huge that his big glasses would scoot up his face. I wanted to run up to him after walking across the stage and give him a hug, saying, "I did it!" My dad would've been so proud. He would have been so full of joy and light it would've looked like he'd swallowed the sun.

I think about the moment Alex asked Mom for my hand in marriage, and how they sneakily found time to go to the jeweler together to pick out the perfect ring. How would it have gone if Alex were to have asked Mom *and* Dad instead?

I remember standing alone behind huge wooden doors that separated me from my soon-to-be husband, my mom, my sister, my family, and my friends, and feeling a twinge of pain swirl into the overflowing excitement, anxiousness, and pure love that I was already feeling. As I stood there in the Italian lace silhouette wedding dress that Mom, Michelle, and my best friend, Rachel, had helped me choose with a long veil draped over my perfectly curled, flowing hair, I thought about my dad. I thought about how much less nervous I would feel if I had his arm to hold on to. After all, I was in five-inch heels, and I was walking down a brick aisle. I wondered if he'd cry. I wondered how he'd feel about watching his firstborn daughter promise her life to another man, while silently mourning the special bond that exists between a father and his daughter, which is no longer theirs to own after that moment of "I do."

Would he tell me how beautiful I looked in a wedding dress? What would our first dance together be? He loved music! He had so many CDs of all genres. I know he would've wanted full charge of our father-daughter dance song and I think he would've kept his choice a secret until the moment we were standing on the dance floor. He would've smiled anxiously in anticipation until I realized what song he'd chosen for us.

I remember the feelings of wonderment over a story never written the day my oldest daughter was born on the night of the blood moon on Sunday, September 27, 2015, at 10:27 p.m. after a long labor and a dramatic delivery. Riley Taylor Valentina Campbell was born with her cord wrapped around her neck three times, and as I pushed her into this world, she slumped, blue and lifeless, onto the delivery table. She gave my husband, the midwife, and the nurse a scare, but I knew everything would be fine. And it was. After all the rushing around had settled, and Riley was deemed happy and healthy, I was finally left in the quiet, dark hours of the early morning with my new girl. I looked down at the tiny face that peeked out of her pink and blue newborn hat, all snuggled in the pastel crocheted blanket my mom had handmade for her first granddaughter. I glanced over at Alex, asleep on the "bed" (read: weird reclining chair), and thought about the sheer joy Mom and Michelle had exuded when they met Riley for the first time in the labor and delivery room at midnight before they were rushed out as visiting hours had ended hours prior.

In the dimly lit recovery room, staring at this new life I had brought into the world, I wondered what it would've been like for Dad to meet his first grandchild. The idea seemed almost foreign. At the age of twenty-six, I had lived more time without a father than with, and while I longed for him to be there, a part of me cringed at the idea too. What would we talk about? Would it be awkward for him to see me in such a disheveled state? Would he hold Riley? My mom had always joked that Dad didn't shine in the newborn phase. She said that he needed to sit in a comfortable position and have a pillow placed under his arm "just so" before he would hold Michelle or me, no matter how badly my mom needed to put us down or what was going on. She laughs about it now, but I can imagine that in the moment, the impatience coming off her would have been palpable.

I remember visiting Michelle in Savannah, Georgia when Stephen, her then boyfriend now husband, was stationed there as an army ranger in July of 2017. We happened to be there for what would've been Dad's sixty-third birthday, and we decided to celebrate by taking Riley Taylor to her first dirt track race as Michelle had a dirt track only thirty minutes away from the house she and Stephen were renting. That night was one of the most beautiful experiences of my life. I watched as Riley said "Hi" to everyone we passed, like long-lost friends, as we found our seats on the metal bleachers. I watched her tiny, almost two-year-old face be glued to the race cars as they zoomed by. I laughed as she squealed and clapped when the winner of each race was announced, as if she knew what any of it meant. I was amazed at the fact that she would scoot just far away enough from me when the races would start so she could pull her ear plugs out and hear the thundering boom of the car's engines as they flew by. (I had been so sure it was going to scare her.)

I felt a sting of sadness, as I knew how much Dad would've loved to share this "first" with her. He would've wanted to explain to her everything that was going on and why the cars would head into the pit mid race. He would've wanted to tell her all about the late model race cars and point to the different parts of the car as they were lined up ready for the checkered flag. He would've been in all his glory as he showed her off to his racing buddies and regulars at the track, and then stopped by the snack stand to get her a pack of Goldfish and a "secret" glow stick lollipop (because he's Abuelo and doesn't have to adhere to Mommy's no sugar rule). And, while we all wish that's how it could've been, we knew how full his heart was for his birthday in Heaven.

When our sweet rainbow baby, Elena Jolie Noelle, joined the world on December 3, 2018, and Alex and I were now "new to two," would Dad have offered Alex advice on how to survive being the only man in a household with three other women? Mom, Michelle, and I were on cloud nine when we learned that the sweet bundle I had finally carried to the five-month mark was a girl. After all, the three of us Riley women had been a powerhouse since February 5, 2001, and now I was re-creating my own girl power club. We couldn't help but think, "Poor Alex . . ."

I know with all the certainty in the world, that Mom, Michelle, and I are who we are now because of that life-defining experience on February 5, 2001, and the journey after. The three of us Riley ladies have been through so much together—from Michelle and I maturing and becoming Mom's sounding board to Michelle and I becoming adults and assuming different roles and responsibilities in the family. Michelle and Mom developed a codependent relationship. I always joke that Michelle is Mom's husband, in which they talk to each other all the time, but they also fight just as much.

I become the middleman for the two of them when they fight, and also have the "last say" in so many things. For example, when Michelle was planning her wedding, she and Mom ran all the decisions by me, no matter how many times I told them that I would be happy with whatever they chose, as Michelle was the bride and Mom was paying. I'm not sure why or how that happened, but that's just the way our family of three works. Mom continues to be what Michelle and I call "Our Ride or Die." She will be there anytime, anywhere, to do anything for us. We were her whole world until Riley Taylor made her appearance, followed by Elena Jolie. Mom is always there to make sure all four of her girls, and now her two sons, have anything and everything they need—even when we don't *need* it and profusely remind her that we can take care of our own families.

Michelle and I will never be able to repay Mom for everything she did for us and everything she continues to do. She taught us to be fiercely independent and to do for ourselves in this world. Throughout my life since that fateful day, she has repeatedly taught me the most valuable lesson. In Spanish, when she talks about my dad's passing, she always ends her story on this note: "An empowered and independent woman must always understand her finances, since you can't rely on your husband to be there for you forever."

CHAPTER TWO

THE IMPORTANCE OF MENTORS

I can't say that I was one of those college kids who just *knew* what they wanted to do with their life. I was certainly not that kid who talked about wanting to be a doctor at the young age of five and then actually grew up to work their way through medical school. Until the beginning of my junior year at McDaniel College, I was what my college advisor deemed "Undecided." I took all my general education studies and hoped on a wing and a prayer that a major would speak to me . . . or at least whisper sweet nothings. Eventually I had to decide what to major in. It was time to pick a course of study that would set the tone for the rest of my life. Or at least that's the pressure I put on myself.

My college advisor, mentor, and good friend to this day, Professor Donald Lavin, was in the college's business school. Our conversation went something like:

"Did you pick a major yet, kid?"

"No, I don't really know what I want to do."

"Have you ever thought about business, or accounting, or economics? Those are all safe bets."

"Yeah, my mom has talked to me about majoring in business. She said it was safe too."

"Well, take a look at the course guide for the business administration major. What do you think?"

I probably studied the hard copy leaflet for all of one minute before I declared, "Yeah, I think I can do this."

I started working my way through the courses to major in business administration and quickly realized that those same courses overlapped with the ones needed to major in economics and accounting, with a couple other requirements layered in. I knew if I kept a full course load and kept my grades high, I could graduate with all three majors under my belt—and I did.

During my junior year of college, we were encouraged to get an internship. I had always loved weddings and planning things for people, or as my dad would call it, "being the ringleader." Once when I was six, there was a huge blizzard and school closed for days. The plentiful snow was perfect for sledding. Our entire backyard was a steep hill and we would sled for hours in our double-seater, hot-pink plastic sled. On one particular day, I decided we needed more of a thrill. I needed to find us a steeper slope. My baby sister had no choice but to tag along for the adventure I had planned.

There was an outdoor concrete staircase that led down to the basement door of my parents' house. I'm sure you already know where this story is headed. . . . I carefully placed our sled at the top of the staircase, which was covered in a thick layer of perfectly slushy snow, and proceeded to put my baby sister right in the front seat. Michelle, per usual, happily obliged and sat there in her giant pastel-pink snowsuit, waiting for me to take my seat behind her.

As I started climbing into the sled, I looked up to see my mom standing there with her arms folded and a smile on her face (clearly, she had been standing there for quite some time and her smile was one that insinuated, "What are these idiots about to do?"). She calmly and quietly, a rarity for Mom, said in Spanish, "But what do you think you're doing?" I proceeded to rationally explain the awesome idea I had for Michelle and I to sled down the steep stairs because we'd go really fast. Mom quickly realized that I had planned this all out so that should this adventure go sideways, *I* would only incur minimal damage, and put a stop to it. Michelle, at the trusting young age of four, had none of this figured out. (I'd like to think that I've grown into a person that can use my skill of planning for good instead of evil, but it may also be that Michelle is a little harder to trick these days.)

All this to say, I've always been a planner and love to watch events or scenarios I've cooked up in my mind play themselves out in reality. I've also always been good at keeping track of money. So, the idea of becoming a wedding planner seemed like a natural fit, as it encompassed my love of weddings, planning, my natural skill set for budgeting, *and* it fit in as an internship for my business administration major. Besides, that was a "girly" business-type career, right?

I landed myself an internship with the events coordinator at a fancy golf course half an hour away from McDaniel and dove headfirst into the wild world of brides, wedding ceremonies and receptions, time lines, and budgets. I enjoyed getting dressed up in business attire and heels on the days I was due in at the golf course, and I loved the events coordinator, Suzanne. She was so knowledgeable and could walk a stressed-out bride-to-be through imagining and committing to the wedding of her dreams, no matter the budget or specifics. I was mesmerized by the entire process, and for the first four months of my six-month internship, I truly thought I would grow up to be a wedding planner, and I let myself indulge in watching J. Lo's *The Wedding Planner*, thinking that was real life. By month five, however, it was starting to sink in that brides were . . . crazy. I'm totally allowed to say that because I, too, was eventually a bride, and I'm sure I had my share of crazy moments.

The realization that I did not want to be a wedding planner hit me in the face like a ton of bricks during one particularly eventful wedding.

The bride was, what we socially refer to as, a bridezilla. She expected *a lot* of everyone around her, and her poor bridesmaids looked both exhausted and excited that the wedding was finally happening and they would be relieved of their duties in a few short hours. The bride was barking orders left and right, and pounding champagne like it was December 31, 1999. I remember being so thankful I was only the intern. Poor Suzanne was in charge of making sure this wedding went off without a hitch, and without everyone killing the bride before the ceremony started.

When the instrumental music indicated that the wedding guests were beginning to arrive and take their seats, the bride went into total meltdown mode. She went from barking orders to full on yelling at her bridesmaids, and then dismissed them all so she could be alone with her wedding planner. For some reason, I was allowed to stay and scurried my way to the corner of the now quiet bridal suite. The bride looked at Suzanne and in an anxious, high-pitched panic said, "I can't do this. I don't think I can walk down the aisle."

Suzanne, such an expert, looked at the bride, took her hands in hers, and in the most soothing voice I've ever heard said, "Let's sit down, turn off the lights, and take some nice, deep breaths." She flicked the light switch to the bridal suite and it went dark except for the sun coming in through the windows. She guided the bride over to a chair and made sure that as she sat, the bride's gown was splayed out perfectly so as not to wrinkle. Suzanne pulled another chair up to the bride so they were face to face, re-grabbed her hands, and said, "Okay, let's just take some nice, deep, calm breaths." The bride inhaled and exhaled deeply and slowly along with Suzanne as I maintained my safe distance in the corner. After inhaling and exhaling about four times in the quiet dark, the bride let out a huge, loud, fart.

I thought for sure she was going to be mortified. I stood there, in the corner, completely shocked at what I had just witnessed—too scared to laugh. Suzanne didn't say a word. Finally, the bride said, "Okay, that's better. I'm ready now." She calmly stood up, gathered her dress in her hand, and made her way to the door of the bridal suite. Suzanne turned on the light in silence, and fluffed the bride's veil. Ladies, that was the EXACT MOMENT I realized I was not cut out for that type of work and turned my back on the wedding-planning scene. I finished my internship program with Suzanne and went on to serve as a waitress and a bartender at the golf course until I graduated.

After deciding I wasn't meant to deal with crazy brides, I realized I didn't know what I wanted to be when I "grew up." One day I talked to my advisor-turned-friend, who I now just called Don, and he brought up that during tax time he helped a local accounting firm with their tax returns, as he's a CPA. He asked if I'd be interested in working there for the summer during their audit season, and I said, "Sure, why not?" Luckily enough for me, one of my best friends from college, JP, was also one of Don's mentees, and Don guided us both toward an internship at the accounting firm for the summer right before our senior year of college.

JP and I had the time of our lives. She was also a Maryland native, so we decided that while everyone went home for the break, we would continue to live in the house that I rented off campus. It was just the two of us in that small house on Main Street for a whole three months. We did everything together and had ourselves on quite the routine: get up, drive to work at the accounting firm together, get a little bit of work done while joking around and eating Jolly Ranchers candy all day, wait until the clock said five p.m. so we could rush to the gym, work out for an hour, and then get back to our little home to make ourselves a healthy dinner and cocktail to enjoy out on the Juliet balcony of my room in the summer dusk. On the weekends, Alex would come to visit from New Jersey, as would JP's boyfriend, and we'd find ourselves on adventures like going to concerts, baseball games, or bars. We lived the dream life during our last summer of "freedom" from the real world, and I couldn't have asked for a better send-off into adulthood.

While we worked at the accounting firm, JP and I both inherently knew we weren't going to be accountants. And, to be honest, we didn't really have to take the job too seriously, as it was a small, local accounting firm, and we knew their intent was to shut their doors within five years as both of the principals wanted to retire. There was a male principal and a female principal, and I had all the respect in the world for Celeste. A short, stocky blond with a curly, pixie cut and blue eyes, Celeste wore kitten heels with her pant suits. Her teeth weren't perfectly straight, but she was always showing them off due to her ever-present smile. Her blushed cheeks were plump, and she wore reading glasses that sat right on the bridge of her nose.

Celeste taught me so much about accounting, but moreover, how to be a respectful and responsible business woman, how to not take crap from a male partner (as hers was constantly dishing it out, but she clearly wasn't standing for any of it), and how to be a smart business owner while still having a kind, genuine heart and being grateful for the people that work for you. Cheryl, the receptionist, was Celeste's cousin, and the two of them would laugh and chat in the mornings together. Cheryl looked a lot like Celeste, except taller and with dark brown hair that made her own crystal blue eyes pop. I think they saw a bit of themselves in JP and me, so they rarely got on our case for our loud laughter in the afternoons or if they caught us sitting at the same desk whispering about weekend plans. They were also acutely aware that some days, there was just not enough work to go around— part of being a small business.

Between Celeste and Cheryl, they made sure that JP and I learned what it meant to be professional business women in a man's world, while also devoting themselves to being wives and mothers.

Cheryl always made sure there was enough petty cash so that JP and I could walk ourselves to Dunkin' Donuts for an office coffee run on sunny days, made sure we never took life too seriously, and checked in on us every morning to make sure we were staying safe and "making good decisions all alone in that house."

Celeste made sure we learned how to hold our own in a male-dominated field while still maintaining a kindness and joyfulness that was unparalleled. JP and I worked at the accounting firm through our senior year of college and enjoyed the weekly paychecks. We also knew that gig was an awesome résumé booster for the real world, which we would be entering in 2010—just two short years after the 2008 recession, which meant we needed all the résumé boosting we could get.

May of my senior year was quickly upon me and I still had no idea what I wanted to actually do with my life. To be fair, do most kids know what they want to do with their lives when they're twenty-one? I felt like I should. In my time working at the accounting firm, I had seen a business card for Joseph Garrison, who worked at Strategic Wealth Management Group, LLC, floating around the office. He had a bunch of letters after his name and I had no idea what any of them meant. That May, Don Lavin encouraged the seniors in his Business Ethics class, which I was a part of, to attend an alumni dinner being hosted by the college. He handed out a hard copy of the agenda for the evening with a roster of all the alumni who would be attending and where they now worked. As my eyes scanned the sheet of paper, I immediately realized I was already on shift as a bartender for a wedding at the golf course on the same Friday night as the alumni dinner. My eyes continued to scan the roster and that's when I saw his name again, halfway down the page: JOSEPH GARRISON, CERTIFIED FINANCIAL PLANNER, STRATEGIC WEALTH MANAGEMENT GROUP, LLC.

Throughout Don's lecture that day, I kept thinking about what it meant to be a Certified Financial Planner™. I had no idea, as I had never even heard of it before. However, I liked the fact that it had the word "planner" in it, and I had already taken a bunch of finance type classes. The more I thought about it, the more I decided I wanted to learn what Joseph Garrison did for a living, and if it was something I'd be interested in. After class ended, I walked over to Don and let him know that I was working a wedding the evening of the dinner, but wanted to get my résumé to this Joseph Garrison guy. Don, per usual, said something along the lines of: "No problem, kid. Get me a copy of your résumé and I'll hand it off to him at the dinner."

Imagine my surprise when about a week later I got an email from Joseph "Joe" Garrison inviting me to have a cup of coffee with him at his office in Columbia, Maryland (about forty-five minutes away from McDaniel). We emailed back and forth a couple of times, set a date, and as they say: The rest is history.

In July of 2010, two months after my college graduation, I said goodbye to my friends and coworkers at the golf course and at the accounting firm, as I was officially starting my career at Strategic Wealth Management Group, LLC as an account representative. I walked into the SWMG offices for my first day on July 6, 2010, and quickly learned about the deep world of financial planning.

SWMG was a small, fifteen-person company with an office in Columbia and an office in Salisbury, Maryland. I acted as the "right-hand man" to one of the firm's founding partners, Jim Griesser—a kind, gentle, man whose client base consisted of retired and retiring couples and widows. Jim expected a lot of me, as he had some of the most complex financial planning cases within the firm. I processed all Jim's clients' paperwork and money movement, emailed back and forth with clients on administrative matters regarding their accounts, and made sure Jim was prepared for all his client meetings. We developed a great working relationship and he pushed me to take on more responsibility, teaching me how he worked through complicated and intensive financial planning matters as he explained his train of thought on subjects I didn't even know existed. It was hard, mind-bending work, but Jim was always patient, and to this day, alongside Don Lavin, he is the best teacher I've ever had.

Because Jim's financial planning cases were so intensive, I quickly realized I was "over my skis" and needed some further education and understanding to keep up. In the fall of 2010, I got a couple of letters after my name, RP®, which stands for Registered Paraplanner, and through that designation learned the foundations of financial planning, or the tips of the icebergs of financial planning topics. While this wasn't enough, it was certainly a good start, and I had a cursory knowledge of what was going on around me and what Jim was helping his clients to do on a day-to-day basis.

Through watching Jim with his clients, interacting with his clients independently, and learning more and more about the business and industry with each passing day, I fell in love with the idea of financial planning and becoming a Certified Financial Planner™. On April 1, 2013, I received my CFP® designation after a year and a half of master's level courses in the areas of financial planning, and a grueling two-day, ten-hour exam with a 50 percent pass rate. During those eighteen months, Alex and I had purchased our first home together, gotten engaged, and brought home our first fur baby, Alba, a sweet female chocolate Lab who became my study buddy, always lying at my feet. Oh, and while studying for the CFP® designation, I also planned our wedding—the event I had spent my entire life dreaming about planning. Looking back, I honestly don't know how I did it all, but I know I couldn't have done it without Alex's support. In the eight weeks leading up to the exam, I had become a hermit—just working and studying.

I found out that I had passed the April exam in May, just two weeks before our June 1 wedding. Alex still jokes that had my exam letter started with the word "Unfortunately" instead of

"Congratulations!" we may have had an entirely different wedding and honeymoon experience. I tend to believe he's right.

After I got my CFP® designation, I was promoted to director of financial planning at SWMG. This meant no longer working as Jim's account representative, but instead implementing best practices for our financial plans companywide. My work with Jim's complex plans had well-prepared me for the role, but I still had so much to learn, not only about financial planning, but what it meant to be a leader. For the first time in my professional career, I had ownership of a department, processes, and procedures, and I was responsible for teaching and leading others. I loved financial planning and the intricacies involved in bringing someone's financial picture to life, but now I was charged with teaching others to do the same. I found such joy in watching someone learn the ins and outs of financial planning, and how to enter data into our software and produce a plan that he/she could explain. I loved when people would ask me tough questions and I would have to scour resources to find the right answer and then walk them through my train of thought. I appreciated the fact that everyone's financial life is a puzzle that simply needs to be organized and put together in a way that makes the most sense for them. Remembering back to Celeste and how she had been such a big-hearted leader, and also relying on what I had learned from Jim about how to teach others with patience, I came to love teaching others this vital skill. I had a coworker tell me once, "Financial planning is a skill you're born with just as much as it's something you can learn to do." I couldn't believe that more.

After my stint as the director of financial planning, I spent a year as the director of portfolio management while I built out our firm's portfolio management system. This part of my story *is* important though because I learned a lesson that will forever impact the way I lead and treat others. Out of respect for the man who taught me this lesson in a way that I will never forget,

I will only say this: I learned that as a young woman standing up for something you believe in, you must stand strong and steady in your resolve. I was called a liar, and my position within the company as a leader was called into question because I chose to stand up for what was right. Harder yet was that everyone around me *knew* I was right, but this person had the upper hand and I truly felt that there was nothing I could do. As everything does, this too did pass, and I resolved to never let anyone have that type of control over my career and future ever again.

During the time that I was acting as director of financial planning and then director of portfolio management, I started to take on my own roster of clients. My book started out with the founding partners shedding off small clients from their books that no longer made sense for them to care for. You know, the sweet little old grandmas who didn't have much left in their portfolios and simply required a check-in call once a year to talk to them about their money, their grandkids, and reminisce with them on stories of a well-lived life. My book also consisted of adult children of current clients—late twenty-somethings and early thirty-somethings who didn't yet have enough money built up to work with a high end wealth manager, but were happy to work with me, as what they truly needed was financial planning guidance and support. With these sweet clients, my firsts, I cut my teeth and earned my stripes. I made mistakes and learned from them. They were so precious to me as they were the proof that I was a financial advisor. They were real clients!

Right after I had gotten my CFP® designation, my friend Rachel went through her divorce. She was married for less than a year and her husband decided he had found greener grass elsewhere (what an absolute mistake on his part, as Rachel is a ten—and I'd say that even if she wasn't my best friend). She came to me one night when she realized there was nothing that could be done to change his mind. "You help people with their money all the time. What does this mean for me?" she asked.

And for the first time in my professional career, I genuinely had no idea. I didn't even know where to start researching in all my resources. I didn't know who I could turn to and ask. I was stumped.

I had to tell her, "I don't know. I mostly help married people." I hated that I had to answer my best friend, and a fellow woman, that way. I hated that I couldn't tell her where to turn. I hated that I truly had no idea, not even a shred of a thought of what this might mean for her. Exactly six months and some studying later, I was conferred with the Certified Divorce Financial Analyst designation (CDFA®). I studied how to analyze the short- and long-term financial impacts of a divorce settlement agreement and learned to work with family law attorneys to support them and their clients in writing settlement agreements that made the most sense for our shared clients. I learned as much as I could so I would never have to tell another woman going through divorce "I don't know" ever again.

A male counterpart of mine once told me after getting this designation, "You can't really do anything with that. You might as well not even put it on your business card. No one's going to know what that is. Besides, you can't market yourself to such a specific niche like people going through divorce. You need to market yourself to everyone. That's good business." While I so appreciated his unnecessary and unsolicited commentary on my career choices, I told him, "I'll see what I can do with it." Again, another life lesson from a male that I was angry and begrudging about at first, but now am so thankful for. I've always been one of those people who works harder when presented with "you can't" or "there's no way," and this only fueled my ambition.

All that to say, by the time I was made partner and was finished doing work *within* the company and was now free to do work *for* the company, as a financial advisor, I was ready and on fire! I started going to as many industry and networking events as I could and was quickly disappointed at how male-dominated all the events were. I was consistently the youngest female in the room and often felt overlooked. I wondered if the more senior women in those same rooms had felt the same way when *they* first started coming to these types of events.

It seemed that at every event I attended, there was a group of middle-aged white men in suits who considered themselves the "grand pooh-bahs" of the committee or organization hosting the event and they were always the loudest voices in the room. They appeared to have all the say in how the event was run, the topics that were discussed, and even took control of the questions being asked. I found it all . . . gross. I then found myself wondering, *If these guys are mansplaining financial planning to women who are financial planners, how are they talking to their female clients?* Were they including their female clients in the financial planning conversations, or was their behavior in a client meeting similar to the behavior they were displaying in front of me? As in, would they sit down in front of a married couple and spend the entire time speaking directly to the husband while the wife stared off into space wondering when the bromance session would be over? What would it be like if my mom, a widow, who didn't natively speak English, went to go see one of these men for financial planning guidance? Would they talk over her? Would they take time to understand what she was saying and to respect her thoughts and values and goals? It was evident to me right away that women who wanted to feel empowered by their own wealth, who wanted to feel financially independent and secure, and who wanted to be taken seriously when it came to her wealth had very few places to turn. Sure, there were a few women in those rooms with me, but nowhere near enough to help all the women out there. And there was no one in those rooms who focused solely on guiding women to their financial independence.

And there it was—the moment everything clicked.

I wanted to help all women achieve their financial independence.

My entire life had brought me to this epic epiphany. From being raised by a financially smart and savvy mother who, after all the trial her life had brought her, still managed to make her life work for her and her daughters without ever being financially dependent on a man. To the extraordinarily defined life perspective I took from my dad's death, which can be described through the memory of seeing my mom sitting at the dining room table hunched over bills and statements, calling banks and companies to try to figure out where everything was after my dad's death. I remember my mom saying things to the adults (in broken English) like "I think he had life insurance . . . maybe the policy is in a box somewhere?" And "I know he gets a pension, but I'm not sure how that translates to us now." Or "He had a retirement account, didn't he? If so, how do we get that figured out?" I don't know exactly how she did it, but she got all of it figured out without disrupting my or my sister's life one bit. In that moment, whether she knew it or not, my mom taught me one of the greatest lessons of my life: *An empowered woman must always understand her finances.* This coupled with working my way through business school and watching the professional women around me excel in their fields, to being told "no," or "you can't" by male counterparts, to leading incredibly smart women during my stints as directors of the firm, to raising my own two daughters alongside my incredible husband, all culminated around the theme of women's empowerment. And I was ready to embrace it.

I became obsessed with helping women to feel financially independent and smart with their finances and wealth. I created a branch of my business that focused solely on guiding women going through divorce toward their own Wealth Empowerment Plans. I educated these women on why it was important to understand what their money meant for them after they signed those final divorce papers. I made it my mission to make sure I never heard another woman say, "I feel so dumb when it comes to my money. I don't know where anything is." I met with widows and helped them to sort through the finances that their husbands had left behind. One widow said to me, "It's not that he didn't want me to know; I just trusted him to do it for us. And now, he can no longer do it for me and I don't know how to take care of myself when it comes to our money."

I made it a point to include wives in the financial planning conversations. I once had a prospective client come to meet with me, and after he was finished telling me why he didn't need me to manage his money because he was doing a great job of managing his funds on his own, he asked when we could meet again for a financial planning follow-up. (Eye roll.) Against all my better instincts, I thought to myself, *If he's so cavalier in speaking with me about his money and how he's so great at taking care of it himself, there's no way he was including his wife in these conversations,* so I said, "Let's find a time that works well for you and your wife to come in." He replied quickly with, "I take care of our portfolios for us. She's busy with work, so I'll be meeting with you on my own." Red flag. I told him I make it a practice of involving both spouses in the creation and execution of their Wealth Empowerment Plan and if he felt strongly about not including his wife, he may be happier with someone else. I refused to purposefully exclude 50 percent of the decision makers at the wealth table.

It became my mission, purpose, and passion to #LevelTheWealth. For myself, for my mom, for my sister, for my daughters, for my friends, for YOU reading this book right now, for all of us women. It is time for us to be seen as the empowered, knowledgeable, and smart women we are. We are ready, willing, and able to take charge of our wealth.

CHAPTER THREE

GUILT TRAPS

How often have you said to yourself:

- "I don't have money to invest. I have bills to pay!"
- "I don't have enough money to warrant a financial plan."
- "I don't have any savings, so why start now? I'm so behind the eight ball. There's no way I'll ever get ahead."
- "I've been fine this long. No need to fix what ain't broken."
- "You only live once! Why should I save my money when I can spend it on something I want today!"
- "I should be spending this money on my family, not myself."
- "I don't understand money, investing, or wealth. Ignorance is bliss."

Until we can start to truly own what it means to be selfish with our wealth, we will never escape the guilt traps that keep us from living in a constant state of wealth abundance, prosperity, happiness, and power. Every single one of us deals with internal guilt that drives our everyday actions as a woman, wife, mother, sister, daughter, friend, employee, business owner—the list goes on and on. But why, in that list, is our name never first? This chapter is to give you the permission you need to start putting yourself first when it comes to your wealth.

Ladies, the more we replay the loop of this self-deprecating, negative self-talk about wealth in our heads, the more this belief becomes our reality. How do these narratives end up playing in our heads in the first place? Society has taught us to "sit still and look pretty" when the men are talking about wealth, pay, and investing. I'm done with the male-centric narrative around wealth. It's boring and it's not what I wake up to passionately pursue every day. We foremost must believe that investing in our future is selfless, so we can begin to craft a strong and commanding narrative around women's wealth, and consequently, our own reality.

Women tend to see money as a pond—a finite source which can be depleted or evaporate at any time. We see it and feel anxious, as if this nonrenewable source could disappear if we sit and contemplate on it for too long. The pond is quiet and still. We fill the buckets of others with our nonrenewable water, constantly putting them first, to ensure that everyone around us is having their needs met—all the while, going thirsty ourselves.

To better illustrate, imagine it's a beautiful summer morning and you're on the bank of a freshwater pond. You've brought a blanket, some snacks, and a small bucket to drink the pure water from. Just as you're starting to settle into the warmth of the sun on your blanket, your daughter walks up with a bucket of her own. You take her bucket from her, fill it, and she slurps it down. You fill it for her again. Now, your husband walks up. He fills his bucket on his own after giving you a sweaty kiss on the cheek. He fills and drinks from his bucket so many times you wonder if he's saved enough water for the fish in the pond. You don't mind though; you'd hate to see him so dehydrated in the sun. Next, your mom arrives. You take her bucket, fill it for her, and watch her drink.

The noon sun is now really beating down and you feel yourself starting to get dehydrated, but you know how many people around you will need water soon, too. If you're feeling hot and thirsty, so are they. You divert your eyes from the bucket next to your blanket—maybe if you pretend it's not there, you won't be tempted to use it.

The day goes on and you continue to make sure everyone around you is hydrated, happy, and taken care of. As nighttime rolls around, you realize you haven't had a drink all day. You're starting to feel sick from the dehydration and decide it's time to fill your bucket. To your surprise, the pond is almost empty! You've been so concentrated on taking care of everyone else that you hadn't noticed the water depleting right before your eyes. Your only option is to find another pond of water . . . but where? You're so tired and woozy, you can't stand the thought of walking somewhere else to find a drink. You end the day depleted, not having taken care of yourself or your needs, wondering who will be taking care of you tomorrow now that you've made yourself sick and have run out of water.

How true does this metaphor ring for us in terms of money and wealth? We want to save money for our future needs in a retirement or investment account, *but*: We need to pay for our son's soccer practice next week; our teen daughter needs a prom dress; hubby's birthday is coming up and he's had his eye on a new golf club for months now; Mom is really in need of a house cleaning service, she's starting to slow down, etc. I could keep going with this list, and I'm sure you have your own curated version, but let's talk about how men tend to view this list, and consequently money and wealth differently.

Men tend to see money as a river flowing and rushing freely with power. They see it swell in times of abundance and fall during dry spells, but the flow and movement never ends. Men recognize that money is a renewable source and live in the knowledge that money is always present.

Imagine a man on a riverbank. Let's call him Mike. Mike has the exact same setup as you do at the pond. He has a blanket to sit on, some snacks to munch on, and is so relaxed as he sits by the babbling river on a sunny summer morning. The river, at some bends, is loud and powerful as the water crashes against rocks and mini white-water rapids form. At other points, the water becomes tranquil and slow and you can barely hear it. In the morning sun, Mike fills his bucket with water and leisurely sips on it. His daughter comes by—the same one as in your scenario—and he dutifully fills her bucket and watches as she slurps it down. Again, and again this happens until she is no longer thirsty. After she runs off to continue playing, he realizes he's running low on water in his bucket, too. He leans over the riverbank, refills his bucket, and sets it back down near the blanket after taking a satisfying drink. Next, his wife comes up and asks him to take a stroll. They walk to a quiet bend in the river—the water washes by the pebbles slowly and pools in the middle of the banks. She reaches down with her bucket and he swiftly takes it from her and fills it for her, not at all worried by the fact that the water in this part of the river is so close to being depleted. Mike thinks to himself, *I have water back at the blanket and besides, if I get thirsty while we're here, the pool in this part of the river will be full again in no time.* After some time, he heads back to his blanket and his brother comes up to visit. He brought his bucket too, and before he sits down, he fills his bucket from the river. Mike walks right up beside him and begins to fill his bucket again. At no point today has Mike gone thirsty or forsaken his thirst to make sure that someone else had gotten a full bucket. Mike acknowledges the free-flowing nature of the river and knows the water will continue to replenish itself as he draws off it.

Men don't wait in line to fill their buckets. They know there is enough water to go around. They know that the water is a renewable source. Heck, Mike filled his bucket while his brother was filling his!

Ladies, just like the water in Mike's scenario, money is renewable! When we can reframe money from a pond to a river in our mind's eye, we will embrace the flow of money's energy. Money is in a constant state of abundance around us. We can, and deserve to, get more of it and have the ability to control how we view it.

We need to stop putting ourselves last when it comes to wealth and money decisions. Why can't we pay for our son's soccer practice *and* put money away in a retirement savings account? It may mean telling someone else "no" or "not right now." For example, "no" to going out to lunch with your coworker for the third time that week, "no" to your kid when they ask for that five-dollar toy at the checkout line, or "not right now" when your husband tries to convince you that it's time to buy that golf club he's had his eye on for the past couple of weeks. Put your wealth first! Be selfish about saving your money. It is the most *selfless* thing you can do!

CASE STUDY: CHERIE

Cherie is a high-powered executive at a large corporation, a wife, a mom, a daughter, and a sister. She spent the beginning years of her marriage with her husband, Rob, just trying to get by. (We all remember that life, or are currently living it—mid twenties—the peanut-butter sandwiches, making sure there's enough money in the account for rent, the feverish couponing at the grocery store, or as my husband calls it "the good ol' days.") During this time, Cherie tells herself that it would be selfish to contribute to her employer's retirement plan. She and her husband can barely afford groceries without a slew of coupons. How could she even consider taking money off their collective table, even ten dollars per paycheck, to contribute to her retirement plan? It's an insanely selfish thought, right? She waves it off and passes on contributing to her plan for the second year in a row.

Through hard work and determination, Cherie starts rising through the company. Her salary increases and both she and her husband decide it's time to buy a house. Now they need to start saving for a down payment. Again, she decides she'll have to pass on contributing to her retirement plan. She thinks to herself, *Rob and I are scraping every penny to put into our down payment savings account. It would be so selfish to block money from flowing into that account because I'd rather put a couple of dollars toward my retirement plan. Besides, what is a couple of dollars going to do for me in the long run, anyway?* So, for the third and fourth year of her employment, she forgoes contributing to her retirement plan.

At the age of thirty-two, Cherie and Rob purchase their first home. They couldn't be more excited. They had saved enough for their down payment and now they are homeowners! The bills start pouring in on top of the mortgage. They have to buy a lawn mower. The bathroom sink starts to leak and they have to call a plumber. Their bank accounts are starting to show the new struggle of "happy homeowner" costs. Cherie thinks to herself, *It certainly doesn't make sense to contribute to my employer retirement plan right now. Look at everything our house needs done! We can't afford to put money anywhere other than bills, the mortgage, and an emergency reserve for house things. It'll be tight for a while around here, but it will be worth it!*

As these things go, nine months after closing on their new home, Cherie and Rob welcomed sweet little Rob Jr. While they were certainly not planning on a baby so soon after the largest purchase of their entire lives, they couldn't be happier. Now on top of the bills, new mortgage, and "happy homeowner" expenses, the past nine months have been spent purchasing cribs, pack 'n plays, diaper bags, bottles, diapers (holy cow, why do they need so many diapers?!), and every other essential item from Cherie's favorite blogger's "Must Haves for New Baby" list. Cherie definitely didn't consider contributing to her employer retirement plan during all this! How could she?! The baby needed things! She didn't have time to worry about her retirement which was, at best, thirty years away!

As it goes, the years pass, life gets busier, and Cherie and Rob welcome a baby girl, Maddie, along their journey. While Cherie continues her climb up the corporate ladder and Rob sees continued success in his business, their salaries continue to grow. But you know what they say: "Mo' Money, Mo' Problems." A bigger house, paying for daycare, fun family vacations, nice cars, and Cherie and Rob's aging parents who need care, amongst all the other fun things a life of luxury can bring, have all created large outflows of cash from their bank accounts. Time has gotten away from them and Cherie has never contributed *a single dollar* to her company's retirement plan.

As Cherie and Rob turn fifty, Rob Jr. is ready to head off to college and the impending doom of a five-figure per year tuition payment weighs heavily on Cherie and Rob as they sit at their dining room table one night trying to figure out how they will be able to pay for it, as they don't want Rob Jr. to have to take out massive student loans. Cherie and Rob commit to "tightening the belt" when it comes to their budget and more years pass in which Cherie doesn't contribute to her employer's retirement plan. At more than fifty, Cherie hasn't put a single dollar away in savings for her own retirement. What an incredibly selfless act, right? She prides herself on always putting her family's needs ahead of her own retirement. After all, that's what a good mom does, and besides, retirement is still many moons away. She'll cross that bridge when she gets there.

After many years of working, Cherie and Rob decide they would like to start thinking about retirement. They finally make time to go see a financial planner. Enter . . . me. After learning all the above, and having them walk me through their wealth story thus far, I have to look at Cherie and Rob, who are now sixty-five years old, and tell them that the only retirement savings they have is the $100,000 that Rob had put into his business's retirement plan.

Cherie says, "Oh, I always thought he was putting more away for both of us. I never saved toward my employer's retirement plan because we always had so much going on with the kids, and life, and traveling, and . . ."

"I always thought *you* were saving too," Rob sheepishly admits. "Business was hard some years, remember? I wasn't always able to put money away toward savings. And that one year that business *was* really good, we took the whole family on that Italian vacation."

Cherie fondly remembers that vacation and says, "Well, I certainly don't regret that."

"Nor should you!" I chime in. "Life is meant to be lived! But, now we have a different problem to solve for—how you can both retire while still being able to have money to live comfortably."

Cherie perks up. "We'll both get retirement benefits from Social Security, right? That should be plenty for us to live off of. People do it all the time."

"You are absolutely entitled to Social Security Retirement Benefit payments," I say. "As top earners with a great income record, you will both receive the maximum retirement benefit. Together, your Social Security Retirement Benefits will be about six thousand dollars per month."

Cherie and Rob look at each other in a panicked state. "Six thousand dollars per month total?" Cherie exclaims. "We spend almost all of that on our mortgage alone!"

After a long discussion, Cherie and Rob decide to keep working for as long as they can. They leave my office sad, disappointed, and wishing they had made different decisions along the way. Did they *really* need to go to that upscale steak restaurant every Saturday night? Did they *really* need to buy Rob Jr. and Maddie brand-new BMWs upon graduation? Had they known the severity of all this, perhaps they would have considered having the kids pay for their own college educations. These are the meetings that I, as a financial planner, dislike most. The ones where I watch as someone's dreams take a different shape. The ones where I wish I could've helped sooner.

They finally retire when they are seventy and unfortunately, Rob passes away two weeks after his retirement party. Cherie is left with a large house, $100,000 in Rob's retirement account, plus the $20,000 she was able to save into her own retirement account since we met five years ago, and social security retirement benefit checks. She ends up having to sell her home and move into a small condo. Rob Jr. and Maddie have already started making plans for if their mom needs special health care in her late years. They know their mom can't possibly pay for a home health care nurse or care at a nice nursing home should she need it, so they wear the burden of this on their shoulders.

While I can go into all the different ways to solve this problem and put the puzzle together, this isn't a wealth management or financial planning textbook. What I will say is this: Unfortunately, I see this all the time—women putting their retirement savings on the back burner because they think they're being selfless. But saving for their retirement and saving for themselves is one of the most selfless things they can do. Since Cherie neglected to save for her retirement, her children now wear the burden of saving money to care for her in her elder years should she need it.

I know what you're thinking. "That would never happen to me." Or "I'm too smart to ignore saving for my retirement forever." Maybe. But the years slip by so quickly and I can promise you that it is never too early to start saving for your retirement.

Now, investing in yourself isn't just about saving for retirement. The above was simply an example. Think about the woman in the first story who was constantly filling everyone else's bucket with water from the pond while hers grew dry as the day wore on. Investing in yourself by way of your wealth can mean *so many things*. Let me give you a few real-life examples:

- Reworking your budget so you can save enough to take that much needed anniversary trip, just you and your spouse, to Europe without taking out a credit card loan. You'll be able to recharge, refresh, relax, and leave the frenzy behind without coming home to a nasty credit card bill with an insanely high interest rate attached.
- Cutting out the daily bought lunch with your coworker from your weekly expenses and instead packing a healthy lunch and putting that money toward a gym membership with a personal trainer. Talk about self-care!
- Resist spending when there seems to be a money surplus! Investing, or even saving this money into an emergency savings account, can help you sleep better at night. You'll gain such peace of mind by knowing that if overnight you need a new dishwasher or boiler, you can just buy one outright with the money you have in your bank account, instead of putting that balance on a credit card.

Self-care shows itself in so many forms—some fun, some peaceful, some just downright responsible. But they all have the same effect: positive energy and no sign of guilt. It's time to start being selfless for yourself. That's a CRAZY way to think, right? Putting your wealth first will not only improve your immediate financial well-being, but think about the longevity of your life. The quality of your life when you begin showing up for and investing in yourself will improve tenfold. Everything is connected.

What changes can you make today that your future self will thank you for?

The moment we can take charge of our wealth and start to be completely selfish in the most selfless way is when the wealth and investing guilt narrative will change. When we can acknowledge that investing isn't all about the dollars and cents, but instead about our emotional state, and reframing how we think, feel, and talk about money, *that* is when we will be a force that cannot be ignored. I'm telling you to invest your wealth *for* yourself in a way that will bring you closer to your own financial independence. Create a guilt-free savings schedule that your emotional self will celebrate and embrace. Watch then as your wealth mindset changes and investing in yourself becomes a vital part of your overall well-being.

REWRITING THE GUILT OF WEALTH

Let's tackle the more existential questions regarding the guilt of wealth. So many of us, maybe even you, feel as though wealth is a "dirty" word. Or you've heard the infamous "money is the root of all evil." You've been taught to believe in a narrative that tells you that you should feel guilty if you have money. And to that extent, you should also not strive to be wealthy.

Come on! *Really?*

Girlfriend, YOU DESERVE TO BE WEALTHY. Say it with me: "I DESERVE WEALTH." So many of us struggle with this universal truth. Why can't we believe the simple fact that we are deserving of wealth in our lives and we are deserving of living in a state of abundance? And let me tell you, whether you believe you live in a state of abundance or not, it's just fact. We *all* live in a state of abundance. Money is flowing all around you every day, and you can be ready to receive it, understand it, and feel empowered by it! Feeling guilty about wealth is not an option for a boss babe ready to take charge of her finances.

Whatever you've regrettably done in the past with money (e.g., misspent it, bought a really expensive treadmill that is now a glorified clothes hanger, went on an insane shopping trip after some guy dumped you, *insert any other excuse here*), who cares! Let go of any guilt and start fresh. We learn nothing from everything in life going perfectly. Let those moments of guilt be a lesson, not the way you define your relationship with money and wealth going forward. Let it go.

Why don't we feel that we deserve to have wealth? Why don't YOU feel that you deserve to be wealthy?

Is it because you feel that if you have wealth, and then by definition are wealthy, that you aren't being true to your roots? You think to yourself, "I wasn't raised that way. My mom and dad scraped every last penny together to feed my siblings and me. I feel guilty saving money while still being able to go on that girls trip that I have planned this weekend." I guarantee that your parents want more for you than what they wanted for themselves. They *want you* to enjoy your life. You deserve to enjoy your life.

Is it because you're worried that other people will think you're snooty and better than everyone else? My best friend in the entire world, Rachel, is a kindergarten school teacher. And my humble opinion, which I've told her on so many occasions, especially after she's been sitting with my oldest daughter going through the alphabet and making funny faces and hand motions to teach her what sound each letter makes, is that she should make no less than one million dollars per year. She laughs and always says, "I didn't learn to teach letter sounds because I thought it would make me rich!" Never once has Rachel made disparaging remarks about anything my wealth has afforded me. In fact, she celebrates every one of my wins—just as I do hers.

If this is a true worry of yours, may I politely suggest that you take real inventory of the women you're surrounding yourself with, and honestly, get better friends. We are who we spend our time with, so make sure you're spending your time with someone who lifts you up, not holds you back. Nobody has time for that!

Is it because deep down you don't think you've done anything special enough to warrant a beautiful savings account with a secure retirement, the means to enjoy amazing life experiences, and the nest egg to be able to afford to stay healthy and take care of your body in the best possible way? I'd be lying if I said I never had this nasty thought enter my mind too. But that's all it is—a nasty thought that creeps into our brains at two a.m. when the house is dark and a little too quiet. Believe me when I say: If you are here and serving the purpose for which you were meant to exist on this Earth, then you are doing something special every single day.

It's all a state of mind—an energy, if you will. To believe you deserve wealth is to put this thought into the universe. To put this thought into the universe is to truly believe it. To truly believe it is to live your life in a way that shows the world you are ready to take charge of the wealth you deserve. Guilt about wealth rears its ugly head in so many deceitful forms. Whether you believe you don't have enough, have too much, don't deserve it, don't know what to do with it, misspend it, feel that you shouldn't talk about it, or fear it's the root of all evil, I hereby give you the permission to stop the *negative self-talk* around wealth and embark on a new, empowering, and self-fulfilling narrative that leaves the guilt you've operated under in the past.

To #LevelTheWealth, we must first let go of this guilt that keeps us trapped in the same vicious cycle that currently gives men the upper hand when it comes to investing and pay. We must decide that we are done with the male-dominated narrative around wealth and leave our feelings of inadequacy behind. We must decide that wealth is not "just for men" and that it is not "unladylike" or "unimportant" for us to engage in crucial conversations about our wealth with our significant others. It is only then that we can start to take the first baby steps to understanding our wealth and why we deserve to have it, how to be good stewards of it, and, above all else, the reason for which we were put on this Earth not to simply exist within the construct of wealth, but to be active participants in our wealth story.

You were not put here to be a workhorse at a nine-to-five job, just hoping to pay the bills and live day by day, praying that retirement comes before the grim reaper does. You were meant for a beautiful journey! You were meant to prosper! The fact that you're even reading this book should be a universal sign to your soul that you're ready to push aside the guilt that manifests itself when you look at your bank accounts, retirement accounts, and budgeting worksheets. Enough is enough. You are ready.

So whether you're new to wealth through an amazing job with an equally amazing paycheck, or you've recently realized that your bank account is now larger than you can manage on your own, or you've got so many accounts scattered all over the place that you're not sure you even know where everything is, welcome.

Perhaps you're new to wealth through a financial windfall: a divorce, widowhood, an inheritance, a winning lottery ticket.

Or you're recently retired and wondering how to make the rest of your life work for you while managing a finite pot of money.

Or maybe you're brand new to the concept of wealth and wish to learn more about how to start on your own journey toward the wealth you deserve.

Everyone's welcome to wealth and will benefit from the guidance to come.

I invite you—yes, you, the person right now reading this book—to first stop and think about why you feel guilty about wealth. Think about the things that have been said to you about money and wealth as you've grown into the radiant, strong, woman you've become. Consider whether those things said were actually directed at you or if, more accurately, they were a projection of another's insecurity, guilt, and fear around wealth. Think about the thoughts that surround and overcome you as you think about wealth. If any of them have guilt or shame laced within them, this is the time to acknowledge those thoughts, thank them for the lessons they've taught you, and give yourself the space to leave these thoughts in the past. Because we've got stuff to do in these next chapters and I can't have you wasting your time and valuable headspace with all that negativity!

CHAPTER FOUR

BABY STEPS TO WEALTH

Now that we've let go of those negative and guilt-filled thoughts and are ready to take charge and feel empowered by our wealth, let's start with some baby steps toward achieving the life of wealth and abundance we deserve. You've got this!

The idea of baby steps is that they're so small you can't fail. They're such itty-bitty changes in your life that can truly happen overnight with a little bit of forethought. They shouldn't feel overwhelming and shouldn't be time-consuming. Eventually, the forethought needed to implement these slight mind shifts won't take any forethought at all; they'll become habits. Again, the goal is for you to take charge and feel empowered by your wealth, not to continue in a state of crippling anxiety, confusion, or wonderment by it.

We'll start with a baby step that seems easy in concept, but will take repetition to make into a sustainable habit.

BABY STEP #1: CHANGE YOUR NARRATIVE

This one really has to do with how we talk to ourselves about wealth. I constantly hear women say things like: "I'm not good with numbers," or "I'm not smart when it comes to understanding my wealth," or "I just let my partner take care of the finances because I wouldn't even know where to start." Ladies, this is the problem! Until we believe that we *are* smart about our wealth, and we *do* make good decisions when it comes to money, men will continue to have the upper hand in investing, pay, and overall wealth decision-making. What if we changed our narrative from: "I'm not smart around money" to "I'm still learning how to manage my wealth?" Even Michelangelo, inarguably one of the most impactful artists the world has ever seen, is credited with famously saying: *"Ancora imparo,"* or "I'm still learning." Even with all he had accomplished: the *David*, the ceiling of the Sistine Chapel, *The Creation of Adam*, I could go on and on, this expert artist still believed that he was in a constant state of learning. Shouldn't it then stand to reason that we're *all* still learning?!

CASE STUDY: LISA

I want to tell you about Lisa, sixty, who came to see me for guidance with her finances after a nasty divorce from her husband of thirty-five years. It was a brutal divorce, complete with a long-drawn-out litigation, name calling, and a fight over every single last dollar. Now she had to figure out what to do with the wealth that she was in charge of for the first time in her entire life. Her ex-husband had always taken care of the finances—which proved to be quite the hurdle when it came to dividing assets during the divorce because Lisa truly had no idea what wealth they had or where it was.

In the beginning of our sessions together, no matter what we started talking about in relation to wealth, she'd say, "Ugh, I just don't understand. I'm so bad at this stuff. This is so embarrassing!" Whether it was talking about her monthly budget, as she was now living on alimony, or talking about her accounts and how I had invested them for her in an effort to meet her goals, or talking about the long-term implications of her financial plan, she was constantly put off by the conversation and relied on self-deprecating humor to get through our sessions together. After giving her the space to work through these emotions, I finally looked at her during one of our meetings and said, "Hey, you are smart with your money. You're still learning, and this is all new to you. How about instead of saying: 'I'm so bad at this stuff' we say, 'I'm still learning this stuff' and know that I'm right there with you. I'm still learning about wealth every single day too.'"

I know it sounds hokey, but it's amazing how the tone and energy of our meetings changed when she started leaning in to this new narrative and vocabulary. She no longer relied on self-deprecation and a cheap laugh to get through our sessions together, and started to really open up and engage in our conversations about her wealth. She even started to smile when she came into my office and got in the habit of saying "I'm still learning about that. Do you mind explaining it to me again?" when she felt stumped on something. She is now a client I absolutely love seeing, and on days I see her name on my calendar, I get excited—it's like hanging out with a friend. She hasn't said she's "bad at wealth" in such a long time. It's honestly hard to remember that sad, broken, lost woman who came into my office three years ago. She understands her wealth and tells me that when she leaves my office she always feels a recharged sense of empowerment around her wealth. She no longer stresses about money and knows that if she ever has a question about it, she can simply pick up the phone and call me. She is still learning about her wealth. We're all still learning. She's learning with the confidence of an expert artist—just like Michelangelo.

TO RECAP: *CHANGE YOUR NARRATIVE.* "I'm still learning to manage my wealth." It's amazing how thinking differently can impact our entire life and the way it unfolds. Changing your narrative has the ability to change our attitudes, our environments, and our perception of life. Next time you feel a negative thought about money and wealth creeping in, silence that voice and let it know that you're still learning.

This next one will sound so common sense that it's going to seem insane that I write about it, but it's one that I talk about with women all the time. Ready?

BABY STEP #2: THINK BEFORE YOU SPEND

I know, I know. I probably sound like your nagging spouse, or frugal friend, or overprotective parent or sibling. But stay with me here, because we're talking about baby steps and this is one you can master!

CASE STUDY: KAYLA

Kayla, forty-five, is mom to one handsome seven-year-old boy, Cole, and wife to a head executive at a large recruiting company in New York City. Kayla is a speech pathologist and her day includes driving from location to location doing in-home therapy with children under the age of five with speech needs. Her days are long and she is physically, emotionally, and sometimes spiritually drained after hours of crawling on the floor with babies teaching them to scoot, making funny faces with a toddler in hopes that they will mimic her back, or teaching parents sign language to help them communicate with their sweet, nonverbal, autistic child.

Did I mention that Kayla, her husband, Rick, and son, Cole, live in New Jersey and Rick works in New York City? He's often gone and on the train by the time she wakes up and starts to get herself and their son ready for the day ahead. Kayla often rises, rolls over to check her calendar on her phone, sees the day is full of back-to-back appointments, and is up and at 'em right into grind mode: get up; get showered; get dressed; throw on some makeup; rouse her son; get him showered and dressed for the day; rush downstairs; feed the dog; throw a frozen waffle in the toaster for Cole; gather his backpack and homework from last night; make sure his school lunch account still has money in it; grab the waffle from the toaster; pick up the book bag, her work tote, and purse; put the dog in the crate; dash out the door; and the day has begun.

In all the rush and hustle and bustle of the morning, as she sits down in the driver's seat of her SUV and makes sure Cole is all buckled in for the ride to school, she realizes this is the third day in a row she hasn't eaten breakfast. She's tried to skip breakfast before, but this always results in a skull-crushing migraine by her ten a.m. appointment. She knows that she'll have to stop and grab something quick at her favorite large coffee shop chain right after she drops her kiddo off at school.

For the third day in a row, she pulls up to the drive-through window, orders her medium-size hot vanilla latte; a bacon, egg, and cheese biscuit; and a slice of lemon loaf for her midmorning snack. She's not proud of what this means for her health, but she's even more embarrassed when for the third day in a row the cashier tells her that her total comes to $17.36. Dutifully, she takes her credit card out of her wallet and passes it through the window to the smiling barista.

She hastily eats her breakfast biscuit and slurps down her latte while rushing to her first appointment of the morning. As the morning turns to early afternoon, Kayla has reached a moment of reprieve—lunch time. She has a few usual spots she frequents and today she decides she'll hit her favorite salad joint. When it's finally her turn to order, she chooses the southwestern chicken salad off the menu (she doesn't have the headspace after the trying appointment to piece together a salad from the "make your own" side of the menu). She decides she needs caffeine since she's on a bit of a crash after the vanilla latte this morning, so orders a Diet Coke to go with it. Kayla's feeling proud of herself. A salad and a Diet Coke for lunch isn't the worst lunchtime decision and, per usual, she swipes her credit card, followed by "Press okay" if $18.47 is the correct amount.

She takes some time to eat by herself at a small table and go over emails on her iPad. She usually finds this relaxing, but today she got a text from Rick saying he has to stay late to work on a pitch and that she and Cole should eat dinner without him. Her mood goes from relaxed to immediately grumpy, but she knows he's been working on this pitch for days and he's rarely late for dinner, so she decides to not let it ruin her afternoon. Besides, it's been a while since she's had a dinner date with Cole, so maybe they'll skip the steak and broccoli she had planned for tonight and take him out to his favorite pizza place.

That night Kayla and Cole head to dinner at the pizza parlor and, after she chooses to add a Caesar salad, garlic knots, and an indulgent slice of tiramisu for dessert, the bill comes to $60.58. Kayla pays and leaves a 20 percent tip for the friendly waitress, making the total for mommy-son date night $72.58.

Kayla hasn't thought twice about spending $108.41 on this random weekday. Life happens, right? Or, the ever famous, "cost of doing business." Kayla hasn't spent her money on anything crazy today. She *needs* to eat. But let's get real—you're reading this book not because you want me to placate you and tell you that Kayla's day was perfect and she was just doing her best, but because you want to change the way you think about mindlessly swiping the credit card on "life's necessities."

Michelle will later dissect why no part of what we just went through for Kayla's day is serving her from a health perspective, but my purpose is to walk you through what happened here from a wealth perspective and help you to create your own baby steps to better navigate this day. We've ALL had this exact day in some form or another and we've all done exactly what Kayla did. But what if we took just one second to think about what we were spending our money on throughout the day?

Using Kayla's day as an example, let's now look at injecting one small thought. What if when she got to her favorite salad spot for lunch, she thought to herself, "I already spent money on breakfast today. I'll skip the Diet Coke and have water instead." Let me break this down for you. If Kayla doesn't spend that extra $2.13 on a Diet Coke to go with her salad (and remember, she eats lunch out every single weekday since she's on the road, so that's two hundred sixty days a year), she's saving $554 per year. *That* is meaningful money! Think about how much you could do with $554 extra dollars per year! All because you stop and think before you spend. The old adage is true: "Every dollar counts." I can't wait for you to read about Kayla's slight mind shift in her daily routine from a health perspective too— the link between health and wealth is undeniable.

TO RECAP: *THINK BEFORE YOU SPEND.* Again, YOU'VE GOT THIS! This is an easy one to implement. You legitimately can't fail. All you have to do is *think* about what you're spending your money on, even if you don't make a change. You may find that thinking about it encourages you to finally skip that diet soda at lunch. But remember, the goal isn't necessarily to implement the change, it's simply to *think* about the change (literally—see what I did there). Easy.

The third baby step I want to talk with you about is one that is much easier said than done, but nonetheless, doable!

BABY STEP #3: REMEMBER, MONEY IS A TOOL

This is another one that seems easy in concept but will force you to take control of your thoughts and feelings around money when you begin feeling stressed out or overwhelmed by it. I sit with clients all the time that are so obsessed with the numbers and how much wealth they have, but I'd argue that that's not the question we should be asking at all. The question we should be asking ourselves is: "What values does having the wealth I deserve service?"

CASE STUDY: CHARLOTTE

Let me break this one down for you by telling you about Charlotte, a seventy-year-old widow who is getting ready to retire from her administrative position with her local county government after forty-five years. Charlotte has been widowed for thirteen years after a loving marriage to her late husband, David. They shared a wonderful, full life and raised three children together—all three of whom are grown and successful in their own rights and merits. Charlotte has two regrets when she looks back on her marriage. First, they didn't get more time together. They were high school sweethearts and loved each other deeply until the day he quickly and suddenly passed from a heart attack. And they didn't get to fulfill their lifelong dream of retiring together to a beach home in Delaware.

As we sat together in my office and reviewed her financial plan on the cusp of her retirement, Charlotte looked at me and asked, "Amanda, do you think I have enough money for someone my age? When you help other women who are as old as I am, do they have more money than me?" Ladies, if you've heard it once, you've heard it one million times: Comparison is the thief of joy. Also, and more to the point, who cares?! I get that people want to benchmark themselves against others to understand if what they're doing is "right" or "normal," but since money is a *tool*, there is no "right" or "normal." There's no way to benchmark yourself and your wealth against someone else's. Sure, there are articles you can find that try to provide blanket benchmarks for wealth. We see the people who have mansions, fancy cars, and designer shoes, and we consider those people "rich," but what about Charlotte? What if she realizes that all her hard work and saving toward fulfilling her own dream of buying that beach home in retirement is *her* version of "rich," and that she's the only benchmark she should be comparing herself to?

I'll give you an example from my own life. Make fun of me all you want, but one of my favorite things to do on this planet is get together with my closest girlfriends, Michelle, and my oldest daughter, Riley, and do a girls wine and craft night. I know, I know—but it's fun, and I honestly don't know if I've ever laughed as hard as when I'm with these amazing ladies talking, crafting, and enjoying a new wine that one of us discovered. We don't all make the same craft. Most of the time I want to paint something, like a cute saying on a wooden board or something seasonal (any other Christmas fanatics out there?), and one of my friends wants to build or create something from scratch. Because of this, we'll end up at the "bring your own bottle" art studio in town. There, I can paint to my heart's desire with all the wooden boards, stencils, and paints in their back room, and my friend can spend time at the glass-blowing station creating another sun catcher or jewelry dish.

The point I'm trying to make is this: Neither of us uses the same tools at all when we're in the mixed-media art studio together. I'll set myself up, as will the rest of our girlfriends, near her glass-blowing station with an assorted display of paints, different paint brushes, stencils, and a wooden board, and she is using a furnace, blow pipe, glass, tweezers, shears, and all the other fun and pokey tools she uses while she's blowing glass. At the end of the night, after all the laughs, a couple of empty bottles of wine, and all the hard work that went into that night's creation, we are all so happy with our end results. She leaves with her glass jewelry dish that she's swirled with purple and will look perfect on her nightstand, and I leave with my red and green "Merry Christmas" sign to hang in the sunroom of my home where we put our Christmas tree every December. We're both so happy with our end result   two completely different ideas of what we wanted to walk out of the studio with, two completely different sets of tools needed to create our projects, and two completely different completed projects that are both exactly what we individually wanted. And truth be told, we're both in awe of what the other person has created!

Wealth can be viewed in the same way!

Back to Charlotte. What does it matter if she's "on track" for someone her age? What does that even mean? I tell my clients all the time: a dollar is a dollar is a dollar—it's what that dollar *means* to you that is the real question. A dollar is a *tool* to help you achieve the life you want. Charlotte's retirement beach home in Delaware coupled with her specific monetary need for her expenses per month are *very* different from a woman who is a seventy-year-old widow that has been working toward a retirement mansion on a golf course in Naples, Florida, coupled with a monthly monetary need for expenses in the five-digit range. So, you see, when you lose sight of money being a tool to live the life you want, you are inviting comparison, and thereby inviting discontentment, into your thoughts and life.

Your idea of "rich" will always be different from someone else's idea of "rich." I personally don't care for use of the word "rich" at all. Again, because it can be interpreted differently from person to person and carries varying connotations based on your background, your life experiences, and your environment. We're all worthy and deserving of wealth, no matter what that means for you specifically. Change your way of thinking about money in a way that will service your wealth values. Stop letting it control the way you feel about yourself and your status in this world. None of that stuff matters as long as you're living life the way you want/need to achieve your financial goals that are ultimately driven by your values (aka, what's important to you).

The beaches of Delaware had always been such a special place for Charlotte and David. They spent summers on those beaches watching their kids grow from sweet babies to high schoolers. What better way for Charlotte to remember David and the beautiful life they shared than to buy her retirement home on the beach and spend summers with her grown children and her small grandchildren. I can think of nothing "richer" than that for Charlotte.

TO RECAP: *REMEMBER, MONEY IS A TOOL.* The next time you find yourself upset over money or feeling overwhelmed by it, remember to say to yourself after a deep breath: "Money is a tool that is helping me to live my best life. It does not define me and does not control me." And remember, this chapter is all about baby steps so small you can't fail. So, even if after you take that deep breath and say that awesome money mantra and you're still feeling stressed out, that's okay! Just continue to keep this thought in the back of your mind and you'll be amazed at how quickly it will be called to the forefront. This baby step is just about a mere two-second thought. You've got this!

The last baby step is one that you can, and will, graduate to.

BABY STEP #4: CREATE SMALL AND ACHIEVABLE WINS FOR YOURSELF

As Plato said, "Never discourage anyone who continually makes progress, no matter how slow." Progress, no matter how small and slow, is what this life is all about and how you will continue to grow meaningful wealth. By creating small, achievable wins for yourself, you are embarking on progress, and in time, no matter how much time, you will see change.

Now, this is NOT the time for major goal setting. None of this:

- "I'm going to save $100 this week by not going out to lunch at all!"
- "I'm going to write down every single thing I spend my money on so I can create an ultra-comprehensive budget."
- "I'm going to walk into my HR/payroll department and ask to increase my 401(k) contributions to the maximum allowable this year!"
- "I'm going to stop myself from buying anything on Amazon for the rest of the month!"

All the above sentences are a quick way to become disappointed with yourself, disillusioned with the progress you're making, and fail at even starting your journey toward wealth empowerment. You're probably tired of me saying it, but this is all about starting with, yes, baby steps so small you can't fail.

Let's think back to Kayla from the beginning of this chapter. Remember when we did the math on her daily diet soda with lunch: two hundred sixty weekdays multiplied by $2.13 per diet soda equaled an expense to her bottom line of $554 per year. What if her one small achievable win, not only for her wealth, but for her health, too, was to cut the weekday diet soda and switch to water at lunch?

I know some of you right now are freaking out and thinking, "Amanda, what?! You said small and achievable! There's no way I'm giving up my diet soda at lunch!" Got it! You may not be there yet and that's okay. *Baby Step #2: Think Before You Spend* is calling your name, chica. You can master it and graduate to this one soon! I know it!

For those of you who are thinking to yourselves, *Okay . . . I might see where this goes, though I'm not sure if I could go a whole week without a diet soda at lunch,* that is fine too! Progress, no matter how slow, is nothing to discourage. What if you restructured the "no soda" rule to only three days versus all five? The math on that is: 156 days multiplied by $2.13 per diet soda for a total of $332 per year. That's a yearlong savings to you of $322 dollars! What could you do with that leftover money? And remember, it's not just about the money of it. As Michelle will explain, cutting back on the diet soda and switching to water just three days a week can do wonders for your health, too!

This baby step isn't just about not spending money. It's also about saving money. What if your savings-related baby step is to simply start by saving just $10 per week? I don't care who you are, what your job is, what bills you have, etc.—everyone spends at least $10 per week on something frivolous and unnecessary.

Think about even as recently as yesterday . . . maybe you stopped off at HomeGoods on the way home from work and ended up buying a pumpkin spice candle because it smelled so good and got you in the mood for the fall, or you ran into Target for "just one thing" and ended up walking out with that coffee mug because it had the most inspirational quote on it to get your morning started off on the right foot—plus it was on the clearance rack so how could you leave it? Or you took the time to pack your lunch for work, but your coworker asked if you wanted to walk over to the deli and grab a sandwich, so you ditched your lunch in the fridge and went out instead.

Again, none of this is to make you feel guilty about those small moments, but to remind you that we all have an extra $10 per week, if not more, that we can be using more efficiently to service our wealth and help us to build the lives we deserve. Ten dollars per week is $520 per year. That's $520 per year that you could put into a savings account at the bank, or an investment account, or your company's retirement plan. I tell people all the time: *Saving something is better than saving nothing!* If you haven't yet retired and aren't saving any of your money, this baby step is for you. Start small—so small you can't fail. You won't miss $10 per week, I promise.

What is one small change you can make in your life right now that can add real dollars to the bottom line? What is one small change that will turn into a real win for you tomorrow, or even today? Everyone has a vice. *Everyone.* No one makes it through the week without giving in here or there. But the point of this is to become more aware of these small moments and make one small change that will turn into an achievable win. You can do it! And be honest with yourself—don't phone this one in. It's a small change that can have a big impact on the way you continue to build your wealth, how you perceive your wealth, and your overall relationship with wealth. Progress is what this is all about, and you're making progress!

> **TO RECAP:** *CREATE SMALL AND ACHIEVABLE WINS FOR YOURSELF.* Set a very small goal for yourself that you know you can achieve! This should be something that you will "win" at today, tomorrow, or at maximum, within a week. Celebrate this small win! Watch as this, and your other small wins, turn into real progress for your continued wealth.

Before we move on, let's revisit the four baby steps in order, the ones that are so small you can't fail and will guide you in the beginning of your wealth empowerment and financial independence journey.

1. Change Your Narrative
2. Think Before You Spend
3. Remember, Money Is a Tool
4. Create Small, Achievable Wins

As you start to take these baby steps in your own life, remember to be patient and to show yourself kindness when implementing these small changes. They're so small you can't fail—just remember that. You can't "change your narrative" in the wrong way. Just thinking about money any way but negatively is the "right" way. You can't "think before you spend" in a wrong way. Just thinking about taking your credit card or money out of your wallet when you go to purchase something is the "right" way to think—even if you still buy whatever it is you're taking time to think about. I think about everything I spend my money on. Some people may find that exhausting, but it's truly just a habit for me at this point. And this doesn't have to be negative! I think about how I'm spending my money on a shared experience when my husband and I put the deposit down for a family vacation. I acknowledge that this is in service of our shared value of family and love. The act of thinking before you spend can be extraordinarily empowering when you are spending your money on things that truly serve your life in the best way possible.

This beautifully transitions me to Baby Step #3. You can't "remember that money is a tool" incorrectly. It's a thought that will over time take charge of the way you view money. It will help you to create a powerful interdependence *with* money and wealth that will ultimately give you the ability to see money as a service to your life, instead of the definer of your life. And lastly, graduating to small, achievable wins. You can only fail at this by setting your bar too high. By choosing to start small, you are telling yourself: "I'm showing up for myself. I'm making myself a priority. I'm in it for the long haul."

Once you begin taking these precise, preplanned baby steps, you will get more comfortable, more confident, and see small changes. You'll think to yourself, "I can't believe it. I'm actually doing it!" These baby steps, or habit changes, will then transform into bigger steps and then bigger leaps that will finally propel you to reach out for the life of wealth and abundance that you deeply deserve.

Now's the time to plan and take those first baby steps. As small as they may seem, these are the steps that will begin to change your life forever.

CHAPTER FIVE

BALANCE

Life is a balancing act—from juggling our roles as mother, wife, sister, friend, employee, business owner, and everything in between, to juggling our expectations, goals, and values within the world around us. There are some areas of our lives that we've learned to balance with such expertise that we no longer even have to consciously think about balancing as an employed skill set, while other areas seem in such disarray because we're overwhelmed, don't understand what we're supposed to be working toward, or we think someone else will eventually relieve us of that burden.

Wealth, and your management of it, is also a balancing act. In fact it's perhaps one of the most complex balancing acts we deal with on a day-to-day basis that has the power to affect the way our lives play out right before our eyes. Balancing your wealth is all about living your life more mindfully while also realizing you're an exquisite human being existing in this world for a moment in time. You're meant to, and deserving of, the day-to-day enjoyment of: brunch with bottomless mimosas, giving gifts to a girlfriend on her birthday, an all-inclusive vacation with your family, and all the other lifetime experiences that make this life worth living and creating the memories that last us throughout our lifetimes. And, you're also worthy, and deserving, of growing old knowing that you can retire without having to worry about the finances. *Life is a balancing act.* You can absolutely learn, and master, the art of balancing your wealth through spending for today, saving for tomorrow, *and* investing for the future.

SPENDING FOR TODAY

YOLO! Am I right? We've all seen those social media accounts that preach the joys of quitting your job and backpacking across every crevice of the planet in search of the perfect picture to post on social media, while doing odd jobs here or there to stay afloat. Or we've seen our friend walk into the restaurant that we're meeting at with a brand-new $2,000 designer purse. Or we've watched as our neighbor put their house up for sale because they're moving into a community of McMansions across town.

Whenever we think about these people, we immediately wonder to ourselves, "What are they doing that I'm not? How are they affording that?" Or: "I wish I had that type of freedom, but I just can't picture taking that leap." And sometimes simply: "They spent THAT on WHAT?!" Admit it. We've all had those thoughts. Even if it's our best friend, our minds can't help but go to that place. It's human. To varying degrees, we're all obsessed with status and what the other person next to us is doing and how they're doing it, why we should also be doing it, or how we can achieve the same things.

In the "perfect picture" society that we currently live in, we only see the highlight reel that someone is willing to post online. We only see the perfect designer handbag and her one-thousand-watt smile as she shows it off to her girlfriends. We only see the perfect family, totally abuzz with excitement, across the street as movers load all their belongings for the trip to their newly built mansion across town.

What we *don't* see is that the twenty-year-old, travel-seeking Instagram influencer had to take a job cleaning fish in the back of a seafood market in Bangkok with a wake-up time of two a.m. after sleeping in a six-hundred-square-foot apartment with four other roommates. She can't wait to get out of Bangkok, but she hasn't yet saved enough for her next flight to the Philippines. You wouldn't know any of that from the overly filtered pictures she just posted of her posing in front of the Wat Arun

Ratchawararam Temple of Dawn at what seemed to be the exact right moment as the first light of the morning sun reflected off the surface of the temple showing its other-worldly, signature, pearly iridescence. While you were sitting there thinking, "Wow, I can't believe she's living that life! I clearly need to change the way I'm living!" she's over in Bangkok thinking, "Wow . . . I can't believe I'm living this life . . . I clearly need to change the way I'm living."

What about your girlfriend that walked in swinging that $2,000 designer purse on the crook of her arm? You have no idea that she bought that purse without any regard to her family's current financial picture. After all, why should she care? She works hard and deserves to treat herself without thinking about anyone else for once, right? Maybe. But before she left her house to meet you at the restaurant, she and her husband had a huge blow-out fight because the credit card statement just arrived in the mail and they had talked on numerous occasions about her spending habits. Her husband pleads with her for the fifth month in a row to stop the over-the-top spending. He explains that he's so stressed out about their credit card statement each month that he's stopped contributing to his employer's retirement plan to ensure they have enough cash to cover the bills each month. She argues that she has a right to buy herself nice things. She does so much for the family that the least he could do is turn a blind eye to her fancy toys. After all, he just bought a new set of golf clubs three months ago! He asks that they simply communicate more when she feels the need to go purchase a big-ticket item so they can make sure it fits within that month's budget. As she walks out of the front door, she rolls her eyes and mutters under her breath, "This is so unfair and is such a double standard!"

And those neighbors of yours that just sold their home to move into that McMansion across town? What you saw was a picture-perfect family beaming with excitement at their next big adventure. What you didn't see was the client I had to discontinue working with within a year of buying their new home. What you didn't see was that between the new furniture, increased utility bills, a need to keep up with their new neighbors, "The Joneses," and the new private school tuition that inherently came with being a member of that community, they had no choice but to clear out their accounts with me to make sure all the bills were being paid. They left my office that day disappointed in themselves for letting their spending get so out of control, and saddened that the wealth they had worked so hard to build was gone in the blink of an eye.

I'm not saying the above three scenarios are a blanket for how all these people live and the turmoil they face, but I am saying I see it A LOT. In today's world of instant gratification and "Look at me!" we often fail to reconcile that while living for today *is* fun and exciting, we must also financially support the person that we will be tomorrow. It's hard to start off every day at zero dollars, or even worse, in the negative. While you're busy living this beautiful life to the fullest and savoring and cherishing all the amazing things and experiences this world has to offer, remember the woman that's going to wake up tomorrow trusting that you made the right decisions today.

SAVING FOR TOMORROW

I'm sure you've heard the good old rule of thumb that you should keep four to six months' worth of your monthly expenses in a savings account for an emergency. I like to call this a "rainy day fund," for when the hot water heater dies, or the car is making that weird sound and the mechanic slides a hefty bill your way after you go in to get it checked out, or the dog eats an entire pack of sugar-free gum and spends four days at the emergency vet so they can monitor his insulin levels. (The vet incident really happened to my husband and me. It's true what they say—Labs eat EVERYTHING. But I wouldn't trade him for the world, even though my husband looked physically ill when we got the bill for his all-inclusive four-day stay.)

Emergencies happen, and you should always be prepared with a hefty nest egg in the bank just in case life spins out of control for a bit. The quickest way to regain control of these situations is to have the peace of mind that you can pay for the emergency outright versus having to put this speed bump on a credit card that you'll be paying off for the next five years.

However, we all know that person who just seems a little too frugal for their own good, right? You know the one I'm talking about. The person who has an awesome job with a great salary, her house is completely paid off, she lives alone, and yet is constantly worried that the world is going to end because "Have you seen the state of this economy and what is going on in the world of politics?" She doesn't trust anyone and will continue to hoard her money away until God knows when.

You try to get her to loosen the purse strings and join you for a night out for dinner and drinks during Restaurant Week. She balks at the $100 prix-fixe menu at the chic new sushi restaurant downtown and lets you know that you're more than welcome to join her at her house for dinner instead. Ugh, dinner at Kathy's again?! You've known Kathy for the past twenty years and she is a dear friend, but seriously, if your only option for the fourth time in a row is to stop at the local liquor store to pick up a bottle of rosé and sit down to another homemade meatloaf and mashed potato (her self-declared specialty) dinner, you're going to scream.

These people tend to have savings accounts at a size you wouldn't believe, but are also some of the most nervous and anxious people I've ever met. They are constantly worried that another economic recession will happen. I'm sure you remember 2008 when the market took a complete dive into the Dumpster and the entire economy slid into a valley that it took a decade to climb out of. These types of people are constantly worried they won't have enough. They are constantly worried that the world is going to crumble around them and the only safety they will have is cold hard cash. Let me tell you something: If the entire world is crumbling around us and the market takes a total Dumpster dive that it can't climb out of, cold hard cash isn't going to save you, and in fact, the zombie apocalypse has probably started, and from what I've seen on TV, they don't seem to care about money.

Some of these people are so busy saving for tomorrow that they're forgetting to live for today. They impose these rules of frugality on themselves in which they alienate themselves from life's most magical experiences shared with the people they love most. These are the people who die with multi-millions in their bank accounts, and you remember them as always at home on the couch watching TV, or walking around the neighborhood, or shopping for the best deal on something, even if waiting for the best deal meant going without something they needed for a couple of months, or saying no to vacations because it's an "unnecessary expense." But wow, those multimillions in the bank really do them a load of good in the afterlife, right?

Ladies, just like how overspending without regard is a detriment to the amazing, secure, and financially independent life you deserve, so is oversaving to the detriment of your life's enjoyment today.

The idea of swinging so far over to the savings side of the spending vs. saving pendulum doesn't just apply to those people with tight pockets and big bank accounts. Think about that young lady just starting out in her career who makes one financial mistake and then completely overcorrects. While correcting is a good thing, overcorrecting is not.

My sister-in-law is the biggest fan of coffee I've ever met. Iced, latte, black, steaming hot . . . heck, she'll even drink it lukewarm as long as it's coffee. She works in D.C., for the United

States Post Office in the forensics department, and is often pulling long hours. Due to the long hours and very early mornings while working on a specific case, she got into the habit of stopping at the adorable, hipster coffee shop right by her office every morning for a coffee on the way in. It was only a couple of bucks here and there, yes?

One evening when she was over for dinner, as she visits every so often to hang out and see her nieces (read: Bring them gifts and spoil them with treats and five different bedtime stories when Riley, my oldest, knows it's usually two), I asked her how work was going. She mentioned that she was still focused on that big project and pulling really long hours. But then she said, "I had to cut out the coffee every single morning, though. I didn't realize what it was doing to my credit card and I'd rather get rid of my student loans."

She has some pretty serious undergraduate and master's degree student loans and they're always at the forefront of our conversations when she confides in me about her finances. She mentioned that she had gone back to making coffee at home and bringing her travel mug with her. Now recall, she *loves* coffee, and trying all the new and seasonal flavors, so I couldn't imagine a world in which she wasn't ever stopping off for a cup of joe that had some razzle-dazzle to it. I'm a financial planner by trade, but a realist and lover of life by heart, so what I said to her next certainly goes against some of the financial literature currently on bookshelves that tells you to "skip buying the latte." I told her, "That's awesome and I'm proud of you for realizing what it was doing to your expenses. But remember to live your life. You don't have to completely stop getting coffee out. It's one of your favorite things to do! Why don't you go back to treating yourself but make it a Friday thing to celebrate the weekend or a Monday thing to get you through the Monday morning blues. You're chipping away so much at your student loans by putting extra principal down each month. Buying a coffee out once a week won't ruin your finances."

She looked at me puzzled at first, but then a look of relief washed over her face. "Really?"

"Really," I said.

This life is for the living and what is the point of saving every single last dollar if you're not enjoying today? When you can balance the right amount of spending with the right amount of saving, your wealth will become a powerful tool that you will have the master skill set to manage on your own, or more preferably, ask for help in managing. Your wealth will become a source of empowerment for you and service your current and future self in a way that creates a balanced approach that will carry you throughout your life.

INVESTING FOR THE FUTURE

Last, but certainly not least, we need to talk about investing for the future. Yes, you need to spend appropriately today, and save appropriately for tomorrow, but what about investing for your long-term future self? What about the woman who you will be twenty or thirty years from now, if not longer? What can you do today and tomorrow to make sure that you are setting her up for the life of wealth and abundance that she deserves? We know it's not spending every last dollar we make. Maybe it's saving every single dollar we make in a savings account at the bank? Nope, certainly not that one either. Saving for tomorrow is smart, but investing for the future is powerful.

Remember Kathy who saves every dollar she makes to her bank account out of fear? The fear of the market crashing, or that she won't have enough, which makes her hoard all her money into a savings account. This can almost be looked at as a self-fulfilling prophecy for Kathy. By saving all her money to a simple savings account at the bank, she is essentially getting no growth on her money. It's not invested in any stocks or bonds and doesn't have the opportunity for any real growth beyond maybe 1 percent per year, if she's lucky, that the bank is giving her in interest. So, every year, she sees her bank account stay stagnant, never growing besides the money she continues to deposit. In retirement, her only option will be to withdraw money from her bank account as she needs it, which will cause the constant depletion of the principal of the account. The account will never have the opportunity to "make back" the money that she withdraws from it. There is no *growth* on the money for her to live off of; she is simply living off the exact number of dollars she puts in today and tomorrow. When you look at it that way, of course she's nervous about not having enough! It's a finite pool of money and she knows exactly how much she's put in and thus exactly how much she will have to live off in retirement.

And to be quite frank, the argument could absolutely be made that she is actually collecting a negative interest rate on this money, as inflation will eat away at these stagnant dollars. We all hear the term "inflation" thrown around, but what does that actually mean? Simply put, inflation is a general increase in prices and therefore a lessening of purchasing power of your dollar. Historically, inflation pushes prices up about 2.5 percent per year on average. A quick example: a gallon of milk today may cost $3.79, but next year that same gallon of milk may cost $3.89. Not overly significant year over year, but over twenty years, you can see how inflation starts to matter. And if prices are increasing, but the cash in your bank is not because you aren't getting a growth return on your money in the bank, you are effectively operating in an environment where your money at the bank is not growing at the rate of the world around you.

Inflation affects not only our dollars, but the entire economy. Think about the price of a house twenty years ago, or the price of a car twenty years ago. In 2000, the price of a midrange SUV was around $20,000. Today, it's easy to spend $40,000 on a mid-range SUV, and that's before you add in all the bells and whistles! So, what if twenty years ago, you decided to put $20,000 dollars away in a savings account for an SUV in twenty years. You would be pretty bummed out to find that your $20,000 in today's dollars could buy you a low-line sedan.

What if you invested that money for a long-term need? What if instead of saving all your money in the bank, for retirement, or a new car or house somewhere down the line, you invested your money in an account in a mix of stocks and bonds?

Let's sidebar for a quick education session. If you know what stocks and bonds are, use this section as a refresher. But if the idea is new to you, I'm going to walk through stocks and bonds in "plain English"—a request I get from women all the time, no matter their wealth!

WHAT IS A STOCK?

A stock is a type of investment that means you own part of a company. When you purchase a company's stock, you're purchasing a small piece of that company, called a share. Your share(s) of stock entitle you to part of that company's earnings throughout the year.

Example: Let's say I wanted to invest in a chocolate company because I love using their chocolate chips for baking (read: eating them straight out of the bag) and believe they have good tenure since they've been around for a long time. I would do my research, make sure I wanted to invest in that company, and then purchase some shares of the chocolate company through a trading platform. Or, more preferably, I would talk to my financial planner about this and we'd work together on picking stock investments that best fit my financial goals.

How do I make money off stock? Using the example above, I would follow the performance of the chocolate company's

100

stock throughout the year in hopes that it does well enough to grow in share price. Let's say I bought stock in the chocolate company for $10 per share, and one year later when I'm ready to sell it, it's trading at $25 per share. Awesome! I just made a $15 per share profit.

That's stock, It's not some insane, crazy thing that needs demystifying. It doesn't have to be a source of confusion. It's simply you investing in a company that you believe in with the hopes that your money will grow for you over time as a way of building your wealth. Stock is generally considered a riskier type of investment since you are betting on the growth and performance of a company.

WHAT IS A BOND?

A bond is a contract between two parties—you (the investor) and a company or government that needs to borrow a lot of money. These companies or governments issue bonds and investors buy them (thereby giving the companies or governments the money they need). At some point, the company or government is required to pay back the money that they borrowed from you with interest attached. Bonds are generally considered a low-risk type of investment compared to stock since there is a "guarantee" of payment. Disclaimer: bonds *can* default, meaning the investor doesn't get paid back. This can happen if funding of a government project is cut short, a company starts to fail, and a myriad of other reasons.

Example: Let's say your county government wanted to issue some bonds in an effort to borrow a large amount of money to fix some of the roadways. The government would issue some bonds, and you, the investor, would purchase some of the bonds which would show you the terms of the loan, interest payments that will be paid along the way, and the time at which the loan must be paid back to you (maturity date). If everything goes well and the roadway project doesn't default (run out of money, lose funding, etc.) then you would get some income along the way (interest) from your county government for letting them borrow your money for a set term. Then, at the bond's maturity date, the money that you loaned out would be paid back to you.

That's a bond—a less risky type of investment in which you loan your money out to a government or company with the expectation of that organization paying you interest along the way along with a return of your original principal loan at the maturity date.

Now that we're finished with that quick education session, let's go back to Kathy. Instead of hoarding her money at the bank, what if she left herself a nice, comfortable cushion at the bank and then invested some of her money in accounts with a mix of stocks and bonds in an effort to grow her wealth over time? Her goal for investment could be to simply beat inflation. Meaning, she mostly wanted to invest in low-risk bonds, with a little bit of stock mixed in, in an effort to make more than 2.5 percent on her money a year. If we look at the stock market from 1966–2015, we see that stocks grew, on average, 9.69 percent per year before inflation. So historically, we know that if Kathy would've invested her money instead of hoarding it at the bank, she should've done well over a 2.5 percent annual return on her money, and maybe wouldn't feel so nervous and scared when she looked at her pot of money. She'd know that her pot of money isn't finite; it is constantly growing (yes, even when the market goes down, it will always come back up, you will just have to wait it out), and this would perhaps give her the peace of mind she needed to loosen the purse strings today because she is invested for the future.

Every facet of life requires balance and this includes wealth. So many women who come to me for financial guidance are taking the first steps to finding this balance for themselves. And honestly, until I meet you and we sit face-to-face and you tell me about your financial values and goals, I won't know what your exact balance should be. The other thing I always tell my clients while we're working through the right spending, saving, and investing balance for them is: "Tell me what day you're going to die and I can have this worked out for you to the dollar!" None of us have a crystal ball and none of us know when our last day on this planet will be. If I had that ability, I would be in a very different profession!

I've watched a client work so hard for retirement and then die two weeks after his last day. I've watched as a woman came into my office completely lost and grief-stricken after her husband suddenly died of a heart attack. I've watched as grown children, and now beneficiaries of their late parents' estates come to me and say, "I wish my mom and dad had met with you. They wouldn't have been so worried about money all the time and could've relaxed a little. I don't need this money from them. I wish they would've used it on themselves."

The only thing we can do is everything in our power to set ourselves up for success today, tomorrow and in the long-term future. For your girlfriend with the expensive purse and the overdue bills, success may come in the form of speaking with her husband regarding big purchases and making a savings plan for these big-ticket items that fit in well with his goal of saving toward his employer retirement plan. For Kathy, success may come in the form of investing some of her money in stocks and bonds for growth which would give her some breathing room when it comes to loosening the purse strings and having dinner out with her girlfriend every once in a while.

The right wealth balance for you and your goals is something that I urge you to work through with a financial planner. The right financial planner will care about you and will want to listen to your financial values and goals. They will want to make sure you're enjoying this beautiful life you've been given and are using your wealth in a way that best serves you. The right balance of spending for today, saving for tomorrow, and investing for the future is a puzzle. It is multitasking at its finest. We all need more multitasking and juggling like we need another hole in the head. However, I believe the saying is true: "If you want something done, give it to a busy woman." You, no matter how busy you are, have the ability to reach out and ask for help to better understand your wealth balance.

From a holistic standpoint, finding balance in your wealth is a huge component to finding overall balance in your health and life. Self-care comes down to the mental state of our health. While yes, having a balanced wealth plan contributes to a large part of our overall well-being, have you ever paused to take a mental self-reflection of what's going on upstairs in that beautiful brain of yours? Do you find yourself so tangled up, overwhelmed by thoughts of figuring out your wealth and finances? Girlfriend, there is nothing more empowering than a solid spending, saving, and investing plan that you can wrap your head around, commit to, and see through to fruition. Start putting yourself first and get this figured out. Your happiness, your health, and your wealth depend on it.

CHAPTER SIX

YOUR WEALTH EMPOWERMENT PLAN

B oss babes, it's now time to get to the good stuff—a full and actionable Wealth Empowerment Plan that will kick-start your journey to financial empowerment. As always, I recommend you work with a financial planner, but the wealth plan below will be a great place to start, refresh, or check in on your current wealth plan, *no matter what stage you're in*, so banish any regretful or negative thoughts of "I don't have that yet," or "I can't imagine getting myself there." The goal is to create and set a plan for continued wealth building. Remember, progress, no matter how slow, is still progress that should be applauded. You've got this! Time to #LevelTheWealth and make financial planning, wealth management, and investing a woman's domain.

STEP ONE: FIND YOUR WEALTH WHY

To genuinely create a plan and stick with it, you must first understand *why* you want to start your wealth empowerment journey in the first place. What values are you serving for your personal or professional self through your wealth?

For example, when I think about wealth, the value I tie it to is family. I am on a mission to make smart decisions in regard to my wealth, because I want to be able to care for my family in the best way possible. I want to enjoy various shared experiences with them. I do not want to be a burden to my children in my old age. My "why" isn't because I want a big savings account, or that I want to go on a fancy vacation to Bora Bora. Those are meaningless and empty reasons to set a goal, and therefore make it so easy to fail. If my goal is simply to go to Bora Bora, I doubt I'm going to put daily, weekly, and monthly effort into that goal since it's not backed by anything real or emotional. But if I reframe that goal with a value like "This year, my goal is to save enough money to take my family to Bora Bora to celebrate Mom's seventieth birthday," then we're onto something. It's going to be a lot harder for me to ignore that savings goal when it serves my value of family.

The "why" that I hear women say most often is, "I just want to make sure I have enough money so I'm not a burden to my children if I have a health event in my old age." Ladies, I get this one A LOT. Especially since, as I discussed before, the average age of widowhood is fifty-nine and the average life expectancy for a U.S. female is eighty-one, as measured in 2019.[2] Widows are often left wondering who will take care of them. They may have just spent the last year of their life caring for their sick and now deceased husband, and it has suddenly occurred to them that they no longer have their husband to do the same for them. See, the goal here isn't "to have a huge retirement account." The goal is "to have a large enough retirement account that the children I love do not have to put their own family financial goals and values on hold to service mine."

Your specific "why" or "whys" can be very different from your sisters', mom's, friends', or coworkers'. It is different and unique in the same way we are all different and unique. It can be so empowering to share your "wealth why" with a friend, but don't compare them. As unique individuals, we are all working to service different values and different end goals. Find *your* "wealth why," commit to it, and stay true to it. You will find that working toward your "why" is a lot more fulfilling (and effective) than working toward an empty goal.

STEP TWO: SET YOUR GOALS FOR WEALTH

Goal setting backed by values follows a simple and easy to remember formula to ensure success. You may even have heard of it before. Set SMART goals. And no, I'm not shouting at you to *wise up*. It's an acronym. SMART goals are **S**pecific, **M**easurable, **A**chievable, **R**ealistic, and **T**imely. Let's get to work on setting some SMART goals as the North Star for your wealth empowerment journey.

CASE STUDY: CHLOE AND STEVE

As an example throughout this exercise, let's focus on Chloe and Steve. Chloe, forty-two, is a high school social studies teacher who makes $75,000 per year, and her husband, Steve, forty-nine, is a superintendent of schools who makes $120,000 per year. They have two kids: Grace, thirteen, and Luke, eleven. Chloe and Steve are experts at living beneath their means, and have been their entire lives, as Steve has always believed in fast-paying their debt obligations. Through their hard work together, they paid off their first townhome and now rent it out to a steady renter, and have recently refinanced their current home of thirteen years down to a ten-year mortgage. Steve and Chloe hate carrying debt and have always focused on getting rid of it as quickly as possible.

In focusing so intently on debt reduction for the past fifteen years, they have come to the realization, as Steve's fiftieth birthday is looming on the horizon, that they haven't been putting away as much as they should've for retirement and now need to kick saving for retirement into high gear. After all, they don't want to work forever and always dreamed of retiring at the same time so that they can enjoy retirement to its fullest, even though Chloe is seven years younger than Steve. Using value-backed goal setting, let's work through their goal of saving more money into their 403(b) plans at work for retirement.

SPECIFIC

An empty and general goal for Chloe and Steve would look something like this: "We want to save more for retirement." A *specific goal* may look like this: "We will each save 10 percent of our salaries into our respective 403(b) accounts at work, so we can fulfill our dream of retiring together at Steve's age of sixty-five."

The more specific you make your values-backed goal, the better. The ingredients to a specific wealth goal are the following: the value you are servicing, the specific account(s) you will be saving/investing to and for what purpose, the dollar amounts you will be committing to servicing that goal, and the time frame to which you will commit yourself to this goal.

For Chloe and Steve, it breaks down like this:

- *Value being serviced*: Joint retirement, love, togetherness
- *Specific account being used for savings*: Each of their 403(b) accounts at work
- *Purpose*: Have enough money in their retirement accounts at Steve's age sixty-five so that they can both retire at the same time and live a comfortable and happy life while not worrying about the finances
- *Dollar amount being committed to the goal*: 10 percent of each of their gross salaries
- *Time frame for goal completion*: Steve's age sixty-five

Now it's your turn. Think about a goal you'd like to build your wealth toward and think through how to make it a specific goal. Write your specific goal down. HANDWRITE IT, as I've always found when clients see it in *their own writing* it's less easy to ignore. And then put your handwritten goal note somewhere you'll see it every single day. Seeing your goal every day will remind you what you're working toward and why.

MEASURABLE

Chloe and Steve will need to come up with a system for measuring their efforts against their desired goal and outcome.

Their efforts are easy to measure in this instance. Either they will each contribute 10 percent of their salaries to their respective 403(b) plans, or they won't.

Their desired goal and outcome of retiring at Steve's age sixty-five may be trickier to measure, but through working with a financial planner on a long-term plan, they will easily be able to see if their savings rate of 10 percent each to their 403(b)s is enough to make their joint retirement dream become a reality.

How can you measure *your* efforts against your desired wealth goals and outcomes? Can you measure on your own, or will you need professional help?

ACTIONABLE

What actions can Chloe and Steve take to ensure they meet their short-term goal of saving 10 percent of each of their salaries to their respective 403(b)s and their overall long-term goal of joint retirement?

In the immediate future, they will be accountable to each other for taking the action of going to their HR department on Monday morning to get the correct payroll deferral form to increase their 403(b) contribution amounts to 10 percent of their respective salaries. For their long-term goal of joint retirement, an action item for them will be to see a financial planner and work through a long-term financial plan to ensure their short-term goal of saving 10 percent is servicing their long-term goal in a meaningful way to ensure success.

Think about what *your* actions for meeting your specific goal(s) will be. What actions will you take today to ensure success in the short-term? What actions will you take today to ensure success in the long-term?

REALISTIC

Is Chloe and Steve's goal of each saving 10 percent of their salary to their respective 403(b)s in an effort to retire jointly in a comfortable and financially sound fashion realistic? Let's examine this in the short-term and the long-term.

In the short-term, this will be fairly easy to assess. If saving 10 percent of Chloe's salary and 10 percent of Steve's salary to their retirement accounts will mean that they can't make their mortgage payment, then the goal is completely unrealistic. However, if they've run the numbers and recrafted their budget appropriately and feel confident in their increased savings level, then they're right on target and their short-term goal can be checked off!

In the long-term, we can assess the idea of this goal being realistic on a more theoretical level. If Steve will be turning fifty and has only ever accumulated $75,000 into his 403(b), and at Chloe's age of forty-two, her 403(b) account balance is $50,000, then we can safely say that the idea of jointly retiring at Steve's age of sixty-five and enjoying their same standard of living will not be attainable over the longevity of their life from retirement into their next thirty-ish years. However, if Steve's retirement account has already accumulated $400,000 and Chloe's 403(b) has accumulated $325,000, with their increased savings to their 403(b)s amongst other factors, the idea of joint retirement at Steve's age sixty-five may be completely realistic in the long term.

For wealth goals, it is extremely important to get help from a professional financial planner, or to get your financial plan reviewed by a professional financial planner if you're more of a do-it-yourselfer, to make sure that you are thinking realistically about your goals and your desired outcomes. Growth rates, expenses, incomes, current accounts and investments (all things I'll discuss later) will tie in to how realistic your long-term goal is.

TIMELY

Most wealth goals will have a concrete time cap on them due to the nature of money being a tool to live your best and most deserved life.

Chloe and Steve have a time cap of Steve's age sixty-five. They will save to their 403(b)s until Steve is sixty-five years old and then they will retire together. Again, through working with a financial planner, they will ensure that fifteen years of their new "high gear" savings increase is enough to make their joint retirement dreams become a reality.

The more immediate time cap however, is making sure they get their payroll deferral forms into their HR department ASAP so Chloe and Steve can start their journey of contributing 10 percent of their salaries to their 403(b)s. If they fail to do this, or take too long to complete the necessary paperwork—and we all know how that goes; the long black-and-white form that HR gives us just keeps getting shuffled to the bottom of the pile— then they will be holding themselves back from starting to achieve their wealth goal and will not have acted in a timely fashion for their wealth success.

QUICK TIP: After about two paychecks, you will barely notice that you've increased your savings to your employer retirement plan and that your net, or take-home pay, is reduced. Yeah, it'll hurt the first one or two paychecks, but after that it just becomes a way of life. Give yourself time to get adjusted to the new actions that will make your short- and long-term goals become a reality, and don't let yourself become discouraged within the first month or two. The short-term goals you fulfill and succeed in today are amazing steps toward the overall progress of your long-term goals in the future. Are the goals you're setting for yourself timely? Will you have time to do the things you need to do for your wealth goals?

All right, now that you've got a SMART goal to work with, let's see how that ties in to your net worth. As I've mentioned throughout our goal setting work together: A value-backed goal is great, but knowing how it fits into your financial plan is what it's all about, sister!

STEP THREE: KNOW YOUR NET WORTH

Sorry, but I'm going to start this off on a heavy foot. Remember when I told you that the average age of widowhood is fifty-nine, as measured by the U.S. Census Bureau? Ladies, this number is shocking and it's real. I give this statistic frequently to my clients and friends and they cringe . . . women and men alike. But it's something that we have to talk about and put some serious thought around.

If something happened to your spouse, do you know your net worth and where all your accounts are located? And do you have access to them (usernames, passwords etc.)? If you're single, do you know where your accounts are? Do you know where all the retirement accounts are? Do you know where all the cash in the banks is? Do you know all your outstanding liabilities: mortgage(s), car note(s), etc.? I don't say this as in "Are there accounts that your spouse is keeping from you?", but along the lines of, have you both sat down to understand your full net worth together? Or, if you're single, have you taken time to hop off the hamster wheel for a minute to really make sure you've kept track of all your pots of money along the way?

So many times I sit down with a couple, and usually the wife will say about the husband, "He knows where all our stuff is . . . just ask him any questions about any of this," or "I'm not good at this stuff and I don't like it." I literally sat down with a woman to help her set up *her* retirement account and she said to me, "Thanks for doing this with me, but I'm just going to turn around and give all my login and contribution information to my husband. I hate dealing with this stuff and I trust that you two are just following through on our financial plan." I verbatim said, "Hey, girl, that is totally fine, I just want you to know where your account is, how much you're contributing from your paycheck, that we have a mix of stocks and bonds set up for you, and you can call me at any time with questions." She was happy with this and I'm happy that she knows where the account is and that there is a methodology in place for how it's being invested.

People always laugh when I tell that story and say something along the lines of, "Weren't you offended you just did all that work for her and she didn't care?" My answer is *always* "Absolutely not!" I know that she was extremely appreciative of me helping her set up her account, she just wasn't going to keep track of it every day. But guess what? I was keeping track of it for her. She knew that if anything ever happened to her husband, I understood their full net worth picture, and I'd be able to help her during a time of need.

Just knowing where your assets and liabilities are is 75 percent of the battle. I truly believe that. I can help you with the rest—but it's going to be extraordinarily difficult and time consuming to find accounts at different institutions when you don't even know they exist.

My client base consists largely of female divorcées, as I am a holder of the Certified Divorce Financial Analyst™ designation, and specialize in financial planning and wealth management for women pre-, during, and post divorce. In the U.S., 40–50 percent of marriages end in divorce, and as you can imagine, the divorce rate for subsequent marriages is significantly higher. I am constantly in the situation of sitting across from a woman who is in the early stages of divorce who feels completely lost. I'll ask a question along the lines of: "Okay, what are we working with here? Let's put everything out on the table so we can start to dive in. What accounts do you and your husband have combined, and separately?" She'll look back at me with a sheepish, confused, and puzzled face, and finally after a long pause say something to the extent of :"I don't know. I have access to our checking account, but I really don't know about the other stuff. I'm so embarrassed. I should've figured this out a long time ago."

It's nothing to be embarrassed about and I remind these women that we'll learn and get through this together, but let's work on preventative care for these situations instead of symptomatic treatment. Instead of "figuring out" what accounts are where during a trying time, let's agree that as women, we should have an active and engaged knowledge of our household accounts, even if we're not the ones directly managing the finances for the household. Knowledge is key.

Another one I see all the time is professionals in their midforties who have job hopped and have left a trail of old employer retirement plans in the wake of all the jobs they've left behind. According to the Bureau of Labor Statistics, the average woman will have held twelve jobs in her lifetime.[3] Twelve! That is the opportunity for twelve old employer retirement plans (i.e., 401(k)s, 403(b)s, TSPs, etc.) that you may have funded with a little money here and a little money there to be floating in the ether that you've completely forgotten about. So many times I will start to work with a woman and during the "Know Your Net Worth" step of our planning together, her memory will get jogged and she'll remember the old 401(k) plan she had from a job ten years ago. It's always fun to find money, but imagine how hard that money would've been to find in another ten years, or God forbid, should anything happen to her. I doubt the beneficiaries of her estate would've even known it existed.

I've made a list of the most common types of assets (what you own) and liabilities (what you owe) and I'd like you to use my list to create a list of your own with real-time current numbers.

Net Worth = Total Assets - Total Liabilities

114

ASSETS: What You Own

Cash Accounts:

- Checking Accounts—In-and-out cash accounts at the bank in which your paychecks are deposited into and your monthly expenses are withdrawn.
- Savings Accounts—Cash accounts at the bank that are accumulated for short-term goals (i.e., emergency reserves, family vacations, big purchases).
- Money Market Accounts—Interest-bearing account at a bank or credit union.
- CD—A certificate of deposit is a product offered by banks and credit unions that offers a guaranteed interest rate at a premium in exchange for the customer agreeing to leave a lump sum of money untouched for a predetermined amount of time (i.e., a one-year CD).

Investments:

- Taxable Accounts—An investment account offered by a brokerage. With a taxable account, you can invest in assets like stocks, bonds, and mutual funds. As your account grows in value based on the stock market's performance, you'll owe taxes each year on your investment income. Types include:
  - Individual Investment Accounts
  - Joint Investment Accounts
- Qualified Retirement Accounts:
  - Traditional 401(k)—An employer-sponsored plan that gives employees a choice of investment options. Employee contributions to a 401(k) plan and any earnings from the investments are tax-deferred, meaning you pay the taxes on

115

contributions and earnings when the savings are withdrawn in retirement.

o   Roth 401(k)—An employer-sponsored plan that is funded with employee contributions of after-tax dollars. This type of retirement investment account is well-suited for people who think they will be in a higher tax bracket in retirement than they are now, as withdrawals on the contributions made to this account and growth on those contributions are tax-free.

o   Traditional 403(b)—Same as a traditional 401(k) except that 403(b)s are used by nonprofit companies, religious groups, school districts, and governmental organizations.

o   Roth 403(b)—Same as a Roth 401(k) except that 403(b)s are used by nonprofit companies, religious groups, school districts, and governmental organizations.

o   SEP IRA—A simplified employee pension is a retirement savings plan established by employers, or people who are self-employed, for the benefit of their employees and themselves. Employers, or people who are self-employed, can make tax-deductible contributions on behalf of eligible employees, or themselves, to their SEP IRAs. These types of accounts have a significantly higher annual contribution limit than a Traditional IRA which makes them very attractive, and they tend to be cheaper to set up and maintain than a full-fledged employer plan (i.e., 401(k) or 403(b)).

o   Pension Plan (Lump Sum Option)—If offered, you may be able to take your pension payout as a one-time-lump-sum instead of receiving a

116

monthly paycheck for a specified amount over time or for your lifetime.

- IRA—Traditional IRAs (Individual Retirement Accounts) allow individuals to contribute pre-tax dollars to a retirement account where investments grow tax-deferred until withdrawal during retirement. Upon retirement, withdrawals are taxed at the IRA owner's current income tax rate.
- Roth IRA Accounts—A special retirement account where you pay taxes on money going into your account and then all future withdrawals on initial contributions and growth are tax-free. Roth IRAs are best when you think your taxes will be higher in retirement than they are right now. You can't contribute to a Roth IRA directly if you make too much money. In 2020, the limit for singles is $139,000. For married couples, the limit is $206,000. These income limits do not apply to Roth 401(k) or Roth 403(b) accounts (you can contribute to a ROTH employer plan regardless of how much money you make).
- Deferred Compensation Accounts—This type of plan withholds a portion of an employee's pay until a specified date, usually retirement. The lump sum owed to an employee in this type of plan is paid out on that date. Examples of deferred compensation plans include pensions, retirement plans, and employee stock options.
- Annuities—There are so many different types of annuities! They can be fixed or variable, have different payout schedules, and can be part of retirement monies or non-retirement monies. I couldn't (and wouldn't for the sake of your boredom) walk you through all the types of annuities, but here's a thirty-thousand-foot overview:
  o Non-Qualified Annuity—An investment that is funded with after-tax dollars, meaning you have

already paid taxes on the money before it goes into the annuity. When you take money out, whether in a lump sum or on a schedule of systematic payments, only the earnings are taxable as income.

- o Qualified Annuity—A retirement savings plan that is funded with pre-tax dollars. When you take money out, whether in a lump sum or on a schedule of systematic payments, your entire withdrawal amount is taxable as income.

- Employee Stock Options—A type of equity compensation granted by companies to their employees and executives. They give the employee the right to buy the company's stock at a specified price for a specific period of time.

- HSA—A Health Savings Account (HSA) is a tax-advantaged account created for individuals who are covered under high-deductible health plans (HDHPs) to save for medical expenses that HDHPs do not cover. Contributions are made into the account by the individual or the individual's employer and are limited to a maximum amount each year. The contributions are invested over time and can be used to pay for qualified medical expenses, which include most medical care such as dental, vision, and over-the-counter drugs.

- 529 Plan—A tax-advantaged savings plan designed to help pay for education. The two major types of 529 plans are savings plans and prepaid tuition plans. Savings plans grow tax-deferred, and withdrawals are tax-free if they're used for qualified education expenses. Prepaid tuition plans allow the account owner to pay in advance for tuition at designated colleges and universities, locking in the cost at today's rates.

Property:
- Real Estate
  - Home
  - Second or Rental Home
- Personal Property
  - Cars
  - Collectibles
  - Jewelry

Business Interests: Your value in any businesses in which you are an owner.

Notes Receivable: A loan due to you from an outside person, party, or organization.

Other

Once you have all these written down with a dollar amount for value next to them, add all of them together. This the TOTAL ASSETS portion of your net worth.

LIABILITIES: What You Owe

Mortgages:
- Primary Home Mortgage
- Second/Rental Home Mortgage
- Home Equity Line of Credit

Loans:
- Student Loans
- Car Loans
- Outstanding Credit Card Balances
- Personal Loans

- Business Loans

Other

Once you have all these written down with a dollar amount for value next to them, add all of them together. This is the TOTAL LIABILITIES portion of your net worth.

Now that you have your total assets and total liabilities numbers, it's time to calculate your net worth.

Net Worth = Total Assets – Total Liabilities

Example: If your total assets equaled $1 million and your total liabilities equaled $500,000, your net worth comes to a grand total of $500,000.

I urge you to take some time for yourself—or if you're married/in a committed relationship take some time together—to sit down and do a deep dive into your net worth in an effort to inform yourself of all the assets and liabilities that correspond with your household. This is an incredibly empowering exercise and a huge step in your journey to take charge of your wealth. You can't create the plans for a beautiful garden without first understanding the landscape. Your net worth is your landscape—it's what you've got to work with in the here and now.

STEP FOUR: KNOW YOUR CASH FLOW

Now that you've got the landscape figured out and you understand your net worth, let's work on understanding your cash flow. Your cash flow will dictate how your net worth either grows or depletes over time. To understand your cash flow is to understand your incomes and your expenses each month, and ultimately, each year. Cash flow is simply the money flowing into your house on a monthly or yearly basis (incomes) and the money flowing out of your house on a monthly or yearly basis (expenses).

I've made a list of the most common types of incomes and expenses, and I'd like you to use my list to create one of your own, with real-time current numbers. Feel free to add categories that you need, and omit categories that you don't. Everyone's cash flow (budget) is different. When you write your list and numbers, let's look at them on a monthly basis and then we'll zoom out to look at these numbers on a yearly basis when we're finished with the exercise.

INCOMES: Money Coming Into the House on a Monthly Basis

- Salary and Bonuses
- Business Distributions
- Required Minimum Distributions
- Annuity Payments
- Social Security
- Pensions
- Rental Income
- Other
  - Alimony
  - Child Support

Once you have all these written down with a monthly dollar amount next to them, add everything together. This is the TOTAL INCOMES portion of your cash flow.

SAVINGS: Pay Yourself First!

(Note: This is considered as money going "out" when we look at cash flow, even though you are putting it aside for use at another time.)

- Bank
- Taxable Account
- Retirement Account
- Education Account
- Health Savings Account

EXPENSES: Money Going Out of the House on a Monthly Basis

- Mortgage/Rent
- Homeowner's Expenses
  - Property Taxes
  - Major Home Improvements
  - Home Repair and Maintenance
- Basic Lifestyle Expenses
  - Food/Groceries
  - Phone/Internet
  - Utilities
  - Clothing
  - Personal Care
    - Fitness and Nutrition Coaching
    - Haircuts
    - Manicure/Pedicure
  - Out-of-Pocket Medical
  - Charitable Contributions
  - Household Help
    - Housekeeper
    - Landscaper
  - Childcare for Children
  - Tuition for Children
  - Dining Out
  - Entertainment
  - Gifts/Holidays
  - Pet Expenses

- Subscriptions
  - Streaming Services (Netflix, Hulu, etc.)
  - Newspaper and Magazines
  - Health Club
- Travel/Vacations
- Insurance Premium Expenses—Property and Casualty
  - Homeowner's
  - Auto
  - Umbrella
- Insurance Premium Expenses
  - Health (includes: dental, eye, etc.)
  - Medical
  - Term Life
  - Whole Life
  - Disability
  - Long Term Care
- Credit Card Payments on Prior Purchases

Once you have all these written down with a monthly dollar amount next to them, add them all together. This is this is the TOTAL EXPENSES portion of your cash flow.

Now that you have your total income and total expense numbers, (be sure to include your monthly savings amount!), it's time to calculate your cash flow.

Cash Flow = Total Incomes – Total Expenses

Example: If your total incomes per month equaled $10,000 and your total expenses per month equaled $5,000, your monthly cash flow comes to a grand total of $5,000 per month *surplus*. A monthly surplus is a means for celebration! You have money leftover in your budget that you can start to allocate toward a value-backed wealth goal!

If this exercise went the other way, as in if your total incomes per month equaled $5,000 and your total expenses per month equaled $10,000, your cash flow total comes to a *deficit* of –$5,000 per month. Any time you end up with a deficit, or a negative cash flow number, you're spending more money than you're making. This is where people get into trouble with credit cards, outstanding loans, and late bill payments.

QUICK TIP: To understand your yearly cash flow, simply multiply your income and expense numbers by twelve, and walk through the same calculation for cash flow above.

You can see how intricately your net worth and cash flow are tied together. The net worth is directly related to how much of your surplus you are allocating to your savings and investment accounts (thereby growing your net worth) vs. how much of your deficit you are pulling off your savings and investment accounts or adding to your liabilities section via credit cards or loans (thereby decreasing your net worth). Your net worth is a snapshot of how your short-term efforts and goals are playing out for you on a specific date. Your cash flow is a living and breathing reflection of how your short-term efforts and goals are working for you today and how they will continue to play out for you in the future.

Just as the net worth is the landscape for your garden, the cash flow is the soil in your garden. Soil for a beautiful and vibrant garden must be rich and nutritious, just as your cash flow must nourish your net worth.

STEP FIVE: BUILD A WEALTH EMPOWERMENT PLAN

Armed with the knowledge of your net worth and your cash flow, you're now ready to build, hopefully with professional guidance from a Certified Financial Planner™, your Wealth Empowerment Plan. To go back to our garden analogy, you are ready to watch as the landscape (your net worth) provides the perfect home to your garden and take pride in the nutrient rich soil (your cash flow) in which you've placed your wealth-empowering seeds.

It's time to have real conversations about your wealth and understand what your money today will be doing for you tomorrow and in the future. It's time to take charge of those small, daily, seemingly innocuous wealth decisions and understand how they will impact your overall wealth picture. It's time to feel empowered by the understanding of your wealth and how all your assets, liabilities, incomes, savings, and expenses come together to create a perfect garden blooming with all the vibrant colors this life has to offer.

If you want to be wealthy (and again, you *are* wealthy, you *deserve* wealth, and you are *worthy* of wealth), you must think wealthy (read the above wealth affirmations again . . . and again, and again until your soul believes it). The wealthy do not employ a DIY strategy for wealth planning. Do you really think Bill Gates DIYs his wealth? Do you honestly think the Kardashians didn't have serious financial planning and wealth management discussions along the way to ensure they were setting themselves up for optimal success? And if you're thinking to yourself, "Well I'm not Bill Gates or one of the Kardashians; I don't have enough money to warrant financial planning help," then you are the EXACT REASON I knew I had to write this book and talk to you.

EVERYONE should have a financial plan, or a Wealth Empowerment Plan, as I like to call it.

Let me say it one more time for the people in the back: EVERYONE SHOULD HAVE A WEALTH EMPOWERMENT PLAN.

I don't care if you're just starting out in your wealth empowerment journey at the age of twenty-five, or if you're well on your way at the age of forty-two and have been a diligent saver and investor, or if you're sixty and wondering if you're behind the eight ball on all this, or if you're seventy-three, recently retired, and lying awake at night nervous that you'll outlive your money.

Ladies, we need to get better at asking for help—in every facet of life, but on our wealth journey in particular. We HAVE to understand how our wealth decisions today will affect us from now until we leave this beautiful Earth. So sit down with a Certified Financial Planner™, and have them analyze the net worth that you've listed out for yourself. Walk through your assets and liabilities with them. You might be surprised at what they find!

QUICK TIP: Are there accounts that can be consolidated? I am forever helping women consolidate all their old employer retirement plans (401(k)s, 403(b)s, etc.) into a rollover IRA, if warranted. So now, instead of five old employer retirement plan accounts from her old jobs that she had laying around without paying attention to them, she has one IRA rollover account that houses all these old plans and is invested in an effort to reach her value-backed goals.

Are there liabilities that should be paid off more quickly than others if cash flow allows? One of my favorite clients is an OB/GYN and surgeon. She is so incredibly sweet and is always doing whatever she can to not only help others in this world, but to help herself to make the best decisions possible. The funny thing about doctors is they start off making peanuts during their residency, (she was making $45,000 living in Atlanta), and they wake up the morning after their residency ends making a hefty six-figure salary with incentive bonuses! It's a total mind shift for doctors, and many of them fall prey to spending every single

126

dollar of their new, exciting salary on fancy cars, houses, and other material things. Which, again, YOU DO YOU, but I will tell you this: I see more paycheck to paycheck doctors than any other profession—with airline pilots coming in a hot second on the list. Again, not all, but I see it a lot.

Anyway, this amazing, modest doctor went from making nothing to making a salary that she joked, "I don't know what to do with all this!" Together, we sat on the phone for two hours and walked through all her assets, all her liabilities, and her cash flow. We decided that now was the time to finally get rid of the $100,000 in medical school student loans that were still showing in red on the liabilities side of her net worth (and had a whopping 10 percent interest rate attached and another ten years until payoff). We ran the numbers, and everything was a go! She got silent on the other end of the line when I told her that she was free to call her student loan servicing company and transact a total payoff. I remember asking, "Hey, Megan! Are you still there?"

Finally, she chirped up and I heard, "Yeah, I just can't believe they're really going to be gone. I've worked so hard to get rid of those things and you're telling me I can be rid of them today. I just can't believe it's really happening."

Listen, I'm not saying that everyone is going to have one of these moments, but there may be something in your liabilities category that has a nasty interest rate attached (think about any credit card balances you're carrying around making the minimum payment on) that with some professional guidance and analysis, you could be free of.

Are there opportunities for more productive savings or investments? That same doctor I was just telling you about is also now putting a solid percentage of her income away to her investment account each month. Through our financial planning, we were able to not only pay off her large student loans, but then with the money that she was putting to her loans every month we were able to redirect that money into an investment account for long-term growth. Or, maybe through understanding *your* Wealth Empowerment Plan, you'll find that you haven't been maximizing your savings to the buckets that will best help you to meet your financial goals.

QUICK TIP: The one I see most is that women are saving all their leftover monies to a savings account at the bank, and are nowhere near maximum funding of their employer retirement plans. So when they come to me, they have a giant nest egg at the bank that they've been building up for years, but they've only ever been saving 3 percent of their salary to their 401(k) at work, which is where she could have been achieving some nice tax-deferred growth for retirement with investments, instead of having her money lay stagnant after taxes. It's absolutely worth making sure you're saving and investing in all the right places to meet your value-backed goals.

STEP SIX: BECOME AN EMPOWERED INVESTOR

To invest your monies in a way that will support your Wealth Empowerment Plan, you must become an empowered investor. An empowered investor is on a path to build her net worth through investing in accounts and assets that she understands. This is the part of wealth building that women tend to shy away from most—the investment part. Why? Because portfolios, investments, and the stock market, are usually being "mansplained" to us by a middle-age white male in a navy suit from behind a desk somewhere on Wall Street.

Boring.

Let's break down investing down into what it is: simple. Again, investing shouldn't be this thing that needs to be demystified. Yes, actually selecting assets to invest your hard-earned money into is tricky, and we'll get to that later, but the actual act of investing your money doesn't have to induce a fear-stricken panic.

There are three basic types of accounts you can invest your money into. Referring back to Step Three, reread the definitions for: Taxable Accounts, Qualified Retirement Accounts, and Roth Accounts.

Hopefully, you have some qualified retirement accounts (401(k)s, 403(b)s, TSPs (if you work for the federal government), etc.) that you are actively contributing to or did contribute to during your working years. And, ladies, as empowered investors who are ready to take charge of our wealth, we must recognize that we can't rely on Social Security alone to fully fund our retirements. We must take an active role in saving and investing for our retirement. There are people out there who have written full books on Social Security retirement benefits and how they work, at what age you will be able to start collecting, how much you're entitled to collect, how those benefits are taxed, and different strategies for how those benefits may be reduced or increased. However, I am not one of those people and this is not one of those books. But Social Security retirement benefits have a HUGE impact on your long-term retirement Wealth Empowerment Plan.

If you're around age sixty, you should start to gain a clear understanding of your Social Security retirement benefit claiming strategy. This is something I help all my clients with so please ask a professional for help if you need it! There are so many intricacies that go into Social Security and it's really hard to "take back" or "undo" your benefits once you've started taking them if you realize you've made a mistake.

For purposes of this book, and giving you the ammo you need to become an empowered investor, I'll talk in generalities about Social Security retirement benefits. In 2020, at your full retirement age, age sixty-seven for people born after 1959, the maximum benefit you are eligible to receive is around $3,000 per month. This amount is permanently increased by 8 percent for every year after your full retirement age that you delay taking your benefit until your age 70 and it is permanently reduced by a certain percentage if you begin taking your benefit before your full retirement age.

I can tell you this much, if my Social Security retirement benefit at my full retirement age of sixty-seven is $3,000 per month, or $36,000 per year, I'm not living anywhere near the life I want to live in retirement off that income! It is up to us to ensure that we are taking an active role in saving toward our own beautiful, and God willing, long retirements!

Maybe you're one of the lucky people who will get a pension that adds to your retirement income, but again, the pensions of today are not what they used to be. In most cases, pensions coupled with Social Security retirement benefits aren't enough to cover all someone's living expenses in retirement.

Let's briefly revisit the nest eggs you have saved up (or are saving toward) for retirement. You have your qualified accounts, or your IRAs, 401(k)s, 403(b)s, etc. These accounts are linked to your retirement and have a 10 percent penalty attached if you decide to pull money out of them before you are fifty-nine and a half. Truly, these accounts are meant for your retirement! The money goes in and should just stay there until you're past fifty-nine and a half or later. These accounts are fully taxable as income to you in the year in which you take a distribution off them.

For example, if you have a traditional 401(k) with $500,000 in it and you take $100,000 from it at your age sixty-five, you will owe full income tax on the $100,000. Using a 30 percent tax rate, your take-home amount of the $100,000 would end up being only $70,000. Of the $100,000, $30,000 will go to the IRS to cover federal and state taxes because remember, this money has never been touched by the IRS. You contributed this money pre-(before) tax to your 401(k) at work and now the IRS wants their piece of the pie.

These nest eggs in retirement are fantastic, however, you need to make sure you have a plan in place for supplementing your retirement income with them so as to not get whacked too hard with taxes. Also, any time you take money out of these accounts, it is counted as income to you in the year in which you took the distribution. So, in that same example above, if you take $100,000 off your 401(k) at your age sixty-five, you are saying to the IRS, "I had $100,000 of income at my age sixty-five." Depending on your tax filing status, it can quickly become expensive to take money off your 401(k) due to taxes and being pushed up the income tax bracket ladder.

And hey, life happens, and sometimes getting whacked with a large tax bill on these things is unavoidable. Maybe there was an emergency and you just had to take a large chunk of money off your IRA and incur a large tax bill. The point is, you should have a plan in place for maximizing these accounts in retirement to make sure you are using your qualified retirement accounts as efficiently as possible.

The other important thing to know about these types of accounts is that the IRS makes you start taking money off them at your age seventy-two. This mandatory withdrawal is called your Required Minimum Distribution and there is a 50 percent penalty for not taking it. So, for those of you thinking, "Well, I don't need the money so I just won't take it and then I won't have a tax bite" . . . not so fast. Remember, this money and the growth on it through investments, has never been touched by the IRS. Eventually, they want their piece of the pie.

The other bucket of money that you may have heading into retirement is called a Roth account. These retirement accounts are special in that, unlike the accounts we just talked about, the money you put into your Roth account is taxed on the way in. Therefore, at distribution, you do not owe any tax on these monies you contributed or the investment growth on these monies. There is also no Required Minimum Distribution on these accounts.

Quick example: Let's say you have a Roth account, and ten years ago, you contributed $100 (after tax) and today, that $100 is worth $200. In retirement, you can take that full $200 as a tax-free distribution. ROTHs are a really neat bucket of money to have in addition to your traditional retirement accounts so you can diversify your tax planning.

The idea of IRAs or pre-tax 401(k)s vs. Roth accounts is that you're taking a risk on predicting your future tax bracket. No one has a crystal ball and can predict how taxes are going to play out in the long term, so make sure you're speaking with your Certified Financial Planner™ and Certified Public Accountant, in tandem, about what method of contribution is best for you in your Wealth Empowerment Plan.

If you are contributing to a pre-tax 401(k), you're saying that today, you are in a high tax bracket and it is too expensive for you to pay taxes on your retirement money now. You'd rather contribute to your 401(k) on a pre-tax basis, not pay any income tax on that money today, and therefore help out your current tax situation since the amount you contribute would be deducted from your gross income on your taxes that year.

Quick example: If you contribute $20,000 to your pre-tax, or traditional, 401(k) this year and you make a salary of $100,000, when you go to file your taxes for the year, you would only end up claiming a salary of $80,000 ($100,000 salary - $20,000 contribution = $80,000 adjusted gross income). But remember, since you're not claiming the income today, you have to claim this income in the future when you withdraw that money from your IRA or 401(k) account. You're taking the bet that you will be in a lower tax bracket in retirement and thus end up paying less taxes on that income, rather than if you paid your income taxes on that money today.

If you're contributing to a Roth 401(k), you're saying that today, you are in a low tax bracket and it makes sense for you to pay taxes on your retirement money now. You'd rather contribute to your 401(k) on a post-tax basis, pay your income tax on that money today, and never pay tax on that money, or its growth ever again. So, this money is "free" in your retirement. Contributing to a Roth account won't help your tax situation today, like a pre-tax 401(k) will, but it will certainly help your tax situation in retirement. Again, you're taking the bet that you will be in a higher tax bracket in your retirement than you are today and that it makes more sense for you to pay taxes at a discounted rate today than to pay a more expensive rate in your retirement when you go to withdraw this money. There are a bunch of reasons to go one way or the other on this. The rule of thumb is that if you're young and in a low tax bracket, you should contribute to a Roth retirement account since it would only make sense that your tax rate will increase. However, like I mentioned earlier, it's really best to speak with your CFP® and CPA on this issue to understand what makes the most sense for your current and retirement goals.

The last bucket of money you may have is taxable accounts. These accounts are usually made up of money that hits your checking account that you invest directly into an individual account on your own, or into a joint account with your spouse. Remember, retirement accounts cannot be joint. Taxable accounts are usually invested in a mix of stocks and bonds, like your retirement accounts. However, you only pay capital gains tax on the growth of these monies.

Quick example: Let's say you bought XYZ Company stock for $100 per share a year ago, and today you want to sell it and it's at $110 per share. You'd owe capital gains tax (around 15 percent depending on your income) on the $10 growth of that share of stock. So, in this example, you'd owe capital gains tax of $1.50. Women are always bummed when they hear me say there's no real way to avoid taxes in retirement. That's just life! But, you can create a Wealth Empowerment Plan to better understand your different buckets of money and how you can best draw off them in retirement to make the most efficient use of your portfolio as an income supplement.

As I've mentioned, you should be sure that your accounts are invested in a diversified allocation, or a mix of stocks and bonds, that makes the most sense for you and your goals. I can't tell you how many times I've had a woman, close to retirement, bring me her retirement account statements and she is 90–100 percent invested in stock and she had no idea. For a rare few, this is fine. For most, this undiversified portfolio is fraught with unfathomable risk. Remember back to 2008—these were the people who got hurt the most.

You should speak with your CFP® to ensure that you have a mix of stocks and bonds in your portfolio that makes the most sense for you and your value-backed goals and allows you to sleep at night!

QUICK TIP: Everyone has different ideas of wealth and their value-backed goals are unique. Therefore, it doesn't really make sense to ask your neighbor how she is invested and just do the same thing.

For example, my mom is sixty-seven and I'm thirty-one. She has less stock in her portfolio than I do since she is retired and uses her retirement accounts to supplement her income in retirement—as in, she is actively using her retirement account to pay for things. Since I'm thirty-one and have many more years left of working and investing, and I have no intention of touching my retirement accounts until I'm retired, I have significantly more stock in my portfolio than my mom does. I'll say this, though. I have several young clients who I work with that are simply more conservative investors by nature. Meaning, that even though they're young and have many more years of working and investing ahead, they can't stand the roller-coaster ride of the market. Because of their conservative nature, and because I want them to be able to sleep at night without worrying about what their portfolios are doing, they have less stock in their portfolios than I do even though we're in the "same place" in life.

There is truly no "one size fits all" when it comes to investing and how you should allocate your portfolio. As the old adage goes, the main goal is to "not have all your eggs in one basket." Take a look at your accounts and how they are invested. Do you have a diversified mix of stocks and bonds that you are comfortable with? What percentage is in each category is up to you, your tolerance for risk, and your Wealth Empowerment Plan. I strongly urge you to seek guidance from a CFP® who can help guide you to find an investment mix that's right for you, as it has been proven time and time again that a portfolio allocation, or your stock and bond mix, is more effective for portfolio growth than stock selection in the long run.

When you think about investing, just make sure you can sleep at night with whatever investment mix you choose. Your portfolio is not your best friend's portfolio! You have to do what makes you comfortable with *your* money, just like she'll do what makes her comfortable with hers.

STEP SEVEN: PROTECT YOURSELF AGAINST LIFE'S RISKS

Now that you understand your portfolio and investments and they are best matched to your Wealth Empowerment Plan, let's talk about protecting your assets, and therefore protecting your dreams and value-backed goals. It's time to address insurance. As an independent CFP®, I do not sell insurance of any kind. However, you'd better believe it's a huge part of your Wealth Empowerment Plan and protecting yourself against risk and liability, so I am constantly referring my clients to smart insurance agents and brokers who can help my clients get the best insurance for their needs. I know the topic of insurance is scary, overwhelming, and quite frankly, boring. But I want to go over some key insurance types and topics so that you feel better prepared to protect yourself from an insurance standpoint and feel empowered to have an intelligent and knowledgeable conversation on this topic.

My biggest piece of advice for insurance is to make sure the insurance broker or agent you're working with truly has your best interest at heart. Insurance brokers and agents make commissions off the products they sell, so if you're not working with someone who you know, love, and trust, he or she could be selling you a product that doesn't best suit your needs, but instead, best suits their pockets.

Before I dive into the different types of life insurance, I want to give you my quick rules on purchasing it:

1. Make a list of all the people you say "I love you" to on a daily basis and are financially responsible for. Chances are, you'll need life insurance coverage on yourself for these people.

2. Make sure the life insurance coverage you take out on yourself can at least cover the mortgage for your spouse or partner should anything happen to you. While this will most likely still not be enough in the way of insurance, it's at least one giant expense that your spouse or partner won't have to worry about after your passing.

3. Do not insure children. I'm sure you've gotten those flyers in the mail before that offer cheap insurance policies that you can take out on your children. These policies are not worth it. I remember a very seasoned insurance professional saying to me once, "You don't insure a liability." Your children are a liability. They cost you money and they're an expense. As sad and unfathomable as it would be to lose a child, I'm sure your wallet would be heavier in the long term. There's a reason the term "DINK" (double income no kids) came

about; they don't have the expense of children! As a mom of two, I can't imagine my life without my girls, but wow are they expensive.

There are so many types of life insurance products and carriers of those products so I'll give you the plain English definition of the most common ones.

GROUP LIFE

This is the type of life insurance you get through work and it usually covers you for one to two times your base salary. Sometimes, there is an option to buy "supplemental insurance" for a nominal extra charge that is deducted from your pay. Your employer may even have an option to buy "supplemental spousal insurance" that would cover your spouse under the group plan for an extra charge. The downsides to group life is that it's usually not portable, meaning after you quit, retire, or are terminated, you don't get to carry the life insurance coverage with you and you usually aren't able to purchase the higher amount of coverage you truly need due to limits. I generally recommend that my clients not only look into their supplemental plans at work, but also take out some private life insurance as a companion to their group life insurance. I'll explain the types of private life insurance below.

TERM LIFE INSURANCE

This type of life insurance guarantees payment of a stated death benefit during a specified term—usually around ten to thirty years. Once the term expires, the policyholder can either renew the term policy for another term, convert the policy to permanent coverage, or allow the policy to terminate.

Example: Let's say I buy a twenty-year term policy with a death benefit of $500,000 and the premium (the amount I pay to carry the insurance) is $400 per year. With this type of insurance, I pay my $400 per year and at the end of twenty years, I can do nothing, get another term policy, or convert the policy to permanent coverage. I don't get any money back if I don't die—the money is simply a "throw away expense." However, if I die within two years of purchasing the term insurance policy and have only paid $800 into the policy for premiums, my beneficiary (in my case, my husband) would still get the full $500,000 death benefit.

Term life insurance is the cheapest type of insurance you can buy since the premium that you pay is a true expense. Remember, you don't get any money back if you don't die before the policy term is up. I typically recommend this type of insurance to my clients because it is cheap and covers you well for a specified time.

WHOLE LIFE INSURANCE

As the name implies, whole life insurance provides permanent coverage for the lifetime of the insured. In addition to providing a death benefit, whole life also contains a savings component where cash value may accumulate. The savings component can be invested; additionally, the policyholder can access the cash while alive, by either withdrawing or borrowing against it, when needed. Because of the savings component and the fact that these policies are meant to cover you for your entire life, they tend to be much more expensive than term insurance policies.

Example: Let's say I buy a whole life insurance policy with a death benefit of $100,000 and the premium is $1,500 per year. Over time, this policy will carry a cash value, or savings account, from all my paid premiums, and I could borrow or withdraw against it, if I needed to. Imagine that after fifteen years, the cash value of the policy was $10,000. That's $10,000 I could take a loan against, or take out of the policy, if I needed to. The loans on these policies tend to have high interest rates, but it does provide a place to go to for cash, in an emergency.

I've been told by several high-end insurance agents that whole life policies are for the wealthy, as they tend to be more of a wealth conservation, or investment play. These types of policies carry high commissions for the insurance agent or broker selling the policy, so be careful and get a second opinion if you're being sold on this type of product. It may not be the best type of life insurance for you.

The below two types of life insurance contain an investment piece within them in an effort to try to cover the cost of insurance—meaning, as you age, the cost of your insurance will increase since there's a greater likelihood of you dying as you get older. Therefore, you become more expensive to insure.

UNIVERSAL LIFE INSURANCE

This is a type of permanent life insurance with a savings element and low premiums like term life insurance. The cost of insurance of these policies is the minimum needed to keep the policy alive. Most universal life insurance policies contain a flexible premium option which will let you skip paying premiums if you have enough built up to cover the cost of insurance in your savings bucket. However, some require a single premium (single lump-sum premium) or fixed premiums (scheduled fixed premiums).

VARIABLE UNIVERSAL LIFE

This type of permanent life insurance allows for the cash component to be invested in an effort to produce greater returns. These policies are built on traditional universal life policies (as discussed above) but have a separate sub-account that invests the cash piece in the market by way of stocks and bonds.

Again, there are so many life insurance products and carriers out there and this chapter isn't to help you pick the right type of insurance for you and your Wealth Empowerment Plan, but rather to help you understand the range available. More than likely, you need life insurance if you have a list of people you love and are financially responsible for. Just make sure you are buying your life insurance coverage from someone you know, love, and trust, and that you truly understand what you're buying.

I'm sure you've heard it before, but from a knowledge perspective, it bears repeating: There's a greater likelihood that you will become disabled rather than die. Therefore, you'd better have some solid long-term disability insurance. You most likely have this type of insurance through your employer which will cover you at 60 percent of your base pay should you become disabled for an extended period of time. If you are someone whose base salary is nominal compared to your commissions or bonuses, you should really consider reaching out to an insurance agent or broker, that you know, love, and trust, to see how much a supplemental long-term disability policy would cost you.

Example: One of my clients is a very high up executive at a large product distribution company. Her base salary is $150,000, but after bonuses, she usually pulls in around $700,000 per year. Her long-term disability coverage through her employer at 60 percent of base salary would only pay her $90,000 per year should she become disabled long term. Knowing her cash flow, her lifestyle, and her Wealth Empowerment Plan as intimately as I do, I knew there was no way she could make her life work on $90,000 per year.

First, we checked with her employer to see if she could purchase extra supplemental long-term disability insurance through them. As suspected, no such luck, but always worth checking! Then, we went to an insurance broker to get some private, supplemental long-term disability insurance which they were able to provide, at a hefty price tag—as private long-term disability insurance is generally very pricey. However, now my client can sleep at night knowing that if anything were to happen to her and she were to become disabled over the long term, her cash flow and Wealth Empowerment Plan can remain intact.

LONG-TERM CARE (LTC) INSURANCE

This last type of personal insurance I want to mention covers the costs that Medicare will not, such as: nursing-home care, home-health care, and personal or adult day care for individuals age sixty-five or older or with a chronic or disabling condition that needs constant supervision. LTC insurance offers more flexibility and options than many public assistance programs.

Most LTC professionals recommend shopping for this type of insurance between the ages of forty-five and fifty-five as it is very costly and only becomes more cost-prohibitive the older you get. Long-term care is usually very expensive, which is why most people need insurance.

Example: One of my sweet, elderly, clients ended up having to go into a skilled nursing home facility at the age of eighty-four for a cost of $250 per day, or $91,250 per year. Thankfully, she had a long-term care insurance policy that covered this expense for her for a little more than three years for an all-in cost of around $300,000. She bought this policy when she was fifty-five and the yearly premium for her policy was $2,500 per year. Meaning, she paid $72,500 for this long-term care insurance all-in over twenty-nine years, but she was able to pay for $300,000 of care with this policy—a lifetime savings of $227,500. This particular client of mine had Alzheimer's, and lived another two years at the skilled nursing home facility after her long-term care insurance had run out, but thanks to this policy, she was able to live happily and comfortably at the high-cost facility that her children had chosen for her for five years. The last two years of her care were paid for by her retirement accounts and savings that she hadn't had to tap into for the first three years of her care. Her children were so thankful that she had the long-term care policy and that their mother was able to be taken care of beautifully without worrying about how they would pay for her care.

Ladies, the research and statistics show that we will outlive our husbands. I've told you that the number one thing I hear from women when I sit down with them after a divorce or the loss of their spouse is, "I don't want to be a burden on my children in my later years." I recommend long-term care insurance to all my clients when the time is right and they're at the age to start really thinking about this. Again, while it is costly, I have seen numerous occasions in which the policy was worth its weight in gold and ensured that the person it was covering was able to be cared for in the best possible way without draining her portfolio.

There are so many different types of long-term care policies and they're all structured so differently, but my main point here is that we, as women, should take charge of these conversations because our future happiness, comfort, and health depend on them. As I've said many times throughout this chapter, please make sure you speak with a very informed and knowledgeable insurance agent or broker when purchasing this type of policy. In fact, there are even agents and brokers that specialize in only selling long-term care insurance! Make sure you know what you're buying and how it will help you if, or when, the time comes.

If you're still with me, good! And truly, I know this is a dry subject, but insurance is the best type of protection you can have for your Wealth Empowerment Plan!

PROPERTY AND CASUALTY INSURANCE

The last type of insurance I want to touch on lightly is property and casualty. Make sure you have your primary home, rental home, automobiles, etc. all covered by insurance. I'm sure you already do! However, remember back to "Knowing Your Net Worth." Another important reason to have your total net worth number calculated is so that you can cover yourself appropriately with umbrella insurance.

An umbrella insurance policy is extra liability insurance coverage that goes beyond the limits of your homeowners, auto, or watercraft insurance. To own umbrella insurance, you must own a standard homeowners, auto, or watercraft policy first, and the umbrella policy will kick in after the regular coverage has been exhausted. If the policyholder is sued for damages that go over the liability limits of car insurance, homeowners insurance, or other coverage types, an umbrella policy helps pay what they owe. In other words, if the dollar limit of the original policy (homeowner's, auto, etc.) has been exhausted, the umbrella policy acts as a fail-safe, so the insured person doesn't have to dip into savings and other assets.

Example: Let's say that I have a net worth of $1.5 million and my daughter has a friend come over to play in our pool. Let's pretend that my daughter's friend slips on the steps of the pool trying to get out and sprains her ankle and her parents decide to sue me for all I'm worth. Let's also pretend my homeowners insurance would cover me for $750,000 of the liability, but I'm on the hook for the other $750,000. If the claim went through, I would have to come out of pocket for the other $750,000 that my homeowner's insurance didn't cover above the limit. Instead, if I had umbrella insurance up to my net worth of $1.5 million, the first $750,000 would've been paid by my homeowner's policy, and the next $750,000 would be paid by my umbrella insurance. I wouldn't have to pay out-of-pocket for this expense (and probably wouldn't have these friends anymore, either).

Umbrella insurance is relatively cheap for the type of protection it provides. I recommend that you call the insurance company that carries your home and auto insurance and get a quote for umbrella insurance that would cover you up to your net worth amount.

There are so many types of insurances out there and I really only hit on a few big ones. The moral of this chapter is to make sure you're covered in all aspects of your life because a large financial hit that isn't properly insured can derail your entire Wealth Empowerment Plan in the blink of an eye. If you don't know where to start with this conversation and this chapter left you with more questions than answers, that's okay! Talk to your CFP® and they will help you get on the right track to ensure that you, your health, and your wealth are covered!

STEP EIGHT: PROTECT YOUR LEGACY

When you think about leaving this world a better place than when you came into it, what do you think about? Maybe it's ensuring that your children and grandchildren have their college tuitions paid for. Perhaps it's leaving behind a large amount of money to charity. Maybe it's leaving behind money for different scholarships near and dear to your heart. There are so many things that each one of us beautiful souls want to do to ensure that others see the beauty in the life we lived, sometimes referred to as "leaving a legacy." What do you want your legacy to be? And remember, this is a question for *you* to answer, not your best girlfriend from whom you copy!

Whatever your answer is, make sure that you have it captured in your estate documents. I know talking or even thinking about wills, powers of attorney, medical directives, and all those other legal jargon-filled documents can be scary, overwhelming, and seem like one more thing on the to-do list. Nevertheless, I can tell you countless horror stories of the women who have come to me after their parents have passed intestate, or without a will, and how hard it was for them to get the estates settled. I've seen even the most loving and stable families go through some really hard times when the parents have passed and now the adult children are left to interpret what Mom and Dad wanted. It's a hard position to be put in and I am never envious of those situations.

In an effort to make sure *your* wishes are known—from how you want to be cared for, to who should be medically and financially responsible for you while you need care and can't speak for yourself, to what should happen with your assets after you are no longer on this Earth—make sure you have legal documents that reflect these wishes. Importantly, if you have kids under the age of majority, you're going to want to make sure you decide who these sweet kiddos are going to if you, or you and your husband/partner/ex, are no longer around.

I am not an estate planning attorney, as you know, but I work very closely with them. Why? Because I would not be fulfilling my duty as a CFP® if I didn't ensure that I spoke with my clients about how important their estate documents are to their Wealth Empowerment Plan. I know it's not a fun thing to do, but set an appointment for yourself, or you and your spouse, to go see an estate planning attorney to create AND execute these documents for you.

I can't stress the importance enough of making these decisions, not only for yourself, but for those you leave behind. Get your estate plans done and take charge of your legacy. Remember, these documents aren't real until you execute, or sign, them. So many times people go through the arduous task of getting these estate documents created and then never sign them. I see this all the time and then I turn into the nagging financial advisor that is hunting my clients down to get them back in to see their estate planning attorney to cross the finish line and get these things executed.

QUICK TIP: As for your retirement accounts and your life insurance policies, make sure the beneficiaries (the person/people you want the monies to go to after you pass) are the right people! Just because you update your will does not mean you've updated your beneficiaries on your retirement accounts and life insurance policies.

I can tell you some horror stories of beneficiaries not being updated and people getting money they shouldn't have, or not getting money that they should have. Yes, beneficiaries can sue and try to "right" the estate that way, but it is costly, and emotionally burdensome. It's your duty to make sure you're doing all the right things to take charge of your legacy.

STEP NINE: KNOW YOUR PROFESSIONAL WEALTH TEAM

You should know every single person who helps to service your financial life and have some type of a real, working relationship with all of them. If you have a CFP®, they will act as the ringleader and ensure that all your financial professionals are working in sync to best service your overall life and Wealth Empowerment Plan. As such, I work very closely with my client's CPAs, estate planning attorneys, business attorneys, insurance professionals, small business advisors and retirement plan consultants, etc. However, it is your job to know and trust these professionals, as they will be servicing very specific needs within your Wealth Empowerment Plan.

If you are married and your spouse is the one that has the integrated relationships with all parties of your professional wealth team, it's time for you to get involved and create relationships with these people too. This is your wealth, just as much as it is your spouse's. You are an active and engaged party to your wealth and you deserve to be chairwoman of your wealth board! Ask yourself, "Do I not know my professional wealth team because I haven't taken the time to get to know them, or, have they not taken the time to get to know me?" And, girlfriend, if it's the latter, it's time to have a real conversation with your spouse about making sure all the members of your professional wealth team see you as an equal half and member of "their client."

I always tell women, "The time to get to know all the members of your professional wealth team is not during a tragedy." I see it far too often: a woman going through a divorce now has to find a new financial advisor and a new accountant because her ex was the one with the working relationship with these individuals. Often, she barely has a name for who these people are. The same with a woman who has recently found herself a widow—she has no idea who services her life from a wealth perspective and now has to begin creating a working relationship with these new (to her) people at a time when she is grieving.

Ladies, make sure you've got a strong seat and a loud voice at YOUR wealth empowerment table. Again, not to beat a dead horse here, but studies prove that we'll be the ones to outlive our spouses and so it will be our job to be chairwoman and lead of our financial lives and take charge of our professional wealth team. Make sure you're surrounded by professionals who know you, want what's best for you, and work hard every day to make your life, dreams, and Wealth Empowerment Plan come true.

You don't have to be a professional in all areas of your financial life—and you shouldn't be! But, you should be working with professionals that make you feel as though you couldn't be in better hands, and as though they've got your back 100 percent, no matter the storm life throws your way.

STEP TEN: SCHEDULE REGULAR WEALTH EMPOWERMENT CHECK-INS

The final step to creating a solid Wealth Empowerment Plan is to set a schedule to make sure you check in on it regularly. Just as life changes, so does your Wealth Empowerment Plan. At least once per year, you should be scheduling time to meet with your CFP® to review your plan and the progress being made to your value-backed goals.

Think of these sessions as your "wealth checkups" just as you would regularly schedule your health checkups. You wouldn't visit a doctor once in your life and then assume you're healthy for the rest of your lifetime! You see the doctor not only when you're sick, but also for your annual well check.

Just as you check in on your health, you must check in on your wealth. You should be checking in regularly as scheduled, and any time there is a major change in your life (i.e., new job, new baby, new house, marriage, retirement, new salary, etc.). Remember, everything you do changes your overall Wealth Empowerment Plan for the better or for the worse. Checking in to know the short- and long-term implications of decisions you make today on your Wealth Empowerment Plan is fuel for your wealth, knowledge, and power.

I know these ten steps to a solid, strong, and purpose-driven Wealth Empowerment Plan may seem overwhelming, but remember: "Rome wasn't built in a day," and neither was your current financial situation. When you start to think about making changes to your wealth and getting your plan in order, just be sure to take it step by step. Begin with SMART short-term, value-backed goals that will lead to progress, because progress, no matter how slow, is how you get to where you're going in the long term.

If you aren't currently working with a Certified Financial Planner™ who manages your Wealth Empowerment Plan, I can't recommend this enough. Just as you go to see a doctor to ensure that your health is on point, you should be seeing a CFP® to make sure your wealth is on point. A person with the CFP® designation is an expert in the financial planning field, just as a doctor is an expert in their field. As a CFP® myself, I can tell you that the information I learned from the required graduate level courses and the two-day, ten-hour-long exam (now it's one day and six hours) is unparalleled. Not every financial advisor is a CFP®, but you can be assured that the ones who are have spent years of their lives making sure they know the ins and outs of a solid financial plan. They are highly trained to show you a financial picture that you can understand and start to take action on.

I can't emphasize this enough—make sure that you're working with someone who has the correct qualifications and is someone who has your best interest at heart. You shouldn't "just be a client" to someone, or "just be another number." Your financial advisor should have a vested interest in seeing you succeed and want to see you flourish in your Wealth Empowerment Plan. I can tell you that I genuinely feel no greater joy than when I see a woman work toward her Wealth Empowerment Plan succeed, and live the life she's dreamed of. These women become my friends, and what's better than seeing your friend live her best life?

CHAPTER SEVEN

FINANCIAL EMPOWERMENT

Now that we've worked through your narratives of guilt and I've shown you how to take baby steps toward creating a Wealth Empowerment Plan that fulfills all your value-backed goals and works for your unique life, it's time to answer the questions that will jump-start the life of abundance and financial independence that you deserve.

- How are you going to start showing up for yourself today so that your future self will thank you?
- How are you going to be a role model for ultimate wealth empowerment and financial independence so you can impact the woman sitting next to you?
- What will you do to pave the way for financial empowerment for the little girl that looks up to you?

I know this won't always be easy, and I know that there will be some speed bumps along the way, but there is nothing you can't overcome with your tenacious spirit, patience, and willingness to learn. This is when we get to the real talk about why *today* is the day for you to feel empowered by your wealth.

FEMALE POWER (WITH THE STATS TO PROVE IT)

WE ARE A FORCE TO BE RECKONED WITH

Women make up 51 percent of the U.S. population and according to the U.S. Bureau of Labor Statistics, 40 percent of U.S. working women now out-earn their husbands.[4] Ladies, as such a prominent demographic we no longer have the choice to sit out of conversations pertaining to our wealth. In 40 percent of households, we are bringing home the bacon! As half of the population and almost half of the out-earning power, we should be involved as a 50 percent shareowner in the wealth decision making process!

WE ARE IN CONTROL

According to New York Life Investments, in 2020, women control 51 percent of the personal wealth in the U.S., an estimated $22 trillion. And this number is expected to increase by 30 percent, to almost $28 trillion, over the next forty years as intergenerational wealth is transferred to the hands of women. According to a State Street Global Advisors' survey, almost 60 percent of women today are solely responsible for making investment decisions. Whether by choice, widowhood, or divorce, we are left with the duty of making the wealth decisions. We are being forced to take financial responsibility and become the sole lead of our wealth management team. Why not take the initiative and be proactive on this front? If you are part of this demographic, then you know how important it is to have concrete knowledge about how your Wealth Empowerment Plan is being managed. If you are not yet part of this demographic, see below.

WE LIVE LONGER

According to the CDC, on average, men will live to age seventy-six, and women will live to age eighty-one. Therefore, we will have five years of having to "figure it out," or "wrap our heads around it," or "feel comfortable with the way the finances and wealth decisions have been managed," and that's on average. Meaning, you may have many more years than that in which you have to take the reins of your financial life if you haven't been an active and engaged member in the wealth decision-making process in the past.

WE DESERVE TO BE UNDERSTOOD

Of women, 61 percent feel misunderstood by the financial services industry and 62 percent of women are walking away from their financial advisor upon the death of their spouse, according to a State Street Global Advisors survey.[5] In my opinion, this is completely unacceptable. Why don't women feel comfortable with their financial advisors—the people who are supposed to be ensuring that they, too, along with their spouses, feel empowered by their wealth? You know I have a theory and some strong feelings on that topic. It's ridiculous to me that women are being left out of the wealth decision-making process by their own financial advisors! It's insane that more than half of women feel that they have nowhere to turn when it comes to solid guidance in managing their wealth. Even more shocking is that this statistic exists considering that 60 percent of us are solely responsible for making investment decisions. So, basically, the same number of women that are carrying the burden of financial independence are also faced with not being able to find good financial help they can trust? Ladies, make sure you're working with a CFP® who knows you, your value-backed goals, and your Wealth Empowerment Plan inside and out. Make sure they have your best interest at heart and will have your back 100 percent in a time of need or during a tragedy.

WE HAVE SIGNIFICANT INFLUENCE

According to *Harvard Business Review*, 93 percent of women say they have significant influence on what financial services their family purchases,[6] but only 20 percent of female breadwinners said they felt "very well prepared" to make wise financial decisions, according to a study done by Prudential.[7] This shows that we influence "who" our families use as a financial advisor, but our influence is undermined by misperceptions around who we are and how we invest. Use your influence to choose an advisor who will listen to you, understand you, and make sure you feel "very well prepared" to make any financial decision that life throws your way, with their help!

WE ARE SMART

Per the Department of Education, women currently earn the majority of bachelor's degrees (57 percent), master's degrees (60 percent), and doctoral degrees (51 percent). Hell yes! And, as today's younger women enter the labor force at higher rates, they bring with them higher levels of education than any generation of women who have come before them, according to the Pew Research Center. The future is female! This just proves that we are able and willing to learn how to feel empowered by our wealth. So many times I hear women say, "I'm not financially smart," or the one I hate most, "Sorry if this is a dumb question, but . . ." Are you kidding me? Look at these statistics again! YOU ARE SMART. WE ARE SMART. And remember, it's okay to still be learning about your wealth. According to these stats, we're fast learners and fantastic students!

WE KNOW THE GENDER WEALTH GAP IS REAL

Because the narrowing, but persistent, gender pay gap still exists, women earn about 85 percent of what men earn, according to a Pew Research Study. Due to lesser earnings over our lifetimes, time out of the workforce as a caregiver (whether that be with small children, or caregiving for aging parents), and the market's performance, the cost of the "investment gap" over a woman's working lifetime can easily add up to $1 million, according to *Money*. What more proof do you need than that to finally put yourself first when it comes to saving, investing, and wealth accumulation?

We deserve to have a nest egg that is just as large as our male counterparts'. We need to take the plunge when it comes to investing through a mix of stocks and bonds that make the most sense for our unique value-backed goals. According to Wealthsimple, women overall invest 40 percent less than men do. This may be a consequence of earning less, feeling misunderstood in the financial industry, or not feeling like we have the education and empowerment we need to make wise decisions, as previously discussed. However, we must start to take action when it comes to our wealth—we're literally losing out on millions of dollars by not investing. We know the gender wealth gap is real, and we have the knowledge to combat it, even with seemingly insurmountable societal contributors.

OUR RELATIONSHIP WITH MONEY IS DIFFERENT

We know that investing isn't about beating the benchmark (i.e., the S&P 500). According to a State Street Global Advisors' survey, women make decisions based on values, and we intrinsically link them to our financial goals and priorities. We're not out to "make a quick buck;" we're out to ensure our investments grow over the long term so we can live a long beautiful life without financial worry. We know we must make financially smart and savvy decisions as we have to make more work with less. Remember the statistics I shared about the investing gap? Think about it this way. We may have less to invest throughout our lives due to the earnings disparity over time, which means we know we have to take precious care of the money we are committing to investing. We don't need to take huge swings in the market and seek to find the next "best stock" to invest into. We feel empowered by knowing that our money is invested in a mix of stocks and bonds that makes the most sense for our plan and that it is growing sensibly, whereas men are typically looking for the next hot stock so they can show off to their buddies. Speaking of showing off . . .

WHEN WE INVEST, WE'RE GOOD AT IT

It has been proven that typically, men's overconfidence in investing leads to women investors outperforming them by a whopping 1.2 percent per year. Crazy, right? Not really. Because women have a different relationship with money and aren't focused on beating the benchmark, they are able to keep a level head during down markets, which means they aren't over - trading in their accounts. This in turn leads to increased performance over time, more awareness of fees, and they aren't as cocky. According to *Money*, women are more aware of financial risk than men, which helps them make informed, rational investing decisions.

So then what's keeping us from investing if all the above statistics are true and we are proven badasses? The likely culprit: fear and a lack of confidence when it comes to making wealth decisions. We don't feel empowered when it comes to our wealth! Men are more likely to take the plunge and start investing earlier than women. Men are putting themselves first and saving in a powerful way: through investments. They are making their money work for them! They know there will be downturns in the market, but they know that downturns don't last forever.

Ladies, it's our turn to take the plunge, start putting ourselves first, and investing in our futures. We have the knowledge to feel empowered by our wealth. We're confident saying we're still learning. We owe it to ourselves to make our money work as hard as it can for us. After all, we're working as hard as we can for it!

UNIVERSAL TRUTHS

Now that we have the statistics out of the way, let's talk about universal truths that we must believe in our souls if we are to change the wealth narrative and #LevelTheWealth.

WE DESERVE AND ARE WORTHY OF WEALTH

I can't tell you the number of times I've sat with a recently divorced woman and she's said something like: "He worked so hard for this money. I didn't work a day in my life when I was with him. Is it wrong that I have half of it?" Wait, *what?* Yes, you deserve half! You were home raising his kids and running the household while he was climbing that corporate ladder. Or how many times I've heard: "I don't know if I'll ever be wealthy. I don't make a ton of money." Girlfriend, YOU ARE WORTHY OF WEALTH. Let me say it again: YOU ARE WORTHY OF WEALTH.

And remember, "wealth" means something different to every single person. The SMART value-backed goals that you created will guide you toward specificity with what you expect from the universe and yourself. You must believe that you can and will succeed in your Wealth Empowerment Plan. You were not born to live day to day, paycheck to paycheck. You were put here to blossom and flourish into the amazing woman you are. You are not a victim of your circumstances. You are on a journey and your journey was meant to be filled with wealth, health, and happiness. You deserve wealth and you are worthy of it. Your mindset and attitude must be in the right place for you to truly succeed.

WE WELCOME WEALTH LIKE A FRIEND

How do you welcome wealth into your life? Over Christmas break 2019, I was sitting with Michelle having a glass of wine and watching Netflix after Alex and I had put the girls to bed. We were chatting about all the things involved with being a woman in business—the passion, the fun, and the challenges. During our conversation, Michelle talked to me about the fortune she had experienced with her business recently, her new booming income, and her curiosity around how to keep things going so well. I sensed her very nervous and anxious energy and, as her sister, I called her out on it. "Well geez," I said, "you're talking about this money—which is a product of all your hard work, by the way—with such fear and anxiety."

I then asked *what if* she started thinking about this money as if it were her friend. If a friend stopped by for a visit and you greeted her with unease and nervousness, she would most likely leave as fast as she could. Instead, what if you welcomed her with calmness, kindness, acceptance, and open arms—like she truly belonged in your home? Are you blocking money from entering your life? Do you greet it with a warm and joyous welcome, or do you sit there wondering why it came to you and how fast it will leave? Wealth is your friend. Welcome it joyously, and with open arms, into your life.

It Is Safe for Us to Be Wealthy

This is one that a lot of women struggle with when they find themselves as the sole person responsible for making wealth decisions. The questions of "Who will come out of the woodwork once I get my financial life in order, feel empowered by my wealth, and start to make smart decisions to continue building it?" or "Who will try to take advantage of me for my wealth?" These are all real fears that we need to have a real conversation about. Believe me, I've heard time and time again about women who find themselves widowed and walk into a bank with their statements and the teller behind the counter is immediately trying to sell them an annuity or a product in an effort to line their own pockets with a big commission check.

That one REALLY grinds my gears. Or, of the savvy businesswoman who has built a beautiful empire for herself only to be caught in the midst of some baloney lawsuit just because someone wants to try to make a quick buck off her fortune.

Ladies, I'd have to believe that these are the exception, not the rule, but to that end, it is imperative that you have a team of people you know, love, and trust on your side to ensure that you're making the best decisions for yourself and your wealth. It is safe for you to be wealthy. The universe wants you to be wealthy. You can empower yourself with knowledge, confidence, and a team of professionals to make sure you feel safe and secure with your wealth. It is yours, you've earned it, and you will continue to build it. It is safe for you to be wealthy.

THE MORE WE GIVE, THE MORE WE RECEIVE

This is one that I can't explain; it's simply a universal truth. The more you put into the universe, the more the universe will give you. I'll use myself as an example. When I first started advising clients, I didn't make any time for pro bono work. I booked myself to the gills with anyone who could fog a mirror as long as they had *something* to invest. I was taking on clients that weren't my target audience left and right, but I couldn't turn down business, right? Ugh. Thankfully, I ended up getting involved with the Financial Planning Association's pro bono committee for the Maryland chapter and was forced to take some time to give back to my community through my unique expertise. Over time, this led to no longer needing a committee to structure this time for me, but being able to commit to and structure this time on my own.

I started taking meetings with women who I knew had nothing to invest and spending an hour walking them through their financial plans. I started giving clients who were not my target audience over to other advisors within my firm instead of hoarding them under my book just to make another dollar. When I started doing this, I noticed that I was getting calls out of the blue from women who needed my help, and were good business for me too! I noticed that my schedule was getting jam-packed with women who I had so much fun meeting. I noticed that work started to feel less like work and I was making more money than I had ever made—with such ease!

Again, I can't explain it, but I KNOW it's real. Giving doesn't just have to be in terms of money. Think about what your expertise is in this life and how you can use it to help others who have nothing to give back to you. You'll be amazed at how good it feels to truly help others and you'll be amazed at how the universe truly helps you.

WE ARE ALLOWED TO LOVE BEING WEALTHY

Wealth is about having options. You are allowed to love being wealthy because it allows you to be the most you can be and do the most you can do—whatever that means to YOU. You have options when you have wealth and having options is powerful. You have the option of leaving a giant tip, or donating to a charity you believe in, or generously giving gifts. You have the option of going on that vacation you've always dreamed of, or finally taking that leap and starting that business that's always been itching at the back of your mind. You are allowed to love being wealthy because it affords you the ability to put your best self into the universe. Being wealthy is not the root of all evil. It is not a sin to be wealthy. Ugh, I am so tired of that weird stigma (and note how it rarely applies to men!). It's all about being a good steward of the wealth you have, and like I mentioned above, using that wealth to better yourself and the world you live in. Love the wealth you've built, make smart decisions to build more, and use it for the betterment of yourself and those around you.

I know that every day we're so bombarded with "gratefulness journals" and "tips for being grateful" and "daily gratefulness affirmations," but this isn't that. What I simply want to say is this: Be grateful for the wealth you currently have and the wealth you have already built for yourself. So much of what I do when I meet a woman and walk her through her Wealth Empowerment Plan for the very first time is to show her all that she's accomplished thus far. I love watching women's faces when I show them their net worth and they see their total. They're often surprised to see how their hard work throughout their lifetime has paid off in such a real way.

So often, we get ahead of ourselves: *How much money am I going to have when I retire? What will my salary be when I get my next promotion? When am I going to be a millionaire?* All great questions, but can we take a moment before we figure all that out to give ourselves a pat on the back for all the hard work we've done to get to where we are today? Look around you. Are you in your own home, or an apartment snuggled under a blanket? Are you on a plane headed to your tropical beachside vacation? Are you just getting off work, exhausted after putting the kids to bed and reading this while eating a cold dinner? Whatever your situation, be thankful and grateful for the wealth you have built that has brought you here. Build out your net worth like I taught you in chapter six. Look at that snapshot in time of your current wealth and be grateful for what you have built thus far. You've worked hard and should be proud of yourself.

WE CAN CHANGE THE NARRATIVE

With women being the driving force over the next decade and decades to come, we are in a prime position to shift the wealth world to include women, understand women, and recognize us as the wealth powerhouses we are. This isn't going to happen overnight, but we can already feel the shift happening around us. It is up to us to stand in front of that bull on Wall Street and let the male-dominated world of wealth and finance know that we are here and we demand that the narrative around investing and wealth empowerment shift. This shift starts with us knowing and standing firm in our Wealth Empowerment Plans. It starts with us truly understanding our wealth and taking the "bull by the horns" when it comes to making wealth decisions and choosing a financial advisor who recognizes who we are, why we're investing, and where our financial priorities lie.

It starts with us having these wealth conversations with our spouses and encouraging our girlfriends to do the same.

It starts with us teaching our daughters how to save and why it is so important for her to understand money.

It starts with us.

There has never been a more important time to #LevelTheWealth. I am committed to do so for myself, my sister, my mom, my daughters, my friends, my clients, YOU reading this book, and every other woman who has found herself taking a stand for her financial independence. We've got to change the narrative and we'll do it together.

PART TWO

MICHELLE TALKS HEALTH

CHAPTER EIGHT

THE VALUE OF HEALTH

My part of the 360° action plan speaks on all aspects of physical and mental health and how we owe it to ourselves to live a nourishing life full of joy, confidence, and the ability to perform in all facets of our day-to-day life. I've made it my life's mission to empower the modern woman through optimal fitness and nutrition. It's my passion to make a fellow woman feel as beautiful, confident, empowered, healthy, and happy as she deserves to be. We have taken the word "fit" and misconstrued it to belong only to women with washboard abs and zero stretch marks, who flaunt around in a bikini while posing on beachfront vacations. It is my mission in this life to change those health standards and transform them into something even deeper that stems from the soul. I am here, with you, to fix the broken system of what women's health is and to empower women to achieve their optimal health through their own physical and mental awareness.

We live in a world where 47 percent of women have jumped into the corporate, business, and entrepreneurial workforce. These women strive for financial stability, elite work presence, and are always looking to break through the glass ceiling. However, these women are also responsible for being spouses, loving mothers to tiny humans, being a superb best friend, amongst all the other thousands of roles we fill on a daily basis. How do we expect to keep up this facade of being an elite woman of business if our mental and physical health are decaying while being put on the back burner?

My dream is to live in a world where women are empowered through their personal health in order to be empowered in their professional health. We look to social media to see how celebrity women are keeping their business, family, and perfect bodies aligned, which they always seem to tie back to some "miracle supplement" that has changed their lives and have given them endless energy and a flat stomach. You know, the "perfection" we all so deeply desire. I call *bull*, as it's my duty to guide us back to the roots of health and wellness and what that really means for you as an empowered, modern female.

As a fellow woman in business I understand the challenges of fitting in the well-deserved time for ourselves as there are so many other important facets of life which call for our undivided attention and time. I am here to tell you that you must make the time for yourself, just as you make the time for work, family, and friends. The Health and Wealth Sisters' ultimate goal is to show you exactly how to create a life in which you can have the best of both worlds in your financially stable career *and* quality of life. The time of running yourself to exhaustion and creating a life of chronic stress and anxiety are over. You were not meant to live this constant life of burn-out, and hustle as if you were going to earn some sort of badge of honor for being the "Busiest Woman Alive." As a modern woman, you are meant to be financially, professionally, and personally healthy in order to be that happy, vibrant, energetic bombshell elite woman who means business.

I am here today as a product of years of training at big gyms, watching as their advertising preyed on vulnerable women who had no idea where to start or how to begin their fitness journeys. Many big gyms take that vulnerability and turn it into big-dollar contracts while these women are left with unused memberships, a pantry full of unused supplements, and the same exact amount of confusion and hesitation they had from day one. While working at countless big box gyms, I never felt like I fit in as one of "their" trainers. I wasn't upselling their products, I wasn't making my monthly benchmarks. I just wasn't what a "real trainer" should be in their eyes. I couldn't bring myself to sell these women products *I* would never use myself, and I wasn't selling as many full-hour sessions as I should have been. Why? Because I understood that these women were barely making it to a training session after a full day of work to get their workout in and then go back home to make dinner for themselves and their family. Instead, I found ways to get them to commit to quick, effective workouts in *just thirty minutes* while seeing amazing transformations, both mentally and physically. I created effective meal plans that they could easily fit into their daily lives and work schedules—supplement free.

However, none of this was good for my sales numbers.

Thank God I quickly realized the big box gym scene just wasn't for me. I couldn't provide these unique, empowering, mental and physical transformations with the constant stress of having to make "x" amount of sales per month in supplements and hour training sessions.

I couldn't sell what I didn't believe.

DISCLAIMER

My mission as an ambassador for a holistic approach to women's health is NOT for the sole purpose of weight loss. If that was your intention for reading this book, then I'm sorry to disappoint. This book is meant for a woman living in modern times, when she must be a main source of income, a mother, a CEO, a friend, a daughter—all while balancing her own presence and self-fulfillment. This is for the woman who needs to be educated on the true meaning of health, which encompasses all things physical, emotional, spiritual, professional, and mental.

We are fortunate to be living in a time where more people are advocating for the true 360° approach to health and how each individual, especially women, must be vigilant and proactive in taking care of themselves.

I am writing this book for you—the modern woman who needs to take back the reins of her life and start showing up for herself in ways she never thought possible. You take care of too many other people, while in turn, neglecting your own health. In this lifetime, you only have this one body, so prioritize it the way you prioritize your career, your kids, and your family. Let's stop taking this precious, vulnerable life and body for granted. All you have is now, and all you're promised is this very moment. It's time to take back the responsibility of balancing your health, your mind, your body, and your soul.

CHAPTER NINE

TAKING CHARGE

My earliest memory of life was when I was three years old, sitting on the floor of our quaint townhome in Eldersburg, Maryland, your average, quiet suburban neighborhood, where we were living temporarily while our home across the street was being built. My sister had a low-grade fever which required her to take Children's Tylenol. This wasn't just any Tylenol; it was a cool, grape-flavored chewable that looked like candy. I was mad because I wanted one too. I mean, I always wanted to do what Amanda did. She was my older sister and I considered her a superhero because she always got to do the "cool" older sister stuff.

After throwing a temper tantrum by the front door, complete with shrieking and flailing, my mom offered me a Flintstones chewable vitamin. Who the heck did she think she was fooling? I knew it wasn't the exact medicine that Amanda had taken. So what did my three-year-old fiery little self do? I swatted the vitamin out of her hand, of course! I was always full of energy, very charismatic, and very adventurous, to say the least. Trying to get me to sit still for more than a few minutes was a challenge, but hey, I had stuff to do . . . things like playing with the long candle lighter by the fireplace and setting toilet paper on fire to just watch it burn on the fresh white carpet of our newly built home. (Needless to say, I got the spanking of a lifetime for that one). Other than that, I only have fun, very innocent first memories of our small family of four.

We were your average suburban family. Mom and Dad worked full-time jobs and Amanda and I would go to daycare during the week. Every morning I was always the one to wake up the earliest and annoy my mom for breakfast. I would creep to her side of the bed and softly say, "Mom, can I have my café and bread?" which was one piece of perfectly toasted bread and a cup of milk with two spoonfuls of sugar and one spoonful of instant coffee. She would blink her eyes open, reach for her glasses, and say, *"Sí nena, un momento,"* and off she went to start her day at six a.m., even on the weekends, to make me breakfast.

I loved our sweet little family of four and we all had our very own nicknames. My dad nicknamed me Chicken, which pretty much replaced my actual name, because I was always the first one up so early in the morning. Amanda's was German because she was always the dictator and bossed me around, but I was her biggest fan so I would do whatever she wanted. Mom was Old Bird because when she first moved to the states from Puerto Rico, all she ate were bird-size amounts of the food that she wasn't accustomed to. And Dad was Old Dog because he was a picky eater and basically survived off hot dogs.

Our weekends were the absolute best. My greatest memories of my father include his true love for old cars and car races, which became a family affair. It was my dad's treat to take his family out for a drive, and when we did, we'd never be going anywhere in particular. It was what people refer to as a "Sunday drive" from "back in the day." We'd drive around in peace and relaxation with nowhere to be. Sometimes on a hot summer day, we'd stop to get a refreshing snowball—shaved ice with flavored sugar syrup on top—from the local produce stand about ten minutes down the road. These were the days I love to remember—the days I realized that true joy comes from "taking it easy" and enjoying the ride, both theoretically and literally. In those moments, I learned a lot about a simple life, one in which true happiness came from being around the ones you love and simply being present while doing things to make others happy.

Another lesson I learned from my father was: "When you have more than you need, build a longer table, not a higher fence." He taught me that you couldn't have enough friends and to always treat them as your own family. These small lessons are the ones I use to this day to always make both my friends, my clients, and really anyone I meet feel as if they've known me for a lifetime. Everyone deserves that kind of connection because we all share this journey of life. It's always good to "feel at home" even if that feeling of home is in someone else's warm smile and acts of kindness.

I have always loved being outdoors, going on outdoor adventures, and having outlandish fun with my friends. I enjoyed the presence of others and the boost of endorphins that surged through me when I was with my friends.

This need of being active and happy translated into my professional presence, which even at a young age, I was fully aware of. My sister and I had been in gymnastics since the age of three. I absolutely loved it and the pure strength it gave me—like being able to stand on my hands for a long period of time, the ability to perform a standing backflip, and I could beat my friends in an arm-wrestling match. I loved my flexibility and the way my body could bend and move into so many different positions. I remember always coming first in the pull-up contest in elementary school, being the strongest girl in my grade, and usually beating most of the boys in said pull-up contests. My body gave me so much strength and confidence.

At the age of thirteen I became a young gymnastics coach and continued this side job until I was sixteen. The human body absolutely fascinated me—the mechanics of it, its vulnerability, and the emotional aspect. I loved the way a little kid would be so excited and happy after I had taught them how to accomplish something so simple as a cartwheel. I was in charge of leading, teaching, and making sure these kids aged three to ten were safe, while building their strength and their ability to hurl their bodies into gymnastics stunts ranging from tumbling, parallel bars, and trampolines. Watching their little bodies increase in muscle, their smiles grow, and their confidence soar, was magic.

MY FIRST CLIENTS

I remember a five-year-old girl named Olivia coming from school to class one day and looking so sad and miserable. Her classmates had made fun of her, saying she wasn't a real gymnast if she couldn't even do a forward roll. After Olivia confided in me, I made it my mission to not only show her how to do a forward roll, but *a forward roll that went right into a cartwheel.* This took a few weeks, but it was my responsibility to make sweet little Olivia a confident little force of energy. I would even stay with her after class to offer some additional pointers for this new trick she was perfecting. She would get frustrated, sometimes even tearfully threaten to give up, but the day came that she finally did it! She kept repeating and repeating her new trick and the smile that appeared on her face radiated from ear to ear. I knew those girls were going to think twice before making fun of her again.

Olivia was one of my first clients and I didn't even know it. She was my first success story, which showed me the power of setting goals, putting yourself first, and understanding how to properly move your body. And how doing so can and will completely change your mood, confidence, and overall happiness.

I might not have realized it then, but I have always known the direct correlation between health and happiness. I also unconsciously established myself as a leader in fitness, starting with this early side job as a gymnastics coach. Because of this fascination, shortly after high school I enrolled in our local community college for my associates degree in science, taking all classes regarding human anatomy, nutrition, and physical fitness. During these years at community college, my relationship with my sister evolved. While Amanda was away at college, only a short drive up the road, we started hanging out more. She would

172

invite me over to her college home and we would make each other dinner, watch movies, and talk about boys—especially one in particular named Alex, who is her husband now. After seventeen years of getting on each other's nerves (as young—and very different—sisters can naturally find themselves), a complete 180 happened. She was not only my sister, but my best friend.

Meanwhile at home, while I was studying at the local college, my mother asked me to join a local women's fitness studio with her. When we joined this studio together, I absolutely loved the interactions that took place between these women. Mind you, I was the youngest one in the studio, being seventeen at the time, so they looked at me like their young daughter or granddaughter. The sense of community, the happy exchanges, my mother's own mental and physical transformation were all so intoxicating to me. I saw that my mom was finally smiling again and exuded confidence as she would strut around the studio in her bright workout clothes. Everyone loved her, her accent, and the way she always spoke her mind. I had never really seen that side of my mother until then, but it was the side of her that was always waiting and wanting to show the world. We stopped yelling at each other and I started to enjoy being around her again. The studio became a symbol for our new happy and healthy approach to our lives and to our relationship.

As my mother and I enjoyed our routine of going to the studio for classes, I continued to be fascinated by the human body. The way my body was evolving both physically and mentally, and how my energy and mood changed with every single workout, became a drug to me. One day, the studio owner sent out an email inquiry to class attendees to enter her certification process of becoming a group instructor. I was absolutely ecstatic. Sure, I was only newly eighteen, but knew this was my true calling. I could be the one teaching those classes, helping women change their bodies, their minds, and the way they felt about themselves when they looked in the mirror. It was my time to take the stage and show the absolute joy I had inside me and translate it into my love for health.

I started teaching classes at the local senior center and boy, did they think I was a laugh riot. These senior women responded so well to my guidance and, of course, I would make it a safe, yet effective workout . . . but there was something else there. One of my senior class attendees, Genevieve, had a slight hunch in her back and used a cane when she walked. She was a widow and would visit the senior center for her social time. Out of curiosity, she took one of my aqua aerobics classes. Genevieve continued taking those aqua aerobics classes for about a year, with me as her instructor. One day in the senior center parking lot, I sensed someone walking briskly up to me from behind. I turned, and was met with Genevieve's smile that radiated through her soul. And then I realized she was walking *without her cane*—the cane she had been using for nearly five years. I was in disbelief. It was like she was aging backward, with her shoulders pulled back and the hunch completely gone.

This encounter was the first time Genevieve opened up to me about her husband's death years earlier and how it not only broke her heart, but made her feel as though she shouldn't be existing without him. She had lost her love and her love for herself—until recently. We both started crying as she embraced me tightly with such warmth. She was finally living again, and living for herself.

This was my client success story number two.

As my love for group classes grew, along with each and every person I taught, my curiosity for more things health and wellness expanded. How could I continue showing people the power of putting themselves first? How could I help more and more people with my love for health? Upon receiving my associate degree I knew I wanted to continue my education and pursuit of optimal health which is when I enrolled in the University of Maryland to receive my bachelor's degree in public health.

Coming from such a small town, I was a bit nervous about how going to a university of more than ten thousand students would affect me and my small "hometown" views of life. But as soon as I was assigned my apartment, I walked in and found my future best friend. Shadé, a beautiful black woman with an enormous white smile that bunched her cheeks perfectly, was sitting on our apartment's brown sofa with her legs crossed, waiting for my arrival. As we got to know each other, we found out just how much we had in common—not only in our lives, but our classes as well. After a few months, our relationship blossomed and she was nothing short of my sister as we did everything together: classes, happy hours, and endless laughter and love. We shortly acquired another roommate, Abbey, who was equally as joyful, vibrant, and also part majoring in public health.

This was my tribe of empowered females throughout my college career. We were truly inseparable as we sat down to adjust our classes so they would all match at the same times, have our bus schedules align, and allow us to share dinner together. The universe has always blessed me in sending the right women to show me just how important building your tribe of equally empowered women truly is. We were there for one another as sisters. I learned throughout those years how big their hearts really were and why the three of us were in all those same classes together. We made it our mission to always encourage one another, give one another sound advice with love, and to make sure we were doing everything we could to help others through the power of preventative health in our communities.

Throughout these classes at the University of Maryland, I was taught the true beauty of protecting the health you have in order to create a life of not just looking a certain way, but creating a life of longevity without having to suffer from chronic disease.

175

I learned just how urgent the need is for communities to understand the importance of preventative health care rather than leaning toward medicine and reactive measures for chronic health issues. It was here that I learned that the number one cause of death, according to the CDC, was and still is heart disease, and that one person dies every thirty-seven seconds from it. Although genetics can sometimes cause this illness, it is usually a consequence of immediate lifestyle choices including, but not limited to: diabetes, obesity, diet, physical inactivity, and excessive alcohol use. I was shocked! *We fully acknowledge that we are slowly nailing the coffin to our graves, yet we still live this life of perpetual risk? How could this happen?* My education in public health gave me so much insight as to how an individual learns behavior, and how we are creatures of habit and results of our environment. I was taught the important and crucial steps of how to change habits, change learned views, and perhaps most critically, how to make these habits sustainable.

As I continued teaching my group classes on and off campus I kept asking the universe what I needed to do in order to help as many people as I could. People mostly think of public health as the CDC trying to find "patient zero" and how to minimize communicable and chronic diseases, but I didn't want to be behind the scenes running the analytics. I wanted to be part of the change. I wanted to do hands-on work and continue educating as many people as I could about the power of preventative health.

My internship during my last semester of college consisted of me working at an adult day care facility and being a public health resource in my community. Shadé's internship was assisting in an occupational therapist facility, and Abbey's was at a local nursing practice. We had no interest in doing research work, as we all wanted to be hands-on and protect and educate our communities. During my internship, I was the activities coordinator for the physically and mentally handicapped adults who attended the adult day care facility. They came from low economic environments, so usually there was no option for healthy foods in their homes or a general understanding that they needed to take care of their health. I would get them outside to kick a ball around as much as I could, help them during their physical therapy sessions, and assist in the kitchen to ensure they were supplying proper nutrition.

It was a true eye-opener to see how much the general population still doesn't know about natural health and wellness. I'm sure you know that smoking cigarettes and eating meals high in fat can contribute to poor health and heart disease, right? But what you might think is common knowledge is completely unheard of and ignored in different socioeconomic environments and populations. I saw firsthand that we truly take for granted the lives we are given, and the benefits of understanding that lifestyle factors play an immediate role in your health and quality of life.

After that internship and accepting a full-time administrative position at that adult day care upon graduating, I knew I wanted to do more. I wanted to give people a true one-on-one experience through guided coaching, education, and creating sustainable habit changes for a longer quality of life. I wanted to use my education in public health to give people the true transformation they deserved from the inside out.

CHAPTER TEN

TRAINER FOR THE MODERN WOMAN

All right, ladies, if you haven't picked up on my sassy Puerto Rican attitude yet, well, here it comes. It's going to get super fiery. My mission in life is to go above and beyond and finally put health fads, trends, myths, and masculine-driven notions to shame. But first let me help you further understand why I am the way I am and why I tenaciously advocate for and help women.

Shortly after attending and graduating from the University of Maryland with my bachelor's in public health I continued working full time as an administrative assistant at the assisted living facility. Although I didn't exactly love this nine-to-five career path, the woman in charge was an INCREDIBLE inspiration. She built her business from the ground up and truly set the tone for all things boss babe in my life. I'm leaving her name out for privacy, but if you're reading this you know who you are and I thank you and love you. She was my boss, my friend, and truly terrifying in the most badass way. She didn't take shit from anyone and showed me what it was like to be in charge of my own life. I watched and I learned, and her sense of empowerment translated itself in my life as the female entrepreneur I am now.

While working this administrative job, I continued to teach group classes, but I felt a growing sense of guilt that I couldn't help these women even more. I loved teaching and wanted to be there all day. I wished to better get to know their needs and then provide help on an even more personal level. It was then that I decided to become a certified personal trainer and shortly thereafter left my nine-to-five desk job for a starting position as a personal trainer at a local gym.

It was there at the gym that I found my passion, my meaning, my confidence to become a trainer who was able to really, really get to know women one-on-one. On the other hand, it was also where I saw the downright ugly aspects of commercial gyms as they used society's views and diet fads to prey on a woman's constant struggle to be not only healthy, but a woman with washboard abs and a thigh gap. I'm not calling out *every single commercial gym*, but let's just say that I've worked at enough of these gyms to know that a majority of them do not have the best interests for a modern woman. And guess what? Interestingly enough, most of them are owned by men with an ego the size of Texas.

It was all about the sales and the numbers. While I understand that every business must make numbers, when did sales become more important than the immediate health of humanity? I guess it's my background in public health that urges these thoughts but *geez*, could we take a step back and take a more holistic and empathetic approach to women's physical and mental health?

I was constantly told to push, upsell, and force people into buying not only sessions but weight-loss products and supplements. They would pounce on anyone who entered those doors and used lures to get them to start paying up. I was quite taken aback by this perspective of becoming some kind of used car salesman for training programs. I saw these vulnerable women step into a gym wanting to do something for themselves and their confidence. I'd watch as they'd look around at all the big, bulky gym equipment with anxiousness and be startled by some beefy guy on the floor who was obnoxiously slamming weights down and grunting as loud as humanly possible. How in the world was she supposed to enjoy coming to the gym if the environment was so male driven and so skewed on health? I was told to sell these women on protein powders and weight-loss supplements that were "sworn" to give them that perfect beach body. Even the very pictures that hung on the walls in the women's locker room were those of women holding supplements with perfectly chiseled abs. I knew I was different and didn't quite fit in with the other trainers or management.

When I started to get the hang of individual training sessions, I realized just how completely different a personal training session was compared to a group class. I only knew the very surface of these women's lives while teaching group classes. As I truly, and I mean *truly*, got to know these women, they would put their lives out on the table—from their careers, their families, their marital problems, to how they thought if they changed their appearance, their partners would look at them differently. I also learned just how little time they had because families were expecting dinner on the table although they had literally just come from their own nine-to-five jobs.

I was these run down, mentally drained female clients' escape, the person they came to not only change their health but to change their mental perspectives on life. These women were so vulnerable, so in the dark on how truly amazing they really were. I knew I had to provide them quick and effective workouts with real nutrition guidance. It wasn't enough for me to tell them to grab a shake after their training session so they could just skip right through dinner.

Again, this approach did not go over well with management and sales, and I was constantly in my manager's office hearing: "Michelle, why didn't you sell Susan the twenty one-hour packs? Why did you only sell the twenty thirty-minute packs?" "You're not going to hit your numbers if you don't sell the bigger packs and the supplements." "We feel as though you're hitting a plateau in your sales and are no longer trying to increase your monthly sales target."

I didn't understand; I was *helping people*. Isn't that what I was supposed to be doing? As I looked around to find the answer in other trainers, I watched more meaningless interactions than true

181

relationships form between the client and trainer. *Where is the engagement?* I thought. *The smile? Where is the warm interaction of a client and trainer who has truly made an impact in their lives?* Don't get me wrong, I know there are wonderful trainers out there, but again, I've worked at countless big box gyms where this kind of relationship is the exception, not the rule.

Through all the management's disappointment and shame, I knew I was doing something very different. Because I had my background in public health, I was able to help my clients make behavioral change, which manifested to their physical change for optimal health. For example, I was bringing one client, Debbie, a smile and laugh that I had never seen before. She told me how much more focused she was at work. How she finally had the courage to ask for the well-deserved promotion that only last year was given to someone else who had worked less hours and had less passion for the work than she did. She was finally able to fit into her jeans from two summers ago, able to come off her high cholesterol medication, and was less anxious than ever before! All of a sudden she not only had time for her family, but made it a priority to take her thirty-minute solitary bath on the weekends and had the confidence to tell her husband to "figure it out" for dinner. I couldn't believe the person I was seeing in front of me. This was not Debbie from three months ago. This was the new and improved Debbie, who started to show up for her own damn self, not anyone else. She no longer looked to her husband, or any others for that matter, waiting for a compliment because she was her own beautiful compliment.

However, my sales still weren't adding up, even though I had been working endless hours to get these training sessions in with these women. I was so unfulfilled in my heart, but so passionate about the lives I was changing. As a woman raised by two other ambitious women, I kept asking Amanda and my mother, "What if I opened my own gym? What if I could offer the group classes and the personal training? What if I could be my own boss and finally have the guts to up and quit?" Of course they were on my side and ready to help and to watch me grow. The three of us Riley women began looking up rental spaces, small business legalities, small business loans, etc. They came with me to almost every meeting with lawyers, property managers, equipment salesmen, and more. As cliché as it sounds, where there is a will, there is a way. And when you have a true burning desire and calling to do what you want to do in this life, there is not a damn thing in the world that can get in your way.

After four years of working for the big box gyms, I finally did it. I opened my very own female fitness studio called Body Oasis. (Shout out to my original Body Oasis sisters. I am here because of YOU and I thank you.) This was finally it—a safe place for women to come and make a true connection to themselves. Not only did I teach group classes, but for those who needed more direction and guidance, I was there to take them by the hand and give them the attention they deserved from a personal trainer. We were a unit, a community, a team of empowered females who helped one another along their roads to true boss babe glory. There was such an amazing energy in the studio that didn't come from selling packages or shoving supplements in people's hands. The power came from the true transformations occurring within those walls, the smiles that would leave the studio every day, the decrease in medications, the friendships that were made, and the lasting habits we instilled in one another to make our lives a healthy and happy one. I continued building my tribe of empowered females who I had slowly been assembling throughout my childhood, my college education, and now, throughout my very own studio.

Unfortunately, it was here that I had to go through my second hardest part of my life—losing one of the beautiful females I had first come to know during my college years. After having my studio doors open with such success, I decided it was time to reward myself with an all-inclusive vacation to the

Dominican Republic with my friend Nikki. We were going to have the girls trip of a lifetime and eat, drink, and simply celebrate what it is to be alive and joyous. I had not a care in the world as we enjoyed crystal clear beaches and colorful tropical drinks. We danced the night away, truly celebrating our friendship.

Upon arriving back to our room after another amazing day, I remember Nikki looking at her phone. We had left our phones in the room that day because we didn't get much service out of the rooms and we were too busy enjoying the beaches and soaking up the sun to care about the outside world. As I plopped down on the bed, a bit tired from all the sun, she looked at me, looked at her phone, looked back at me, and then covered her mouth with her hand. Anxiety began to fill every inch of my body. I jumped up from the bed, my heart racing. "What's wrong? What's wrong?" I kept repeating.

"Michelle, please sit down, please just sit," she said.

I begged her to spit it out, as that same gutted feeling I had when I found out my father had died started churning in my stomach.

"Shadé is dead; she was shot," Nikki blankly stated.

My world was turned upside down . . . again. I let out a painful yell that came from the pit of my stomach, from the spot in my chest that was once my heart. My mind started racing: *Why? How? When? Where?* I couldn't process any of it. She was so joyful, so pure, always willing to drop everything and help another in need. My best friend who had just started her dream job as an occupational therapist, who I had seen only weeks before, *was dead?* Why was I being thrown through this kind of trauma again? Why did life feel the need to serve up another helping of death? Why did it have to be someone so close to me?

Why did the universe have to be so cruel?

I later learned Shadé had been shot and killed by her ex-boyfriend who had a laundry list of assault charges and

184

restriction orders against women. Shadé and I never talked much about this boyfriend of hers, which was a little strange to me because we would talk about everything under the sun. I found it odd, yet didn't pay much mind to it and left it alone. The last time I saw her, she told me she was no longer with him and we left it at that. I had no idea that he was capable of such evil.

Shortly after that incident, I dreamed about Shadé. It was so vivid. I was lying down in my bed and she was standing over me. Her brown eyes looked right into mine and once again I saw her big beautiful smile and her black braided hair flowing over her shoulders. I was in disbelief as I exclaimed, "Shadé, I miss you so much! Where are you? What are you doing?" As I felt a wave of sadness fall over me, she eased my emotions and began telling me that she was so happy where she was and not to worry about her. She told me she was doing what she loved best, which was shopping with her friends, and that soon she would start her journey to help others transition smoothly to the other side. Shadé told me she couldn't wait for me to come there and see how beautiful it was. "Well hopefully not too soon!" I interrupted and we both laughed. She told me she loved me and then tickled me on my side.

The dream felt so real to me—as real as sitting down with your friend across the dinner table. I've dreamed about Shadé a few other times since then. And Dad, too. I had all the proof I needed from Shadé that she was okay, she was happy, and that she was thriving on the other side where I will meet her once again.

Although Shadé's passing was heavy on my heart and the hearts of her friends and family, I came out of this experience a little stronger than I had been before and with a renewed sense of purpose. I knew I needed to be surrounded by the tribe of women I had built at my studio, and I knew they needed me too. I had to keep building this community of women who need to feel empowered, to know they're not alone in this journey, and my studio had to be a safe haven where they could come and talk in times of need. Shadé showed me that, as women, we must stand together and refuse to be overshadowed by fear. I decided to honor her by setting sail in a different direction and leaving my own troubled seas of failed and toxic relationships behind.

On the heels of declaring myself a "single and independent woman who don't need no man," fate stepped in with a plot twist that changed my entire life. Over lunch one day with Heather, my very close friend and fellow fitness instructor from the studio I had first worked at, she only part-jokingly said to me, "Michelle, once you're done dating a**holes, you're going to meet my nephew and you two are going to date."

Ladies, when I say build your tribe of empowered females, I MEAN IT! They will not only call you out on your B.S., but they will always give it to you straight. Because when you surround yourself with like-minded women operating on the same flow of energy, they will be there to not only support you, but to watch you grow. As I admitted, I had a track record for dating men who I knew didn't hold my best interests at heart, and that wouldn't help me flourish into the beautiful vibrant woman I knew I could be.

A few months later, I took Heather up on her offer and she coordinated an entire semi-blind date with herself, her nephew, and her husband at a local Italian wine bar. I say semi-blind because she proudly showed off the pictures she had of her extremely handsome nephew who had just graduated from West Point, and she had secretly done the same with him.

As I pulled up to the wine bar on a warm summer day, I remember my heart fluttering as I gazed upon a tall drink of water who had perfectly coiffed strawberry-blond hair. As if he had been sculpted by the Greek gods themselves, I could tell he was perfectly chiseled under his slim-fit navy-blue T-shirt. I remember he was standing outside by himself, as Heather had texted me saying she and her husband had gone inside to find a table.

As I walked over to him, he smiled, extended his hand and shyly said, "Hi, I'm Stephen." At the entrance he chivalrously held the door open for me. I laugh now because Stephen was, and still is, so completely opposite of me. I am outgoing, loud, so much of an extrovert, and he couldn't be any more opposite. Throughout the evening he said a few words here and there as Heather and I did most of the talking. I thought he was so handsome and found it intriguing how quiet he was, wondering what was going on in that square-jawed head of his. I knew I had to find out what made this cool, calm, and collected guy tick.

The very next day, he texted and asked me out on a date. I was happily surprised since he was so quiet and hard to read the night before. This time, it would be just the two of us. As we sat down at our upscale steak dinner, he spilled an entire glass of water all over me while reaching for his drink. Later, he would confess that his nerves had made him more clumsy than usual. I remember a man from the neighboring table leaning in and asking, "First date, huh?" Stephen sheepishly nodded and proceeded to clean up the table. Even though he decided to drench me in water during our first date, I instinctively knew there was something different about him. He was kind, calm, and respectful. His quietness quickly grew into effortless flowing conversation. We had so much in common even though our immediate personalities were complete opposites.

Deep down I knew Stephen was my match. I know how crazy this is going to sound, but I had found someone whose features and traits reminded me of my father. They were both of strong Irish descent with strawberry-blond hair, pale skin, and bright blue eyes. And just like my father, Stephen too had a calm personality with such humble intelligence. I was amazed at how the universe aligned itself so perfectly to bring Stephen into my life at just the right time. We spent our first summer together falling in love while traveling the beaches of the east coast. As it always does, summer ended too soon and Stephen had to move south for the beginning of his military career as a post-graduate. So there we were . . . dating long distance, since I had my flourishing studio in Maryland and he had his blossoming military career at his first station in Georgia.

After about a year and a half of long-distance dating, I knew I had to follow my heart to Georgia. I took a huge leap of faith and closed the doors to my Maryland studio for the last time. While I cried enough tears to flood the studio (or at least it sure felt like it), I knew my journey as a health and fitness coach wasn't going to end just because my studio's journey had wrapped. I knew I could re-create the experience I had given to my tribe of women in Maryland. But how was I going to keep changing lives knowing military living has you moving every few years from one location to another.

We moved to Savannah together and had the absolute best time of our lives. It was there where I continued to help women and rebuilt my business. You're crazy if you think for one second I was going back to work at one of the big box gyms where my mission would be smothered. I transitioned as best as I could, dabbling with virtual classes for my Body Oasis women. I wanted to show the women back home that even though I couldn't be there for them physically, I was still able to help them achieve their health goals—even if it was through a screen.

While in Savannah, I started my traveling training business. I had so much fun visiting my clients' homes, training these women where they were most comfortable and confident, and touring the charming "Hostess City of the South." It was here that I realized just how sheltered I was in my one-dimensional small town in Maryland. Going into the homes of these women and training at local parks under Savannah's beautiful Spanish moss trees, I was exposed to new communities and women who had been dealt completely different cards in their lives. These women had different careers, stressors, and aspects of life that they needed help and guidance with to become the empowered females they knew they could be. I was able to continue fine-tuning my business mission by tailoring my workouts, programs, and coaching in order to help these unique women, who were coincidentally mostly made up of small business owners. I learned *so much* from these women who were striving to make their passion their business at a time in which I was doing the same. We learned so much from each other as we helped each other grow our businesses and understand the meaning of being a self-sustaining woman in charge. Many quickly became my close friends.

Just as I started to get into the swing of things and had fallen madly in love with Savannah's charms, it was time for another military move. Damn. Together, Stephen and I moved to Columbus, Georgia. This time I had a ring on my finger and we had our fur baby, Mildred, a crazy, spunky Australian shepherd, in tow. It was in Columbus that I realized just how different each military town can be. Coming from such an incredibly dense, female working population in Savannah, to a quieter town with less working women, was quite the adjustment. I continued my same advertising to promote my traveling training business, but the population just wasn't the same and my business suffered. I was at a loss for how I could continue following my passion and mission in life within all the constant moving that is demanded of a life in the military. I still had so much more to offer and more women to help through their journeys of optimal health and wellness. It was as if the carpet was being ripped out from under me, as I had no control in this military world. My passion for what moved me was dimming.

As I sat one day exploring my social media feed, all the sudden I saw a trainer talking about his online training success. *LIGHT BULB* The epiphany came to me that I, too, should begin converting my training business online in order to help as many women as I could through the power of preventative health. It's crazy the way the universe shows up once you allow yourself to be open and vulnerable. The universe was telling me not to give up and to keep transforming my business to not only work for the women I needed to help, but for myself and my new military lifestyle. As I began researching and educating myself on how exactly this kind of training worked, I let it settle in and marinate so I could enjoy my beachfront wedding in Puerto Rico with my soon-to-be husband and closest family and friends.

Under the gaze of our guests, I locked arms with my strong, amazing, beautiful mom to begin walking down the aisle. I held tightly to the beautiful handmade seashell bouquet my sister and I had made together for my special day. At the base of my bouquet, I tied a small framed picture of our father walking down the aisle on his wedding day. I wanted him to be there. As much as I know deep down in my heart that he was there in the warm salty breeze, I wished he himself could walk me down the aisle. Questions kept spinning around my head. *What would he think of my soon-to-be husband? Is he proud of me and where I am today? Would he cry from the corners of his deep blue eyes as he gave me away?*

The sandy aisle was sprinkled with tiny starfish Riley, my niece and flower girl, had dutifully strewn about. I looked ahead and saw all our family and friends that had traveled to be with us on this day. And finally, I zeroed in on Stephen's smiling face. He looked like a groom straight out of a bridal magazine in his light blue suit. Heather, his aunt and our matchmaker, stood next to him waiting to commence our wedding ceremony and join us together as husband and wife. As I got closer, I looked into Stephen's eyes and couldn't help but smile myself, as I knew I was exactly where I needed to be.

As my mother gave me away, Heather asked, "And who is here today giving Michelle away?"

With a cracked voice of mixed emotions, my mother responded, "John and I do." I knew with my entire being that Dad was right there, giving his daughter away to a wonderful man he had handpicked just for me.

Returning from my fairy tale wedding, I knew it was time to get back to figuring out exactly how I could make the transition to help women online all around the world. But good Lord, have you seen what is online these days? I'm not only trying to force my way to be seen, but I am competing against half-naked models holding up some kind of fit tea or promoting a diet shake. How in the world was I supposed to compete with that? Were my ten social media followers going to give me a precious moment of their attention so that I could tell them that none of what they were seeing was real?

As I began doing all the research I could on how to train online, how to increase my online presence, and how to still authentically connect with women behind a cell phone screen, I started to become desperate. I felt angry and annoyed that I couldn't help the women who I knew needed me. I was frustrated with the oversaturation of misguided nutrition information and the use of half-naked models to promote fitness which ultimately led to poor self-body image.

At a point in my life where I started to look around for other jobs and made excuses for why my business was sinking, I began practicing meditation, which led to many incredibly vivid dreams, and even ones with guides who helped me on my journey. I learned to ask for what I need and what I want to achieve in this life—that just saying it in your mind's eye is enough to plant the seed of positive intention in order to manifest those intentions into reality. At first, meditating was hard. I kept thinking about how I was going to get my new business up and running and that if I wasn't on my computer working, I wasn't going to be successful. One day during meditation, it finally happened—what I call the "in-between."

The in-between is where your consciousness is separate from your body, where you are surrounded by unconditional love and you are able to receive messages from your higher self, your loved ones, your guardian angels, your spirit guides, and the universe, or God, if that's what you like to call it. This place is detached from the inner voice in your head which is fueled by guilt, shame, and judgment.

If you're reading this thinking, "Michelle must have been hitting the peace pipe a little too hard," I'm not mad at you for it. This is simply what I believe and what has helped me to understand who I really am and why I've been put on this Earth. When I was finally able to reach this place, I could hear messages like: "LET GO, BE AUTHENTIC, BE LIMITLESS." I had never been one to have this kind of positive mindset by myself, as I was always looking to others to give me the reassurance I needed. But here I was, in a town where I wasn't able to take the easy road, looking into myself for the answers I needed to get me to where I am today. I was able to change my perspective on how to find true confidence in myself. I found the confidence to listen to my heart, to know that my audience would grow, to trust that I would say the exact words needed for that modern woman to hear and to trust.

That's when it truly came to me. In order to stand out from the rest, I had to let go of control and be my authentic self. I needed to show the world that the reason I stood here today was because of all my experiences in the past including: my father's suicide, my empowered female force of a family, my own desire to be the very best I could be, the traumatic death of my best friend, and the need to show women why their health shouldn't be put on the back burner of life. I needed to use all these experiences as fuel and as my platform to help as many women as I could. I had to stand out and make an impact even if it was behind a computer, on how to help women understand that they can be in charge of their health and that they *deserved* to be both healthy and happy. Most importantly, I needed to show them that they weren't alone on their journey throughout this incredible life and that we all have scars and experiences that we must grow from and use to help the woman sitting next to us.

With my newly charged acknowledgment of higher purpose and consciousness continued vivid dreams which helped to guide my path. One of these dreams was of my father, whom much like Shadé, I assure you is thriving and doing what he could not physically or emotionally do here on this Earth. In my dream I asked why he left us. He told me he wasn't made for this lifetime and he was on the other side aiding people going through what he went through and helping them understand how much more there is to life than sadness. He told me he was sorry and that he was still looking out for all of us girls, just in a different way. I've had a few other dreams about my father and I know he is happy. Happier than I ever saw him on this side of life. I learned from this dream that the road to healing is hard, but that I must practice like my father and continue to help others here, on this side of life, to put their happiness through health first. We must end the stigma of mental health and be able to talk about it openly and freely. I know my job here is to help others find joy in their own happiness, joy in their ultimate health, and the real joy found in the beauty that begins in the mind, not the body. I needed to continue being my authentic self and share my story.

Another powerful dream which guided my path was with an energy healer by the name of Emma. In my dreams, my favorite thing to do is to fly. I am weightless, limitless, and free. I flew over snow-capped mountains to a luminous cave where I was greeted by a woman with blond hair who told me to lie down on a stone bed. I asked her name, and she responded, "Emma." I asked if she was one of my spirit guides and she replied, "Yes." It was so matter of fact, like she was saying, "Duh, Michelle, we talk all the time."

I laid down and she placed her hands on my shoulders. The energy that surged through my body, from her hands, was indescribable. If pure serenity and peace had a feeling, this was it. It was almost as if she was surveying me. She told me I was very right-side dominant, which was my masculine side and harbored my strong ambition, tenacity, and feeling of needing to get ahead. Emma told me that although these traits were wonderful for my current life, she'd like me to try to balance these sides and put forth more energy into manifesting my feminine side.

I woke up from that dream thinking, *What the heck? What is the right side and left side of my energy body and why am I having these intensely vivid dreams?* Needless to say, even I thought that I was a little looney tunes. I decided to do my own research and there it was: feminine energy resides within the left side of your body, promoting a state of flow, intuition, and calmness, while male energy, which resides on the right side of your body, harbors your confidence, self-motivation, ambition, and action taking. I know how crazy this sounds and if you're as confused as I was, look it up. It's real.

I wondered, *Why was I receiving this dream? How could I put this into my own mission of female empowerment and my own life?* So many thoughts floated around my head . . . then it came to me. I was meant to show myself, and show other women, that you can most definitely be a hardworking, ambitious woman while also nurturing your need to let go and simply be. We are in a serious energy shift in the world. Females are beginning to rise up, become more self-sufficient, and have more independence than ever, yet we are not balancing these two states of professional and personal life effectively, resulting in manifestations of poor health, poor sleep, mental health instability, lack of confidence, and more. But that's exactly why I had this dream and why I need to show women they *can* have a balance of both energy fields.

I work at pairing my energy fields daily, and I still find myself sometimes worrying, working around the clock, and not focusing on myself. It's a constant challenge to get into the state of flow. But once I'm there I truly see the balance between having the best of both worlds in my professional and personal health and quality. For that reason, this dream has been one of the most important and impactful lucid dreams that I've had with my spirit guide. I will say this—no matter how crazy you think I am, start talking to the universe. Ask what you need with complete faith and trust, and you shall receive; it's as simple as that.

Backed by the universe, I set out to transform my business into one that ran solely online. My mission was to reach the modern woman who desperately needed to find balance in her life and who needed to put her health first. She is the woman who is living in a time where she makes her own salary, who has her own career, who has a busy work life and perhaps a family at the same time. She's the woman who wakes up day after day seeing the same tired face in the mirror looking back at her, thinking, "Is this it?" She's the woman who might not have the luxury of dropping everything and getting to the gym for a quick workout. I knew I had to be there *for her*, to fight for her, and to be her voice.

I knew I had to set up an online training system that would fit perfectly for someone like my late client, Amy, who worked a nine to five with an entire family and a full day's worth of tasks, all while trying to increase her own happiness and confidence. I needed to take it a step further and give these women the transformations they deserved with proper information on both fitness and nutrition, which ultimately led me to acquire my nutrition coaching certification.

As I continued to trust myself, the universe, and regain my confidence, I spoke to my small, yet growing audience with my authentic voice. My strong voice promoted all things mental and physical health for the modern woman. Through this, I began to stand out. I didn't have to flash my muscles or model half naked on my social media in order to get the attention of the women who needed me. I spoke from my heart, which led to one client, then another, and another. I slowly started building my very own tribe of women who needed my help and needed to be taught to love themselves through proper fitness, nutrition, and self-care. As I slowly began building my online presence and my online business, I began to see the mindset shift of the women I was training and coaching. They were doing it, and I was doing it! I was providing these women with the tools they needed to transform themselves into the beautiful, vibrant, and confident women they knew they desired to be, not for anyone else but themselves. I was giving the exact same hands-on approach that I had built my journey upon, even while being states away.

The most important lesson I learned from my online coaching service and continue to learn to this day, is that these women weren't learning new, groundbreaking information on how to become healthy and happy. *Instead, they were finally able to push "mute" on the negative self-talk.* They were able to quiet the bully in their heads telling them they weren't good enough, the noise in social media saying that they could drop "x" amount of weight with diet pills, the noise of other people telling them they couldn't do it . . . They finally shut all of it out. Again, I simply provided these beautiful women with the tools they needed to be their own superheroes.

It's my purpose and job in this lifetime to find these women and show them they are not alone in their climb to selfless health initiatives. They don't need to sacrifice their health, energy, and vibrancy to live the life of a successful modern woman. In order to run at peak professional performance, they must invest in their immediate mental, physical, and spiritual health. We are living in a different time here, ladies—a time where the modern woman is in charge of her finances, her career, her family, and her complete well-being. We are part of a truly amazing moment in which women have the upper hand, the resources available, and the means to be the superiors.

As a trainer and nutrition coach for the modern woman, it's my passion and life's work to continue empowering these women, much like yourself, and watch them blossom and grow into some of the world's most professional and personally successful people ever seen. Together we are the powerful voices and strong advocates for not only health but for all things women empowerment. This is the time we must grow together as women and celebrate our health and our bodies. We must be authentic to ourselves, which is why at the beginning of this section I told you this is not a program designed for weight loss or how to get washboard abs. This work and my mission are designed to show you that no matter where you are in life, you are and must be in complete control of your own health. It's our time, ladies, and it's your time to start showing up for yourself the way you do for everyone else.

CHAPTER ELEVEN

GUILT

This chapter is to give you the permission you need to start putting yourself first. Why do we struggle with internal guilt as an employee, a mother, a friend, a spouse, etc. who tells us we should always be looking after others and putting our careers before anything else? We believe it's selfish if we do something for ourselves. How dare we even think for one minute that we are allowed to give ourselves the quality time and self-nourishment we need in order to function at such a high level of performance? As a female climbing the professional ladder, it would be absolutely shameful to think about anything other than your job and your family, right?

Let me paint a picture that's about to hit you so hard to your core that you'll think, "My gosh, how have I not seen this myself?" Imagine it's a new day and the sun has yet to dimly light the dark night sky. Your alarm goes off at six a.m., and with a groggy head, you blink your eyes open and immediately, without even thinking, turn to your phone on the bed stand and start scrolling through all your emails and notifications for work that appeared overnight. Preparing your mental checklist, you are already feeling scattered, wondering how you're first going to get everything done that was left over from yesterday and why you're already "out of time" before the day has even started. You quickly scramble out of bed and start getting ready for the day ahead. In the mirror, you see your tired eyes looking back at you—a shell of what once used to be a bright-eyed, bushy-tailed bombshell ready to take on the world. As you rifle through your closet to find something to throw on, you ready yourself to wake up the kids and endure the morning battle to get them ready and out the door on time for school. Your husband has already gotten himself ready, quickly plants a kiss on your cheek, and is on his way to work. Meanwhile, you're scrambling to make your morning cup of coffee, as this warm cup of joe has been your only saving grace to get you through your morning routine while getting the kids' lunches and book bags together. You have barely even taken a sip of your coffee and you're locking the door behind you.

Great, another day without a packed lunch but it's okay because you made your spouse's lunch and the kid's lunches the night before. You take solace in the fact that you have that café across the street from work where you can sit, eat, and continue finishing the proposal that needs to be submitted by one p.m. With your mental schedule ready, you drop the kids off at school, and you're ready for a day at the office. Within minutes of stepping into the office, your coworker stops at your desk, saying they need help with a client problem. Without hesitation, you dismiss the fact that you need to concentrate on your proposal. You're ready to help with the situation at hand without even thinking about yourself, the fact that you haven't had time to settle in, that you haven't had any breakfast, and the fact that you still have to submit your own proposal.

A few hours go by and you've helped your coworker find a solution and your boss is happy, as is the client. It's now past noon, still no breakfast, and your proposal hasn't been completed. Many have already gone on their lunch break, so you quickly run out to the café and purchase your usual BLT sandwich with some chips and a soda. Instead of taking the time to eat and finish your meal, you move quickly to put the finishing touches on your proposal. With just ten minutes to finish your lunch and head to the office, you click *submit* and feel a wave of relief wash over your body. As you hurry back to your office, you discover there is a heaping pile of new tasks your boss has put on your desk since you've been gone. More hours fly by and you look down and realize it's already five thirty. You were supposed to be on your way home by five p.m. in order to go get the kids, make dinner, and let the dogs out because they've been inside all day. Ugh. It's time to hustle and bustle. You think about calling your husband so he can get dinner started, but remember that he is currently at the gym and you'd hate to interrupt his workout. So, after picking up the kids a little late and finally coming home from your extended work day, you walk through the front door, unpack, let the dogs out, help with homework, make a frozen pizza for the family, and *finally* get to settle in. It's time for you to relax, grab a glass of wine, put the kids to bed, and watch some Netflix with your husband, as this is your only quiet time together. As you head to bed and lay your head on the pillow, you're already mentally preparing yourself for tomorrow. Wash, rinse, and repeat.

Sound familiar?

While you've been spending days, weeks, months, or years in this cycle you realize your energy is draining. The light within you that once shined so brightly is fading. You have the saddest thoughts come to mind which really put you in a deep funk. You are gaining weight in places you never have, and you rely on Advil to get your achy joints through the day. However, you think to yourself, "Hey, this is life. I need to do whatever it takes to make sure my family and my career are thriving. It's all for the best and there's no need to focus on myself because that is downright selfish. Besides, there is just not enough time in the day for myself."

Whoa. Even I need to take a deep breath after going over that incredibly stressful series of events. Unfortunately as a woman, this is pretty normal, right? We live in a world where women have always been pushed down. They are the caretakers and must always be there to help someone else, often neglecting their own climb while they act as the stepstool for someone else's. To top it all off, that same woman is expected to be in pristine health both mentally and physically. How in the world is that something that we think is normal or that our society thinks is normal? I am here to tell you to wake up and to start taking back your birthright to put yourself first in all aspects of life. In order for you to bust through that glass ceiling and be the very best woman in business who means business, you must do what it takes to show up for yourself every single day, to be that high-earning, healthy, happy, and fearless woman you know is waiting to shine.

The entire scenario above was based around guilt. It's the guilt that ensures you constantly put your needs behind those of everyone else around you. Guilt that you don't deserve to put yourself first because you are a mom, a caretaker, and an employee with obligations, and there just isn't enough time in the day to get everything done for everyone.

Let me show you some common deteriorating thought processes that seem so harmless on the surface, yet are self-sabotaging. These thoughts form the voice inside your head, often disguised as your "best friend," but in reality, is an ugly monster you have created in your own mind keeping you as far away as possible from a healthy life.

GUILT IN DISGUISE

Do any of these statements resonate with you?

- "Taking time for myself to work out would be taking time away from doing all my work and spending time with my family."
- "I'm so unmotivated to work out, but I'm ashamed that I look and feel the way I do."
- "My family's health history is already bad. Who am I to think I can change this with a few workouts and salads?"
- "My partner loves me just the way I am. Why would I give up our nightly Netflix "date" just to do a little workout?"

- "It would be selfish of me to spend that kind of money on healthy foods, a gym membership, or a massage. I need to use this money for other things."
- "I'm not good at sticking to a workout plan. Why even bother if I'm always going to be so flaky?"

These are only some of the ways that guilt and its hideous face can disguise itself and form that voice in your head telling you that you're *not good enough* to live a healthy life. You might even think to yourself, "Who do I think I am, trying to change the person I am today?" Society reinforces this misguided self-talk by telling you to have a seat and be the polite girl the world wants you to be, helping others before you dare think about helping yourself. We've ingrained these thought patterns as our norm and thus are left caught in a vicious cycle between wanting to be healthier, yet feeling guilty about putting our own health and happiness at the forefront of our precious lives.

Perhaps you feel guilty about not being in your best health. You feel guilty that you should look a certain way and that you've been neglecting yourself. You think, "Why start now if I'm already like this? I'm still here, aren't I?" This then becomes one heck of a self-defeating trap of wanting to work out and not wanting to work out due to lack of motivation, which you also feel guilty about. I've heard this exact monologue more times than I can count. We are constantly trying to balance this internal, male-driven narrative that society has ingrained into our brains. It's time you get out of your own way and finally show up for your beautiful self, kicking those past narratives of guilt to the curb and out of your life for good! We can either continue feeling bad for ourselves or we can finally wake up and change this deteriorating mindset. By changing our ability to look after ourselves the way we so eagerly look after others, we will have the platform we need to fight the internal voice whispering, "You're not good enough."

Perhaps you think that if you take those thirty or so minutes for your workout, self-care, or preparing a healthy meal than you're being selfish. You're taking away time you could be doing work, getting on the phone with a client, hanging out with your family and friends, or cuddling with your pup. You automatically think, "I just have too much to do and that wouldn't be fair to everyone who needs me." I'm here to tell you, it *can* wait! We're always going to be busy, pulled in eighty directions at once, going from meeting to meeting, and so on. Why can't you give to yourself the way you selflessly give to others?

By constantly letting your internal guilt and others depict what your optimal life should look like, you're devaluing yourself and basically telling your body, "I don't care if you suffer because my physical and mental health aren't important to me." Your body responds in turn by throwing you through a whirlwind of symptoms, including but not limited to: anxiety, depression, weight gain, mood swings, chronic illnesses, and more. Well, no wonder, girlfriend! Your body and your health are suffering because you aren't making yourself a priority.

I want you to think about something. Why does this guilt seem to be coming from some deep, dark, place in your heart? The self-reproach that fears if you start working out, your friends and family will say backhanded comments like, "Oh well, since Sandy's been in her new 'health craze,' she definitely won't come out for Ice-Cream Tuesday anymore." Or even worse, when you do eat a sweet treat, your friends and family are the first ones to comment, "Oh, Sandy, I thought you were on a *diet?*" I mean, c'mon . . . how rude is that? If this is your environment, the guilt also stems from the insecurities of the people you choose to surround yourself. Are you worried that if you start investing in your health that these people will not only have negative comments to say, but that they will altogether disappear? Guess what? Time for you to take a mental inventory and ask yourself if these people have your best interest at heart. Are they people who will support your journey to optimal health? If you answer no to any of these questions, then *why* are they in your inner circle in the first place? You deserve to live in a state of true health and happiness. The resources are all around you. It simply comes down to a shift in mindset and perspective to acknowledge and receive them.

Speaking of mindset and perspective, ask yourself:

- Do you feel as though you deserve to be healthy and happy?
- Are you worthy of this incredible gift of health you can give to your current and future self?

If you answered yes to the above questions, then what is holding you back? So what if healthy food costs more money? So what if that training program is double what you've ever spent on gym memberships? Make healthy foods and a training program a part of your budget and follow Amanda's Wealth Empowerment Plan to help enable this switch to become part of your life. I'm telling you right now, the only person standing between you and that healthy woman full of life, is you. Get out of your own damn way and show the world, show your boss, and show your family that *you mean business* and will no longer stand behind the destructive feeling of guilt. Prove to them, and yourself, that you are ready to invest in your health and your happiness and will stop at nothing to become the confidently healthy and vibrant boss babe you know you can be.

Start being selfless for yourself. That's a crazy way to think, right? Putting your health first will not only improve your immediate physical, emotional, spiritual, and professional well-being but think about the longevity of your life. The quality of your life when you begin showing up for yourself and investing in yourself will improve tenfold. What changes can you make today that your future self will thank you?

Ladies, the moment we can take charge of our health and start to be completely selfish in the most selfless way is when the health guilt narrative will change. When we can acknowledge that a healthy life isn't all about treadmills and kale, but instead about our emotional well-being and reframing how we think, feel, and talk about our physical and mental health, we will be a force that cannot be ignored.

Make time for yourself, invest money into your new selfless lifestyle, and create a guilt-free routine that your mind and body can celebrate. Watch then how that healthy and confident woman will be more poised for job promotions and opportunities, how she will be cleared on her annual physicals, or be the life of the party at every event. You might think the sudden joie de vivre is random, but deep down you know it's because you have finally banished those feelings of guilt and are telling the universe: "I AM HERE AND I AM READY. BRING IT ON!"

INVESTING IN YOURSELF

Investing in yourself by way of your health can mean so many things:

- Visiting your local farmers market to find and purchase fresh fruits and vegetables that will nourish your body instead of relying on overly processed, pesticide-ridden produce at the commercial grocery store (plus extra kudos for investing in your community).
- Using that sudden burst of energy on a Saturday to get up and move your body, instead of mindlessly scrolling on social media.
- Getting in shape so you can freely walk around an amusement park with your family and friends instead of feeling winded all the time and having to take plentiful stops, etc.

- Taking the initiative to finally join that annual employee 5K and feeling great about it, rather than dreading it and feeling worried you won't be able to finish.

I promise, as soon as you make this commitment to yourself, all the sudden you will see your priorities shift. Thirty-minute time slots become available, a new affordable healthy meal kit hits the market, an awesome Groupon deal on that hot stone massage you've been wanting for the past year becomes available. The universe plays a huge role in this, my friend. Once you make changes to your narrative, opportunities will arise all around you. They've been there the whole time, but now you are open to receiving these little gems of love from the universe. Say it with me: "I AM DESERVING AND WORTHY OF HEALTH."

Taking this discussion of guilt one step further, I want to describe the law of attraction. Even if you don't believe in it, what's the harm in following along? The law of attraction states that positive or negative thoughts bring positive or negative experiences into one's life. I live by this law and it's seen me through my own past experiences with guilt. As cliché as it sounds, you truly are your own worst enemy. We are stuck in this notion of life that has us placing our own health and happiness on the back burner so we can watch others grow and succeed in life. Then *we resent* those people for the life they've created for themselves. But what did that person do so differently from you? It seems like they are always in the right place at the right time. The true secret for their success is the fact that they decided to prioritize their own needs above anyone else's. I'm telling you, it's the only way you're going to finally understand the way this whole law of attraction works. If you truly believe deep in your heart and soul that you are deserving of living this ultimately healthy life, then you are opening yourself up to receiving it.

Our thoughts are incredibly powerful, as they emit energy waves into our consciousness. The energy waves that are emitted through the body act as magnets to attract like energy from the universe. If you're having low-energy thoughts such as: "I don't deserve to work out and feel good about myself," then undoubtedly you will attract those low-energy vibrations to perpetuate your feelings of being undeserving. Equally, if you have high-energy thoughts such as: "I'm so grateful I can be in charge of my own health and make time for my own workouts," you will attract high-energy vibrations and perpetuate your feelings of gratefulness. These energies manifest themselves into your physical reality, which can either be positive or negative manifestations. For instance, if we think of ourselves as undeserving of a healthy life, we will physically manifest these thoughts into symptoms like weight gain, poor self-esteem, or perhaps even chronic illnesses due to lack of preventative health measures. On the opposite side, if we think of ourselves as deserving, worthy, and grateful to be able to preserve our health, then we will see this positively manifest into better heart health, better body compositions, healthier mental stability, and more due to following those positive thoughts with actions that promote those positive energies and a healthy state of being.

Now, I know it's easier said than done to completely change the mindset that's been your safety net all these years, but what if there was a way to train your mind to think more positively about your current state of health and happiness? What if we could retrain our brains to think about our own stories of life on a more positive note? What if you could *think your way* to a healthier life? I'm not saying that having one thought of: "I'm the healthiest woman in the world!" is going to give you that immediate state of optimal health in the blink of an eye. But we need to talk to ourselves in a more positive light. Rather than saying "It would be too selfish of me to take thirty minutes to work out," say: "These thirty minutes are going to change my mood for the rest of the day, so I'm able to be more present and help myself *and* my family even more." One thought can cause a positive or negative ripple effect that begins in your consciousness and then translates to reality.

CHAPTER TWELVE

BABY STEPS TO HEALTH

Now that you're ready to create a guiltless journey to your optimal health, let me give you a head start with simple, actionable steps that are so small, you cannot fail. No one simply wakes up one day with a completely different mindset. That's overwhelming and frankly unrealistic. First, we must ask ourselves: "In order to live the vibrant life I want, what are the steps I need to take in order to get there?" And then break them down into achievable baby steps.

CASE STUDY: KAYLA (REVISITED)

Remember Kayla from Amanda's section? To refresh your memory, she's a speech pathologist, mom to seven-year-old Cole, and wife to Rick, a head executive at a large recruiting company in New York City. Let's look at her life from a health perspective—but first some déjà vu to reset the scene. Kayla's long days include driving from location to location for in-home therapy with children with speech needs under the age of five. She is physically, emotionally, and sometimes spiritually drained after an exhaustive day of crawling on the floor with babies teaching them to scoot, making funny faces with a toddler in hopes that they will mimic her back, or teaching parents sign language to help them communicate with their sweet, nonverbal, autistic child.

Kayla and her family live in New Jersey but since Rick works in New York City, he's often gone and on the train by the time she wakes up and starts to get herself and their son ready for the day ahead. Kayla often rises, rolls over to check her calendar on her phone, sees the day is full of back-to-back appointments and is up and at 'em right into grind mode: Get up; get showered; get dressed; throw on some makeup; rouse her son; get him showered and dressed for the day; rush downstairs; feed the dog; throw a frozen waffle in the toaster for Cole; gather his backpack and homework; make sure his school lunch account still has money in it; grab the waffle from the toaster; pick up the book bag, her work tote and purse; put the dog in the crate; rush out the door, and the day has begun.

As Kayla sits down in the driver's seat of the SUV and pulls down the mirror to check her hair and makeup, she sees a tired woman looking back at her. "I've really let myself go," she sadly thinks. Her stomach begins to grumble as she realizes this is the third day in a row she hasn't eaten breakfast. She's tried to skip breakfast before, but this always results in a skull-crushing migraine by her ten a.m. appointment. She'll have to stop and grab something quick at her favorite large coffee shop chain right after she drops her kiddo off at school.

Now for the third day in a row, she pulls up to the drive through window, orders her medium-size vanilla latte; a bacon, egg, and cheese biscuit; and a slice of lemon loaf for her midmorning snack. She's not proud of what this means for her health. She knows her breakfast of choice contains a high calorie, fat, and sugar count that she'd rather ignore. She'd also rather ignore the dent it puts on her credit card for the third time this week.

Kayla hastily eats her breakfast biscuit and slurps down her latte while rushing to her first appointment of the morning. Not only does this hurt her stomach because of how quickly she ate it, but heartburn is starting to creep up her throat. She's struggled with heartburn for quite some time now, so she keeps a stash of antacids in the center console to pop in between meals. As the morning turns to early afternoon, Kayla reaches a moment of reprieve—lunch time. She has a few usual spots she frequents and today decides she'll hit her favorite salad joint because she wants to make up for the unhealthy breakfast. When it's finally her turn to order, she chooses the southwestern chicken salad off the menu (she doesn't have the headspace after a trying appointment to piece together a salad from the "make your own" side of the menu). She also decides she needs more caffeine since she's on a bit of a crash after the latte this morning. As a compromise, she orders a diet soda. Kayla's even feeling proud of herself. A salad and a diet soda isn't *the worst* lunchtime decision, even if the salad is made up of iceberg lettuce, two small slices of tomato, buttermilk fried chicken tenders, and loaded in her favorite ranch dressing. But it's a salad, right? It's not like she stopped at her favorite burger spot and got her usual number three combo of burger with extra cheesy fries. She saves that for Fridays—her designated cheat day after a long work week.

Sitting at a small table, Kayla eats the salad and the baguette slices it comes with as she simultaneously reads and responds to work emails. She usually finds this relaxing, but earlier that day she got a text from her hubby that he will need to stay late at the office to work on a pitch and that she and Cole should eat dinner without him. Her mood goes from relaxed to immediately grumpy, but she knows he's been working on this pitch for days and he's rarely late for dinner, so she decides to not let it ruin her day. Besides, it's been a while since she's had a dinner date with Cole, so maybe they'll skip the steak and broccoli she had planned to make and take him out to his favorite pizza place. Honestly, if Rick won't be home for dinner, it'll be easier to just go out to eat than deal with getting dinner on the table on her own while ensuring Cole finishes his homework. "I've already had a salad for lunch," she thinks, "a few slices of pizza tonight will be all right."

Kayla hasn't thought a thing about all the empty calories, high sugar, processed and chemically enhanced foods and drinks she's already consumed on a random weekday. But life happens, right? Or, the ever famous, "A girl's gotta eat." Not so fast. I want to change the way you think about eating in a manner that is not just set up for survival mode, but is instead for optimal fuel for the body. In Amanda's section of this book, she dissected why no part of Kayla's day is serving her from a wealth perspective. *My* purpose is to walk you through what happened here from a health perspective and help you to create your own baby steps to better navigate this day. Because in one form or another, we've ALL had this exact day and made the same kind of easy, unhealthy choices.

Remember, it's all about taking steps so small that you can't fail. That's what your new beginning is all about—making these minute changes that will create a ripple effect throughout your entire life. Baby steps are put in place, again, to ensure your path to success is as smooth as possible.

So what does this look like starting out? Instead of the self-destructive mentality of "go big or go home" (which usually turns into a big flop), think about replacing or changing just a few new habits at a time. Recall all the times have you been gung ho about starting a new diet or a new workout. For about one month, you're doing great. You see your body composition change. You're getting compliments. And yet, something is still missing. You feel depleted because the particular diet you're on demands that you eliminate all dairy, meat, eggs, carbs etc. Or pounding headaches occur because the new intermittent fasting cycle lands right around lunch time. You're staring at your computer screen while your grumbling stomach is telling you, "Hey, can you please feed me already?!"

These diet fads really amp you up in the beginning with promises of a flat stomach and limitless energy, but what they are really doing is taking your money and setting you up for failure. Not only will you stop the regimen in a few short weeks or months, but you'll likely gained the weight back *plus more*. The reason behind this is because you deprived your body of nutrients all at once, sending signals to your body that you will not eat again so it then goes into starvation mode. Once you do begin eating the way you did prior to the crash diet, your body says, "I never want to go through *that* again!" so it restores the previous balance (weight) in the body and adds more room (weight) for reserves, just in case. None of those diet fads explain this. They're looking for the "get rich quick scheme," preying on vulnerable women who are fed lies and myths about how this program differs from others.

This is exactly why we must start out small and steady, creating small habits, or baby steps, that promote a sustainable lifestyle for years to come. Do not overwhelm yourself all at once. The first step in creating a healthy happy life is not even an action. It's the *pre*-action, or the small changes that begin in your brain, that eventually manifest to your physical actions.

BABY STEP #1: CHANGE YOUR NARRATIVE

You know that "mean girl" in your head who loves to tell you that you're already too fat, too busy, too old, or not good enough? This, my friend, is the absolute biggest barrier standing between you and your healthiest and happiest self. Every time you're ready to make a change, that bully in the back of your mind is waiting and ready to shout something so mean, so cruel, that you decide to stay in your old ways. It's time to kick that evil bully to the curb and stand up for yourself! It all starts with reframing those past feelings of guilt and negative self-talk into more profound, actionable measures. Any kind of change starts by planting little seeds of positive affirmations and positive self-talk in your mind that blossom into physical motion (much like the aforementioned ripple effect). But just how can we reframe those self-destructive feelings and negative self-talk? How can we kick that mean girl voice out of our heads once and for all?

It's about perspective and setting mental intentions. What if instead of saying something like: "What's the point? I don't have time to eat healthy," we said something like: "My health is important to me, so even if I have to eat at this coffee shop, I'm going to choose something more mindful for my body." If that's a stretch, why not start by replacing your negative self-talk with just *one word* that will change your internal dialogue or your internal guilt? What if instead of Kayla starting her day by looking at herself in the mirror and thinking, "I've really let myself go," she instead thought, "This girl needs some serious TLC and I'm excited to start putting myself first." Yep. Hear me out.

Do these following examples ring a bell as to how you might be talking to yourself without even knowing it?

- "I have to go work out today so I can just get it over with."
- "Ugh. I'm so bad at working out and eating healthy. How am I going to do this?"
- "How am I going to afford this new program?"
- "How long is it going to take before I can wear my old jeans again?"

I'm sure at least one of those above statements hit close to home. Watch now as just a few word changes and placements can shift your self-talk entirely, creating a more positive perspective that you can feel good about.

- "I get to work out today and have those thirty minutes all to myself."
- "I am still learning how to work out and eat healthy but I know I will get there."
- "I'm excited to finally cut out all the extra spending in an effort to make my health a priority."
- "I can't wait to fit into my old jeans again!"

See how these very small changes to your internal dialogue can change your mental mindset? Think about talking to yourself the way you would your best friend. The one who just got out of a terrible relationship. Remember how you told her how awesome she was, how beautiful she was, how she needs to pick herself right back up and get back out there? Talk to yourself just like that because you are your own best friend! If you're not cheering yourself on throughout life, then who will? Are you going to wait for someone else to give you all the daily pep talks you need? If so, girlfriend, you're going to be waiting a long time.

Shifting those past negative self-statements into a positive light will send out some serious subliminal messaging to your brain. It's amazing how much your self-talk truly manifests into your own reality. I know it's not always easy to be bright and cheery, but the more you change your inner talk, the easier it becomes, and the more positive affirmations you will give your brain. Begin in your mind and soul and your physical body will follow.

BABY STEP #2: THINK ABOUT YOUR OPTIMAL HEALTH

This is not the time to go back and think about every poor decision you've made against your health, nor is it time for you to feel guilty. This baby step is solely for the purpose of being more mindful in your own approach to living your most vibrant, healthy life. So many of my new and excited clients start ranting off the eighty things they're going to change in their lives *that day* in order to be on the road to healthy living. While I think it's absolutely amazing that they are so motivated to begin putting these actions into place, I have to remind these women to pump the breaks and to cut themselves some slack. Again, it's about taking small, yet profound, steps in building your optimal health.

Let's return to Kayla's story. By just pausing for a moment to think about her optimal health, what are some ways that she could have changed her day entirely? Since Kayla is the mother of a seven-year-old, what do you think optimal health even means to her? Does it mean having enough energy to come back from her busy workday and still play in the backyard with Cole?

Does it mean not having to suffer each day with episodes of heartburn while on the way to another appointment for work? Could it possibly mean just putting aside thirty minutes for herself to clear her mind, move her body, and feel good both physically and mentally?

I challenge you to do the same, as we are all different people with different lives and different agendas. Picture your healthiest and happiest life. What does that life look like? What do *you* look like? You are both worthy and deserving of living this optimally healthy life that you just pictured. We can't wait on the sidelines for permission from some higher power. We have to give ourselves permission to embark on this ever-rewarding journey.

By thinking about your optimal health, you are both subconsciously and consciously making small changes in your life and your day-to-day routine. Going back to Kayla's story, what if instead of rolling over to look at her phone first thing in the morning, she laid there with her eyes closed just for a few moments to set one positive intention for that day. That intention could be something like: "Take good care of my body." Done. Remember, these steps are so small you can't fail. That one intention she set for herself will now ripple throughout Kayla's jam-packed day. When ready to order at her favorite chain coffee place, she thinks back to her intention of taking care of her body and instead of getting her usual sugary latte, she opts for a hot green tea with a dash of honey. Again, nothing radical here; it's just a more mindful choice.

Let's roll over to lunch time when Kayla still goes to her favorite salad place. But this time she *does* take the time to build her own salad. She chooses the fresher greens, the lighter dressing, the grilled chicken over the fried. All these small little changes just because she set that five-second intention earlier in the day. Her intention can be noticed as she scrolls over her emails during her lunch break. Today, instead of diving right into multitasking the second she sat down, she paused, took a few moments to breathe deeply and be present in that moment, without thinking about work.

By taking the time to simply think, you are giving yourself a choice—a choice in every moment to be more mindful in your approach to healthy living. You haven't even made any radical changes here; you simply started by throwing the small stone into the pond to create a ripple effect for the benefit of your own life.

BABY STEP #3: TAKE CARE OF YOURSELF BEFORE TAKING CARE OF ANYONE ELSE

Remember the preflight safety rule: "Put your oxygen mask on first before assisting others"? The same concept applies here. This baby step is about shifting your mindset so that you can mentally and physically begin to put yourself at the top of your daily to-do list. It ties back into our unhealthy relationship with guilt, but remember, if you don't take care of yourself, then who will? As women, we want to be able to do it all, as if we're proving something to the world. But what are we trying to prove? That we work our butts off so we're dead tired and feel like crap all the time?

Picture the range of roles you've seen in your own home—perhaps with your partner, your husband, your friends, or even your parents. In no way am I trying to call out any one of your loving friends and family, but take a minute to look at their dynamic from a distant perspective. Does one partner kind of "call the shots," while the other falls in line? Perhaps you've witnessed a dynamic in which one partner is a bit more "hands off" with parenting, leaving the other to pick up the slack and make sure both the home and children are fed and clothed?

We both know these lopsided relationships exist, yet it's viewed in such social normality that it doesn't get a second thought. In Kayla's scenario, she's the one who is in charge of getting both herself and Cole ready throughout the day and even after her long work day. Her husband is not a bad guy, it's just that Kayla is the one responsible for the well-being of herself and their child, as she has kind of always assumed that role.

As we revisit Kayla's day, let's see how implementing this baby step in one event could immensely change her day without sending anyone's life in a complete tailspin. Let's go back to when Kayla was rushing around to make her son's breakfast and lunch. If Kayla were to put herself first, do you think she would have entirely skipped *her* breakfast? No, she would have grabbed something for herself first *and then* continued her morning, knowing she was her own top priority. Now I'm not telling you to leave your kids out to dry, I'm simply stating the mind shift of prioritizing your own well-being first. The one small step could have entirely changed her morning. Think about it. If Kayla ate her breakfast before heading out to work, she wouldn't have had to stop at the local coffee shop, saving her extra calories and money. Maybe she wouldn't have had to pop an antacid because she wasn't eating her breakfast in such a hurry. Such a small change that can lead to a different chain of events, all because she decided to put herself first in one task.

In your own life, what are ways that you can put yourself first? Is it finally sticking up for yourself and not letting your boss or coworkers bombard you with their issues as soon as you step through the office door? This might help put boundaries in place to protect your mental health so you don't feel so stressed and anxious first thing in the morning. Is it telling your spouse you need thirty minutes to yourself after coming home from work before the kids come rushing to you with a never-ending call of "Mom, Mommy, Mom . . ." Or taking those first waking moments in bed to silently set intentions (which I will cover more in depth later). By taking care of yourself before anyone else you are making yourself even more available and capable of taking on the day (or evening) ahead of you without feeling as drained.

Remember to start small here. Even just taking a five-minute breather before making dinner for the family is a wonderful way to take extra care of yourself first.

BABY STEP #4: CREATE SMALL, ACHIEVABLE WINS

The final step is about taking your first small initiatives toward living your optimally healthy life. This is not about "big picture" goal setting, not even close. Remember, it's *steps so small you can't fail*. As referenced before, people can be so adamant about starting their healthy habits that they jump right into them. And while they may stay on track for a good two months or so, they soon after fall off due to lack of adherence to the intense restrictions of many extreme diets and programs. The reason these plans weren't successful is because the goals were simply too big, too much to bite off at once. Nobody likes to fail. That's why for change to "stick," we have to take smaller bites we can chew. Bites we can feel good about and celebrate. Not everyone's progression is the same, but you still must celebrate each win, each small step in the right direction. Make this process slow and steady. Remember the tortoise and the hare? Slow and steady wins the race, my friend.

For this step in action, let's go back to Kayla's day. What if when she got to her favorite salad spot for lunch, she thought to herself, "I'll get the dressing on the side and only one small (two-tablespoon 140 calories per serving) cup of dressing instead of my usual two." It's time for some math. If Kayla doesn't get the extra two tablespoons of salad dressing five times a week for an entire month, she's saving 2,800 extra calories per week. Wow, that is a lot of extra calories. Empty calories that she is eliminating from her daily diet and eliminating from her overall weight. All because she stopped, thought, and made one super small change to her daily routine.

Or what about Kayla's diet sodas? What if she just stuck with drinking water rather than the chemically-processed sugar added to those "diet" sodas. In one single twelve ounce can of a typical diet soda there is approximately 125 milligrams of chemically made sugar. These "fake" sugars go by the name of aspartame, sucralose, saccharin, sorbitol—the list goes on and on. They have the catchy advertising schemes of being "calorie-free" and "sugar-free," yet they fail to mention the chemical processing that goes into the manufacturing of these items. As a nutrition coach, I advocate for good ol' H_2O's natural nourishment to your body. Since 75 percent of your body is water, and water is used in almost all cellular functions of the body, it is important we hydrate naturally to assist these everyday bodily functions rather than make the body work harder to break down chemicals that can, over time, lessen the effectiveness of our body functions.

This is not to say you can never have a soda again, but in Kayla's scenario, if she were to only drink that soda once a week rather than every day, she would be saving her body from having to break down fake sugars as well as saving her wallet.

Another small, achievable win may be taking that thirty-minute lunch break to get up and do just one lap around the office before getting back to lunch. Or maybe closing your office door to shut off the lights by your desk and taking a five-minute breather before getting back on the desktop. I'm not telling you to start packing your gym bag and hit the gym first thing in the morning. Simply start putting in these small actions to create a positive ripple effect in your healthier life. Now remember, everyone's steps are different and this is not the time to compare. These are all small steps that must fit into *your* life, not anyone else's.

And one more thing. *Celebrate these wins.* The more you give yourself positive reinforcements, the more you will want to continue these achievable wins and then grow from them.

Before we move on, let's recap the four baby steps in order—the ones that are so small you can't fail. Altogether, they will guide you in the beginning of your journey to empowerment in your health.

1.   Change Your Narrative
2.   Think About Your Optimal Health
3.   Put Yourself First Before Anyone Else
4.   Create Small, Achievable Wins

As you start to take these baby steps in your own life, remember to be patient with yourself and to show yourself kindness when implementing any small changes. Once you begin taking these precise, pre-planned baby steps, you will get more comfortable, more confident, and you will start seeing small changes. You'll think, "I can't believe it, I'm actually doing it!" These baby steps, or habit changes, will then transform into bigger steps and then bigger leaps that will finally propel you to reach out for the life of health and abundance that you deeply deserve.

Now's the time to plan and take those first baby steps. As small as they may seem, these are the steps you must take to begin to change your life forever.

CHAPTER THIRTEEN

BALANCE

E verything in life is a balancing act—from juggling our multifaceted roles as a mother, wife, sister, friend, employee, business owner, and everything in between, to juggling our expectations, goals, and values within the world around us. There are some areas of our lives that we've learned to balance with such expertise that we no longer even have to consciously think about balancing as a skill set. And there are other areas that seem in such disarray because we're either overwhelmed, we just don't understand what we're supposed to be working toward, or we think someone else will eventually relieve us of the burden.

Health, and our management of it, is a balancing act too—perhaps one of the most complex we deal with on a day-to-day basis that has the power to affect the way our lives play out right before our eyes.

Balancing your health is all about living your life more mindfully, while also realizing you're an exquisite human being existing in this world for a moment in time, in which you're meant to, and deserving of, such day-to-day enjoyment as brunch with bottomless mimosas, indulging in a girls weekend full of wine tasting with chocolate pairings, and leaving the world behind to treat yourself to a spa day full of massages, facials, and a mani-pedi. These experiences make this life worth living and create the memories that last us our lifetimes.

Balance is the keyword and tactic that so many of us ladies are missing when we are super excited and motivated to begin a new lifestyle change. We buy the gym membership. We purchase the twelve-week detox program we saw our friend praising and selling on social media. We seek out only all fresh, organic produce. And maybe start buying trendy new gym clothes and some pieces of at-home gym equipment. We even start leaving work a little earlier to head to the gym and enter week two of the new 21-Day Shred boot camp. *This is it.* You're ready to start living this new life. You're doing your juice cleanses, and even got some of your friends at work to start the program with you. You're so amped, knowing this is exactly what you need to get your butt off the couch and into this new way of living.

But what happens after the first couple of weeks, or months? You catch yourself considering how many more days and weeks you have of this program, because all you want to do is EAT A DAMN BAGEL WITH CREAM CHEESE, but this diet gives you a hard "NO" for thirty days. Or perhaps you've been going to the gym for three weeks straight, no days off, then one day you take a break . . . which turns into another day, and another. All the sudden you see four months of paid yet unused gym membership on your back statements.

In this chapter I'm going to give you real-life tactics to use when creating and managing your own version of an empowered, healthy life, while giving you the permission you need to understand that just as in life, optimal health is all about BALANCE, baby.

Oh, and that occasional bagel and cream cheese is yours for the taking.

CASE STUDY: STACY

Let's chat about my girl Stacy. Stacy is a thirty-year-old, full-time hairdresser with no kids, who lives with her husband and two adorable rottweilers. The hair salon she works at just posted their second annual one-month health challenge where the hairdresser to lose the most weight in four weeks wins the big grand prize of a full-paid day off, money in the pocket! It may not sound like a lot, but to a hairdresser, paid days off don't otherwise exist. She did okay last year and was only three pounds shy of winning the grand prize, which was given to another hairdresser who used the money to go on a beautiful cabin stay by the mountains with her boyfriend. Stacy was so envious of that vacation and down on herself for losing that she stopped going to the gym entirely and gained back all the weight she had lost plus more. "But not this time," she thought to herself. "I'm going to double down this year. I'm going to win it, no excuses!"

Stacy was ready and more motivated than ever. Right before the four-week challenge, she started going back to the gym directly across from the salon and putting her unused gym membership back to use. She told her boyfriend that he needed to keep her accountable. She rigorously searched low-carb, low-sugar meal plans on the internet and looked to social media to see what the fitness models were doing on their accounts. Just as she thought, everyone was doing low carbs, low sugar, and the results they showed were amazing. She even got her favorite social media fitness model's meal replacement shakes and specially formulated teas promising a slim waist and a curbed appetite. Stacy put together her own weekly meal plan of drinking two meal replacement shakes twice a day, only teas and water between meals, and then a leafy green salad with a thin slice of chicken breast on top for dinner. "I can do this, it's only for four weeks," she thought.

The challenge began that following Monday. Armed with her shakes, teas, and newfound love for the gym, she was set. Each day she would wake up, pack her gym bag, and reach for her two already made shakes in the fridge. Out the door she went and had her first shake in the car, working her back-to-back hair appointments always resisting the urge to eat the packaged snacks and cupcakes provided by the salon for free. Between shampoos and blow drying she would go to the back, chug her "fit" teas and get right back to work. During her lunch break, which was only five minutes, she would slurp down her second shake then wave over another client to come sit in her chair. After all her appointments were done, usually around seven p.m., she would grab her gym bag and head right to the gym where she hit the cardio machines. She knew this is where she burned the most calories, where she would get the most sweat. Heck, last year she went from 150 pounds down to 138 pounds just by doing one hour on the cardio machines five times a week! This time she did even more. If she had an hour break between hair appointments (which happened on the occasion), she was back off to the gym. These days she would fit in not just one, but *two* workouts, which made her extremely proud.

In the evening, Stacy would come home after the gym to her two dogs who were always so eager to go outside and get in their walk. She thought to herself, "Even though my feet are aching, it's still another workout." So off she went for her daily walk with the pups, knowing this would be her year. Afterward she would make her baked chicken breast on top of her leafy green salad. Her boyfriend, although supportive, was not a fan of this bland meal. She would usually make him his own side of potatoes, or noodles, or rice to go along with it—sometimes sprucing it up with a steak instead of chicken. But not for her—she had her eye on the prize!

She continued these patterns every day, every week, and never stopped on the weekends. She quickly started seeing the weight come off. She weighed herself once a day, and if the scale didn't comply, she would sometimes skip the chicken breast for dinner and just eat the salad.

One night the girls from the salon went out to their favorite Mexican restaurant for one of the other hairdresser's birthday. While all the girls ordered their favorite dishes loaded with rice and cheese along with one of those mouth-watering margaritas, Stacy simply ordered a side salad, no dressing or croutons, with water to drink. Her friends looked at her with a hint of sadness, as they usually were the girls to go out, gossip about their high-

228

maintenance clients, and enjoy their perfectly salt-rimmed margaritas, stress-free. Again, Stacy didn't want to lose the grand prize this time. "It's only for these four weeks," she thought. "We'll go out again and I'll make it up to them."

A couple weeks go by and Stacy is in the lead! She chose to skip the usual Sunday family dinners with her boyfriend and his family because they tend to be a carb-loaded buffet of Italian foods and she just couldn't afford to indulge in the pasta and bread. Of course she loved the food and missed the company, but would be too tempted to overindulge if she went.

Week four began and another hairdresser, Hannah, is right with her, neck and neck for the lead. Stacy is *not* taking any chances. With one day left to announce the winner and do the final weigh in, she decides to fast for these next twenty-four hours and only drink her fit teas and water.

The time comes for the final weigh in and guess what? She's done it! Stacy won! The full paid day off is hers and she is over the moon. Not only did she win the grand prize but she also lost a whopping twenty-five pounds in the short span of four weeks. That's even more than last time! She was so proud upon booking her favorite cabin stay for the weekend with her boyfriend and two pups. She deserved this; she worked so hard.

While at the cabin, Stacy and her boyfriend went out every night to celebrate. She enjoyed her favorite sugary cocktails and even splurged on dessert because she hadn't touched any of it in four whole weeks! After an amazing trip at the cabin she came back to work. She knew she still wanted to go to the gym but thought to herself, "Well, if I just go two or three times a week, I can definitely maintain the weight I'm at." Instead of packing her two usual shakes for lunch, she now packed just one, but man, those snacks and cupcakes in the breakroom looked so good, and they were free. Why not just have one? Work kept her too busy to bother preparing food at home for a packed lunch, so she went back to getting takeout from her favorite sushi place or her usual Chinese order. She knew she had her meal replacement shakes in her bag but she wanted something good, more satisfying. Chinese takeout it was.

Stacy gathered the girls one night after work to make up for last month's absence of "Fun Stacy" and they went back to their favorite Mexican restaurant. This time Stacy enjoyed every last bite of her cheesy enchilada dish and bottomless chips and salsa, washing it all down with her favorite jumbo margarita. This time she wasn't missing out on anything.

Work got so busy that she would come home, feet aching, and while her dogs were waiting by the door for their walk, she would simply open the backdoor so they could play in the backyard. "I'm just too tired," she rationalized. "Last month was exhausting and I just need a break." Dinner soon turned back into a quick frozen pizza or a boxed pasta meal because she was tired of eating those bland chicken salads.

A few months of skipped gym and poor nutrition later, Stacy had regained all the weight *plus* five pounds. She thought to herself "How could I have let this happen? What do I do now?"

Well ladies, here is the happy part of the story. Stacy is my friend and my hairdresser. I watched as Stacy started this journey and watched as she posted on her social media how much she was doing and how much weight she was losing so quickly. But I, being a friend and a trainer, bit my tongue until she was ready. I remember getting the text saying, "Michelle, I NEED your help!" And that my friends, is where I showed Stacy what she was missing. That the missing ingredient to her never-ending cycle of yo-yo dieting was balance.

I'll break it down for you the way I broke it down to Stacy, into the three main parts of optimal health: fitness, nutrition, and self-care.

FITNESS

Diving back into Stacy's story, she went entirely overboard with not only the amount of time spent at the gym but focused her time on only one component to her fitness: cardio. Her priority of going to the gym for one hour, sometimes more than once a day, just to burn a certain amount of calories, unintentionally set herself up to fail. You might be thinking, "But isn't going to the gym for one hour, five times a week *good?*"

It's time to debunk the common fitness myth that our workouts must be at least an hour's length to be beneficial. Coming from a background of teaching hour-long group classes, I'll admit I too believed this was just common knowledge. I didn't understand the truth until I attended a fitness seminar which discussed how working out, no matter how long, depends on that person and their perceived level of exertion. For example, if GIRL A was to do a thirty-minute high intensity workout and GIRL B was to do a one-hour lower intensity workout, who do you think would be exerting the most energy? Actually, *both* women would be exerting almost equal energy as GIRL A was simply exerting herself more in a shorter time frame while GIRL B was steadily exerting herself over the span of a longer time frame.

The "go big or go home" mentality is a common pitfall from establishing lifelong habit changes. Perhaps if Stacy had thought of the long haul rather than the four-week grand prize, she would have cut herself some needed slack. It all comes back to balance and cutting yourself a break. Try putting sustainable and steady habits in place, something you can stick with and feel good about, and you'll be helping to set yourself up for success.

The other mentioned aspect of Stacy's rigid workout plan was the never-ending cardio workouts. There's even the term "cardio bunny," referring to women who only hit the cardio machines, hoping to sweat off their body fat. These ellipticals, treadmills, bikes, and running in general most often take centerstage in what women consider to be fitness. Not to mention the fact that these machines are less intimidating than the dumbbell rack shoved in the corner surrounded by the typical "meatheads," forcing us to take to the machines to "look busy." We think it's all about how many calories we burn, or how high we can get our heart rate and stay in the "max heart rate zone." While yes, it's great to sometimes work at higher intensities, it's also important to balance this cardio with resistance training. Resistance training has been proven to help build muscle while burning fat. When you perform resistance training you are creating microtears in the muscle fibers. That may sound awful but is a good thing. These muscle fibers need to be repaired in order to grow leaner and stronger. The body breaks down fat cells and turns them into fuel for these muscles, which creates an increase in lean muscle tissue and a decrease in fat cells.

By just doing cardio, you are not only working for the short-term change, you are putting higher stress on these vulnerable bones and joints that need to be protected by strong muscles. When you implement a resistance training program into your daily routine you are building and preserving these muscles that help with sustained weight loss rather than quick calorie burning cardio workouts. As women we must be striving to balance these two components of fitness.

So what did I tell Stacy? I told her that in order to achieve—and sustain—her results, she must understand that it's okay not to go to the gym one hour five times a week. I told her, and many of my other clients, to do thirty minutes four to five times a week. One thirty-minute workout being a cardio workout (elliptical, running, rowing, biking, etc.) and the next day to alternate to thirty-minute resistance training (weight lifting, barre, Pilates, etc.). Why thirty minutes? Because I want you to know that you don't have to kill yourself at the gym for hours on end. I mean c'mon ladies, we're only human and we got other stuff to handle. Balance your fitness plan and don't beat yourself up for not going all in or nothing.

This is a hard one. We live in a world where we turn to social media to see what celebrities are doing, what the latest diet trends are, what magic weight-loss supplement is out there to help us get that flat stomach. Sorry, ladies, but there is NO magic pill for weight loss or that will help supplement real food. Looking back at Stacy's journey we see that she not only started using weight-loss supplements and fit teas, but she also was skipping meals and not eating enough calories to keep up with her highly demanding workout load. She was essentially depriving herself of real food, real energy to help her through her workday and workouts, which is why as soon as her four-week challenge wrapped she was so quick to fall back into her old habits.

Women fall victim to these supplements and detoxes promoted through a petty face on social media, but it's these very diets that lead to such self-sabotaging behavior. They promise that if you stick with using their supplements for two weeks, you, too, will get a flat stomach like some Instagram model posing in a skimpy bikini on the back of a yacht. We are blinded by the facade of what these women look like in our social media feed. We lead to almost starving ourselves just to try to look like what we see every day online. It's not fair to do that to yourself and you are better than that. We exist to enjoy the luxuries of this life and have it be okay to indulge here and there.

I stand by the 80/20 rule, stating that 80 percent of the time you should be eating more mindfully and 20 percent of the time it's okay to indulge. Now I'm not telling you to go off the deep end here with the word "indulge," I'm just saying that if you've eaten more mindfully and you want to treat yourself to that cupcake in the window on a Friday, go for it. Restrictive diets and detoxes leave no room for flexibility, and it's in these inflexible diets that women set themselves up for failure. You must have balance in means of your nutrition that leads to your overall quality of life. Stacy most definitely could have enjoyed an evening out with her girls and not have to feel bad about it. It would not have undone everything she did. In fact, it might have averted her from falling completely back into her old ways because she was giving herself that simple savory meal and not mentally punishing herself for it. Stick with the 80/20 rule so you, too, can unwind those past feelings of guilt, shame, and punishment for wanting one of your favorite cocktails out with the girls at the end of a long work week.

When we put together Stacy's meal plan, I told her to ditch the meal replacement shakes. She was working much too hard and too many hours to try to sustain her energy with a simple shake. She needed real food, real nutrients to fuel her body. Instead of getting takeout for lunch, I guided her on how to make easy packable lunches, along with some fruits and veggies as snacks in between meals and clients. As for the weekends, I told her verbatim to "enjoy mindfully." What this means is that instead of going through the entire weekend on her health kick, to enjoy those wings and beer with her boyfriend at their favorite spot. Perhaps pass on the fries with the wings and just get an extra order of carrots and celery sticks. Perhaps limit those drinks and make sure to have a full glass of water in between each. Do you see where I'm going here? It's about *balancing* your meals, your nutrition, and ultimately your new healthy and happy life.

SELF-CARE

As women, we have so much stuff to balance on our plates between work, family, being a parent, being a friend, etc. We're being pulled in so many different directions that we too often forget to focus on the most important part of our optimal health: ourselves. We are busy being fierce ladies who want to grow in our professional lives, keep up with social appearances, and still leave quality time for family. As crazy as this may sound, whenever I'm putting together one of my client's fitness and nutrition programs I always leave equal room to discuss their self-care routines. Stacy, much like my other clients, laughed at first when I brought this up, then I heard the soft pause in her voice when she said, "I guess I never really thought of that part."

Self-care comes down to the mental state of our health. Yes, having a balanced fitness and nutrition regimen contribute to a majority of our well-being, but have you ever paused to take a mental self-reflection on what's going on upstairs in that beautiful brain of yours? When I asked Stacy to tell me which part of her four-week journey she was able to enjoy for herself, there was almost a full minute pause between her responses.

"Well I, um . . ."

"Well I was doing, um . . ."

"Well definitely when my boyfriend and I got to enjoy the weekend in the cabin, it was so relaxing and just what I needed."

"So you're telling me you never really felt happy, felt good about yourself throughout those four weeks? Only after?" I replied. I already knew the answer in my head; I just wanted to hear her say it with her own words.

"That was the worst four weeks of my life," she sheepishly replied, almost as if confessing to a priest. "I was constantly drained, always hungry, always pushing myself to go to the gym even when I didn't want to. I turned down outings with friends that would bring me so much joy . . . just to get to a dumb number on the scale."

And that, my friends, is how self-care gives another third of the pie to overall optimal health. In Stacy's story there were so many missed opportunities for self-reflection and self-affirmation. She never balanced the workload, the workouts, or the diet with any kind of positive self-reinforcement. Yes, she was looking to the big picture goal of her romantic weekend getaway, but what about the journey getting there?

As a trainer and nutrition coach, I know that getting into these routines can be a little tough, but this journey is not one to make you unhappy, to cost you your sanity, nor to be about giving up all the joys in life. It's to empower you while you celebrate your wins and give yourself the rewards you deserve in your waking life, making this incredible transformation to your most ultimate, beautiful, vibrant, and healthy self. You are a hardworking woman and you deserve to treat yourself like the absolute queen you are. Instead of always thinking ahead to the outcome goal, why not take a moment to reflect? This self-reflection can be an array of different things: meditation, being mindful, being present, maybe even treating yourself to that special spa day (because hey, your body needs that extra TLC). These small acts of showing kindness to yourself—the way you show kindness to everyone else—make an incredible impact on your self-image, your self-worth, your confidence, and your overall mental health. There's absolutely no need to embark on a journey that you're not happy about. There's no need to do a two-week detox program which restricts you from all the things you love in this life, even if it is the occasional glazed donut you treat yourself to on a Friday morning.

Balancing your physical state of health with your mental state of health is one goal that is commonly overlooked and under-appreciated. If running on the treadmill for thirty minutes seems like absolute torture, well, you're not alone. Find another way to get your heart rate up that brings you joy and happiness; maybe a dance class, a walk in the park with your dogs and/or your kids, maybe even going for a swim. Stop pushing yourself to do things that mentally drain you and deprive you of the beauty in making your optimal health your top priority.

So you might be asking yourself, where the heck Stacy is now? Well, I'm glad to report that Stacy no longer only drinks two meal replacement shakes and a frugal salad for dinner. Training and coaching with me for the past six months has given her the self-empowerment she needs to understand that she is allowed to enjoy her girls nights out while living her most healthy and happy life. She now finds joy in going to the gym for her usual thirty-minute workouts, using it as a time to give back to her body and take a load off from work. She comes home and takes the dogs on their usual walk, using this as her quiet time to think about her day, reflect inward, and feel good about herself. It's funny, she actually passed on the most recent four-week weight loss challenge and told me, "It's just not going to make me happy." Well said. She is now at a body composition that is comfortable and healthy for her. She no longer looks at the scale daily, but rather tracks her health by how she is feeling inside. Stacy is the true embodiment of what balancing a healthy and happy life looks like as she has adopted these new habits as a way of life.

So how are *you* balancing your life? Are you making the appropriate boundaries in your personal, work, and family life to establish your happiest and healthiest life? Remember these few tips when creating your empowered healthy life:

- Make working out a time for yourself, not a chore.
- Interchange these workouts with both resistance training and cardio, thirty minutes four to five times a week is great.
- Mindfully nourish yourself following the 80/20 stance; 80 percent of the time eat more quality foods and 20 percent of the time mindfully "treat yo-self."

And last but most definitely not least, check in with that smart girl upstairs, your brain. How is she feeling? Do you need to show her some extra love? Everyone's balance looks different. The right balance for you and your goals is something that I urge you to work through with a healthcare professional who holds your best interest. The right health coach will care about you and will want to listen to your health values and goals. They will want to make sure you're enjoying this beautiful life you've been given and are establishing healthy habits in a way that best serves you.

The right balance of fitness, nutrition, and self-care is a puzzle. It is multitasking at its finest. We all need more multitasking and juggling like we need another hole in the head. However, I believe the saying is true: "If you want something done, give it to a busy woman." You, no matter how busy you are, have the ability to reach out and ask for help to better understand your balance. This is something you need to do. Start putting yourself first and get this figured out. Your happiness, your success, and your health depend on it.

CHAPTER FOURTEEN

YOUR HEALTH EMPOWERMENT PLAN

All right, boss babes, this is it! The time where we can finally put all these empowered steps of health into an actionable, achievable plan. I will give you the exact breakdown and tools you need throughout this action plan so you can start this journey on your own as soon as possible. I highly recommend you use a separate notebook as we go through this plan, so you can doctor it to make it specifically yours. Write it down so you can easily take this tangible action plan with you as you begin your new journey of optimal health.

As a certified personal trainer and nutrition coach, I created this plan so that whoever fills it out will still be in charge of their own approach to optimal health and wellness. This approach is not one size fits all, which is why I highly recommend that if you need specific guidance due to previous injury, specific food preference, etc., that you reach out to an expert in the field. Remember, you are deserving and worthy of putting your health first, so don't hesitate to outsource when needed.

STEP ONE: FIND YOUR "WHY" FOR HEALTH

Earlier, we worked through letting go of the guilt or shame you feel about health due to your past. This book is all about moving forward on a new and empowering health journey. To genuinely create a plan and stick with it, you must first understand why in the heck you would want to start the journey in the first place. What values are you serving for your personal or professional self through your health?

For example, when I think about health, the value I tie it to is "longevity." I deserve and am worthy of health, and am on a mission to make smart decisions in regards to my health, because I want to be able to care for my mind and body in the best way possible. I want to have enough energy to bring my A game to work while also being the "energetic" mom, daughter, and friend who is always ready for an exciting adventure. I want to avoid having to take various medications and lowering my risk of chronic illness by taking as many proactive steps in my preventative health that I can.

My "why" isn't because I want washboard abs, or I want to fit in size four pants for the rest of my life. Those are meaningless and empty reasons to set a goal and, therefore, make it so easy to fail. If my goal is to get washboard abs, I doubt I'm going to put daily, weekly, and monthly effort into that goal since it's not backed by anything real or emotional. Now, if I reframe that goal by backing it with a value like: "This year, my goal is to work on my stamina, so I can have enough energy to enjoy our annual family vacation hiking in the mountains of Arizona," then we're onto something. It's going to be lot harder for me to not work toward that health goal for the shared familial experience when it serves my value of "longevity."

It works in the same way when I hear women say, "I just want to be able to feel better." I'd say more than half of the time this is the true reason why women want to begin their health journey. As I stated before, the modern woman is now responsible for "bringing home the bacon" while also having been crowned as family caretaker. It's a lot of pressure we're under, but it doesn't have to be like that. Just as I mentioned in Baby Step #3, take care of yourself first! This right here is how you're going to be able to feel better about yourself, how you're going to bring your best professional presence to work, and how you're going to show up for yourself day in, day out. Now, having this gem of knowledge in mind, I want you to find your "why" deep down inside when making mental and physical health a priority in your own life.

The goal here isn't to "eat healthy so I look good at my friend's wedding." The goal is "to create a quality of life in which you can feel your best while preserving the vital life force you have inside you for years to come."

Before we move on I challenge you to create your own "why." Write it down in a notebook, somewhere you will be reminded each day as to why you want to create your most healthy life. Once determined, we're ready to move on to step two.

STEP TWO: GOAL SETTING

There's absolutely no way you can get to your end destination if you have no idea where you're headed. Just as when you get in the car to go on family vacation, I'm sure you pull up a map before doing anything else. It would be pretty interesting to watch someone try to get to their weekend getaway cabin on hopes and dreams alone. We have to get really technical here. The more specific we get with our goals, the more efficiently we will reach them, as we always have the end destination in mind. Now just to be clear, these goals do not have to be set in stone. They can change. They can become more detailed or they can change altogether—whatever makes you feel the most empowered. After all, they're your goals, not anyone else's.

First, we must establish the long-term goal, which is the big picture. As the saying goes: "Rome wasn't built in a day." Just as the Romans had their own blueprint to the empire of Rome, we must do the same to draw our own path to optimal health. In order to get to that big-picture goal, let's break it down into short-term goals, the stepping stones. Some may be bigger

241

hurdles than others but you must set these benchmark goals so you can see your achievements, big and small.

Now there's one more critical thing before we start developing your big picture goal. Let's make sure this goal is exactly what you want and need so you feel empowered to take on this amazing achievement without setting yourself up for failure. We do this by establishing our long-term goal by following the SMART goals breakdown. (You'll recall this formula from Amanda's related Wealth section.) SMART goals are: **S**pecific, **M**easurable, **A**chievable, **R**ealistic, and **T**imely. This is where goal setting requires some real self-reflection. I will walk you through each one as you complete this process with me. Now let's get to work, *hermana*.

LONG-TERM GOAL

Example: Kelly's goal is to feel good in her clothes and have more energy for summer in four months, then continue her healthy habits after summer is over.

Okay, now it's your turn.

My Long-Term Goal:

_____

_____

_____

_____

Great. Kelly's put together a big picture goal that follows seamlessly to the SMART goals breakdown. I'm going to show you why Kelly's long-term goal follows the template, but as I go through Kelly's, make sure you are mentally analyzing yours to then do the same.

SPECIFIC: Kelly didn't just say I want to "feel good." She wrote that she specifically wanted to feel good in her clothes and have more energy for summer. Remember, the more specific, the better. When you write these goals, I really want you to picture what you will look like and how you will feel inside once you achieve these goals, as if you've already achieved them.

MEASURABLE: How will you measure this goal and outcome? It does not have to be physically measured; you can simply set up weekly self-reflections. In my opinion, ditch the scales for these goals. That stupid number on that scale is not the determining factor as to how far you've come in your journey to becoming the best version of yourself. That number will not encompass all the physical activity, the nutrition, the amount of sleep, and the other actions you've been implementing in your life to get you to your end goal. Example: Week two after implementing this program, Kelly was able to have enough energy to walk the dogs after work and she noticed her pants, once snug around the waist, had a little more stretch.

ACTIONABLE: Ask yourself, what actions can you put in place to achieve this goal? For instance, Kelly's goal may have actionable steps like going for twenty-minute walks each day, substituting more fresh produce in her diet over salty/sugary snacks, or something like drinking more water throughout the day.

REALISTIC: Make sure it's something you can stick with and feel good about. Is your goal realistic? Good Lord, I've had a few women come to me saying they want to lose twenty-five pounds in one month. This may be possible using extreme, drastic measures . . . but it's not realistic if you don't want to set yourself up for failure. Just as I mentioned before, be clear on your "why," which will lead to more valued goal setting. Kelly wanting to feel good in her clothes and have more energy is very realistic, as she is not drawing such extreme black lines in her playbook.

TIMELY: I'm not saying you always have to set a concrete time cap onto your goal, but for some, having that end time helps light the fire under their butt they need. Now, because I have my background in public health, I am not a fan of those thirty-day fads. Yes, you have the time component of this goal (thirty days), but you're not giving yourself enough time to make these actionable steps part of your everyday lifestyle. According to behavioral health theory it takes approximately six-plus months to create and change a lifestyle habit to one that becomes part of your daily routine without having to think about it. What I'm saying is to cut yourself some slack. Having a time cap to your goal is great but also make sure it's a time cap that allows you to make these changes permanent and ones you don't have to think about. Why not start by giving yourself a timely goal of at least three months when creating your own Actionable Health Plan?

It's back to your turn. Going over all the aspects of your long-term goal compared to its counter SMART goals approach, how is your goal withstanding? Remember, this goal does not have to be set in stone. You can change it at any time—tweak it, enhance it, or even just roll it into a ball and toss it out the window and start from scratch. This is the beauty of creating YOUR very own journey. Now go ahead and give it a shot because I know you've been conjuring your own big picture goal.

Your SMART Goals Breakdown

SPECIFIC:

_____

_____

_____

_____

MEASURABLE:

_____

_____

_____

_____

ACTIONABLE:

_____

_____

_____

_____

REALISTIC:

_____

_____

_____

_____

TIMELY:

_____

_____

_____

_____

SHORT-TERM GOALS

Now that you have created your SMART long-term goal, let's break these down into smaller, more bite-size pieces to give you the self-efficacy you need to achieve your big-picture goal. Think about it as monthly benchmarks. Use these benchmarks as your own check-ins to keep you accountable and motivated. Continuing Kelly's example, I'm going to construct short-term goals that will flow and bring her to her long-term goal of wanting to look and feel good for summer and the months to follow.

Month One: By the end of month one Kelly wants to be able to have enough energy to walk the dogs right after work and drink sixty-four ounces of water per day. Great, we've established a short-term benchmark goal for the first month. Small, bite-size, and doable.

Month Two: By the end of month two Kelly wants to be able to say she has completed thirty workouts and has been eating more mindfully throughout the week. Another great bite-size benchmark goal. Notice how I haven't written "drop four pants sizes in two months." I want you to continue writing these benchmark goals in a way that empowers you to take action in these goals, not one that will shame you or deter you from accomplishing your long-term goal if you're not able to achieve it.

Month Three: By the end of month three Kelly wants to feel stronger and sign up for the local Summer 5K. This benchmark goal may seem so simple but that's the exact point. Treat yourself with kindness when writing these short-term goals for yourself while slowly building on them each week, month, year . . .

Month Four: By the end of month four Kelly wants to feel good about how she feels in her clothes and have enough energy for summer. That's the end goal stated from above but it's still part of her short-term benchmark goals. See where I'm getting here? Now, you can continue breaking these goals into even smaller, more bite-size pieces such as weekly goals. Perhaps even something as simple as: "By end of week one, I want to have prepared five meals at home." Going back to your inner dialogue, notice how these goals are not taking jabs at your physical body. They are goals which give you actionable intentions when completing them. Be kind to yourself when writing these goals and make sure they are realistic.

Keeping yourself accountable for these short-term goals is another way to document, evaluate, and track your progression as you approach your big picture goal. Use your journal. Write down these short-term goals and use them as a checklist. You'll be blown away each day, week, and/or month as you check in with your benchmark goals and see just how far you've come. One step at a time, my friend. Your journey to health is your own unique and beautiful path.

STEP THREE: CREATING YOUR FITNESS PLAN

I can almost hear your anxious thoughts. *Here it comes, the part where Michelle tells me I need to start running three miles a day, four times a week.* Oh, heck no. Even as a trainer, running long distances is not my favorite. So guess what? I don't do it. *What? A trainer who doesn't run miles and miles?* Yep, and you don't have to either. If you like it, go for it. If you don't, then don't. Simple. Creating your fitness plan must be specific to you, your body, your schedule, and making sure you are not doing anything that creates injury or leads to inflammation of past injuries.

Here is my weekly five-day workout plan. Each workout can be done right in the comfort of your own home using just a set of dumbbells. Edit these workouts as you see fit. I just want to give you a tangible workout agenda you can take with you to start implementing as soon as possible.

Just as I said in previous chapters, give yourself thirty minutes. Thirty deserving minutes to give back to your mind and your body while alternating between resistance training and cardio for optimal results and health.

DAYS ONE, THREE, AND FIVE: RESISTANCE TRAINING

Now this one is where I get all the questions. Women especially, want to focus on one part of the body. I'm sorry to say but there is no such thing as spot-reduction training. You must work the body as a complete unit to build lasting strength and to change your body composition. Many of us want to tighten the core so we spend hours doing back-aching crunches and holding planks for what seems like an eternity. Sorry, time to squash this myth too. In order to get that tightened core you must work the extremities of the body, which all stem from the core. For example, say you're doing a basic squat. Believe it or not, that squat movement is not just stemming from the legs, but rather working your core in an equal effort to keep your body in the correct form and position for that squat without falling over. Continuing the core component; say you're doing the seated bicep curl machine. (You know, the one where you have to sit first, adjust those weird levers, then make sure you're seated high enough to reach those handles that look like two poles sticking out of the seat.) Okay, so when you're doing that seated bicep curl, you're taking away the need to acquire the use of the core because you are most likely hunched over trying to get enough leverage to curl those weights to your face. See where I'm getting here? I like to interchange the words resistance training with functional training. Resistance training must be done using the entire body in order to properly distribute the resistance of the working muscles. I'm also an advocate of using more free weights as those machines can be very confusing, very puzzling, and complex at the gym.

As women, functional resistance training is important for those day-to-day tasks. For example, let's say you're doing something as simple as picking up a box. Instead of hunching over and risk slipping a disc, you have the basic strength skill set to know to squat down, embrace the core, then use the power of your legs and core, not your back, to lift that box. So, just as you're working on resistance training and building those muscles, you're also working on the functionality of your body. When resistance training, opt for those free weights and even doing a body weight workout such as Pilates, yoga, and/or a barre workout. All these are forms of resistance training. You are resistance training with the weight of your own body, promoting muscle stimulation and growth. Pretty cool, huh?

All right, so for your resistance training I'd like you to work with full body circuits. In order to get these workouts done in about thirty minutes we must work the body head to toe. Here's a quick example workout you can tweak and edit so it's just right for you:

Full Body Resistance Training Circuit
- Legs: ten squats (with option to hold dumbbells by your side)
- Arms: ten standing shoulder presses (Press dumbbells overhead while embracing core)
- Core: Hold a thirty-second plank on hands and feet or modified by holding on knees

Now, do this circuit three to four times through for that thirty-minute full-body resistance training workout. If you're extra crunched for time, you can even break it up further by doing two rounds one part of the day and two rounds another part of the day.

DAYS TWO AND FOUR: CARDIO

The dreaded "cardio" word. I know, I know . . . being sweaty and out of breath doesn't sound like very much fun, but the beauty of this is that you don't have to be a trained runner in order to get your heart rate up. When talking to clients I soften the blow of the cringey word "cardio" by saying "interval training." Interval training allows you to work hard and have periods of rest. Pretty amazing, right? Your heart rate is being sent on a roller-coaster ride while you are working hard for an amount of time, increasing the perceived rate of exertion followed by a shorter period of time to catch your breath and allow for your heart rate to come back down. This break allows for more powerful bursts of workload in comparison to someone who is running for an hour straight.

For interval training let's use a general forty seconds of medium to high energy (work), followed by twenty seconds of rest. This short time frame of harder workload gives you an achievable amount of time to increase your perceived rate of exertion while then giving you a shorter rest period to not only rest, but to build back the stamina needed to get you through another bout of hard work. You can really use any kind of timing breakdown but the point is that you can work at that higher rate of perceived exertion without exhausting yourself and making you feel as though you can't get through it because you have that time of rest to renew your energy capacity.

Now in order to get your heart rate up in those thirty minutes, you must be willing to exert yourself with high energy. Notice how I said high energy, not high intensity. High energy is all about your own level of exertion while completing these cardio workouts. I'll say it again and again: Every woman is different and every workout is different, and that's okay as long as you're doing exactly what's right for you and your body. Another misconception is that cardio means a lot of jumping. Why would I have my client Kelly with a past injury of a torn meniscus jumping around and putting more strain and pressure on that meniscus? Doesn't seem enjoyable to me, and doesn't seem like it would be something she could stick with. Instead, think of interval training as forty seconds of work, followed by twenty seconds of rest done repeatedly in the span of about thirty minutes.

This forty seconds of work is different for each person. For example, my client Kara, who used to be a college runner, loves the way running makes her feel. But after having her first baby her right knee always seems to give her a bit of pain when she would hit the three-mile mark. I told her she didn't have to give up running completely. On her cardio days I give her a workout that looks something like this: forty seconds light running or jogging, followed by twenty seconds of a brisk walk. She's exerting her body for those forty seconds and getting her heart rate up, shortly followed by giving herself and her knee the twenty-second break to let her heart rate come down in order to build back the stamina to go back to another forty-second workload.

You might be asking yourself, "What about someone who doesn't want to run, walk, or jog at all?" I got you, my friend. For clients who truly disdain running, I give them the option to do bodyweight exercises in those forty seconds, no weights needed. Here is what a thirty-minute interval training workout might look like for you. Again, edit, tweak, and transform this cardio workout for yourself to implement into your actionable fitness plan.

Interval Training Workout

- Forty seconds jumping jacks (No-jumping option: alternate leg tap out to side)
- Rest twenty seconds
- Forty seconds squat jumps (No-jumping option: take out jump from squat)
- Rest twenty seconds
- Forty seconds jog in place (No-jumping option: march in place)
- Rest twenty seconds
- Forty seconds jump rope (No-jumping option: shift body weight on toes side to side)
- Rest twenty seconds
- Forty seconds alternating side hops (No-jumping option: step side to side)
- Rest twenty seconds

Use your stopwatch and repeat this circuit six times to bring you to thirty minutes total.

Now that we have both resistance training and cardio training workouts, let's put them into a real-life weekly plan. Take out your calendar or even use your phone for this next one. My recommendation is to fit them in like you would any other non-negotiable appointment in your schedule. If life throws some curve balls your way, simply move a workout to the weekend. You wouldn't want to skip a doctor's appointment, so treat these thirty-minute workouts as little appointments for yourself and your health. Block out the time needed and see where exactly you can put those thirty minutes in place.

You might be thinking, "Michelle, I'm just too busy." If working out to benefit your health is a priority, I promise you will find the time for these precious thirty minutes. If it helps, use the alarm feature on your phone to go off about ten minutes before your workout so you know it's coming up. Utilize anything that will hold you accountable and motivate you to put in the deserving quality time for yourself and your body.

STEP FOUR: CREATING YOUR NUTRITION PLAN

Salads only, right? No way, woman! We work much too hard to only fuel ourselves on leaves and grass. This general nutrition plan is one that allows for wiggle room and uses the 80/20 stance to give you the flexibility you need to enjoy mindful eating. For my ladies who would rather punch themselves in the head rather than cook, I got you covered, too. Now, I know there are diet trends coming from every direction. Let me assure you, this nutrition plan has been created in its simplest, most natural form. For specific nutrition planning, it is extremely important to get help from a professional in nutrition, or to get your nutrition plan reviewed by a professional in nutrition if you're more of a do-it-yourselfer, to make sure that you are thinking realistically about your goals and your desired outcomes. And I am not going to sit here and try to sell you on different supplements or shakes because I do not advocate for that. I am an advocate of eating whole, natural foods that are more bioavailable for your body to break down and use for quality fuel.

I also understand that as a busy female, sometimes being able to eat a healthy meal on the go is just not feasible. But there are always options and you always have choices. In regard to nutrition, I want you to be able to naturally choose and make mindful food decisions that you can feel good about while increasing your energy, work quality, and professional presence throughout your day. I started implementing this nutrition strategy called the Three Ps (Plan, Prepare, and Prep) when I began training and coaching a nurse by the name of Sarah. She worked twelve-hours shifts for four days straight, followed by three days off. Her workday began at six a.m., dashing out the door with a microwavable breakfast sandwich to eat in the car. This was immediately followed by back-to-back patients, zero lunch break, staff meetings, floor changes, and so on. In between patients she would down a protein shake or quickly grab a bagel with cream cheese from the staff room, then she was onto the next patient. When she needed a quick pick-me-up, she would usually stop by the administrative desk where they had a bowl of packaged chocolates, and grab a handful to shove into her scrubs. There was no time for dillydallying, these twelve hours were hard and long.

When Sarah would finally get in the car to come home, she was always starving. She hadn't listened to the grumbles of her stomach throughout the day because there was just no time. The time she did get to sit down she was usually transcribing patient charts to have them reviewed by the doctors while popping a few of those chocolates from earlier. Sarah was ravenous upon coming home and would literally eat anything she could, usually feeling bloated and full before bed, but she was starving and needed the food. Then up and at 'em again for days two, three, and four.

On her days off, Sarah just wanted to relax, kick her feet up, catch up on her favorite shows, and get some well-deserved rest. This usually resulted in takeout, frozen pizzas, and heavy snacking. Sarah knew these meals were not the healthiest and the excess headaches, body weight, and lethargy were a direct result from improperly fueling her body. Needless to say, Sarah was one busy bee, and upon reaching out to me for nutritional help I knew I couldn't direct her the way I would another client who had the freedom of coming home at a normal time and preparing their own meals. I thought long and hard about how to give nutritional advice to a full-time nurse and this is where my Three Ps tool for nutrition was born. I'm going to break down the Three P's while referring back to my client Sarah, but I want you to also be considering how to adhere these three Ps into *your* nutritional action plan.

PLAN

I know how busy you are between work, family, and friends. But let's not forget our values behind our goals which is ultimately to increase our quality of health. Plan your weekly meals just as you plan your work week. Pull out a weekly calendar and write down all your meals for the week ahead. While this may seem tedious, I promise that once you start getting the hang of it, it will only take you five to ten minutes tops. You can do this while you have some downtime at work or even on a Sunday afternoon before your workweek.

Write down your breakfast, lunch, dinners, *and snacks* on this weekly template and don't forget to give yourself some wiggle room. For my clients, I advise they write down their Monday–Friday meal plan, then leave Saturday and Sunday blank to allow

254

for more mindful eating, even if it's at your favorite bar. For Sarah, she knew work days were sometimes tough to get in her meals but she would write down what she knew she could eat quickly in between patients and save in the staff kitchen. She even wrote down her favorite fresh-packaged delivery meal that required zero cooking (which I will get to in a second). Remember to give yourself some flexibility and allow yourself to indulge in a taco night out with the family. If your nutrition plan is too rigid, there is more room for "falling off the wagon."

PREPARE

Now that you have your weekly meal plan written down, use this same plan as you prepare your grocery list on a separate piece of paper. For example, if Monday your breakfast is eggs and strawberries, make sure you have written these ingredients down on your grocery list. As for more complex meals which require a recipe, write down any ingredients needed after checking what you already have in your own fridge or pantry. Now remember when I said Sarah even wrote down her pre-packaged foods she would get? All right, you're about to love me forever for this one. There are so many new, healthy delivered meal services that will be shipped right to your door. They're online everywhere now and you can pick and choose which menus you'd like to be delivered. Most of these companies even now have the selection for healthier meals or specific dietary preferences, which is amazing. You might be asking yourself, well what about a quick frozen dinner? I'm sorry to say, but most of these frozen dinners are high in sodium content as well as preservatives because they need a longer shelf life. They may have the alluring "lean" and "low fat" trendy words written on their packaging, but it doesn't avoid the fact that they are still frozen, which also leads to less nutrient quality.

Okay, so now that my non-cookers are all set, let's move to our last P.

PREP

You might be thinking to yourself, "Seriously? Prep my meals in Tupperware and store them in my fridge for the whole week?" Nope, not even! But if that's what you enjoy, do it! Prep simply means preparing yourself for your weekly meals. Do you have the ingredients you need? Do you have your plan set somewhere you will see it each day? For Sarah, she actually used a weekly calendar magnetic whiteboard and would write down her meals so she could see them right on her fridge each day. No thought needed as to what she was eating or what she was going to prepare. I recommend you do the same, especially if your partner and family are always asking what's for dinner. It's a great timesaver for yourself and for the family. And by using your grocery list from your weekly meal plan, visits to the grocery store will be far more efficient. No more aimless strolls around the store pondering, *What should I get this week?*

"But, Michelle, I literally have zero time to go to the grocery store." Girl, I got you. Look online at your local grocery store. They most likely have a service in which you use your phone or computer to select all the ingredients and produce you need, then *voilà*, it's brought to your doorstep in just a few hours. Man, what a time to be alive. So for my busy gals on the go, use your five-minute break at work to utilize your already prepared grocery list and have that healthy food delivered right to your house.

QUICK TIP: For those who like to prep, go for it. By taking the time to quickly chop up some fruits and veggies to have in the fridge, they'll be easily accessible (and extra appreciated) for grab-and-go. Prep smarter, not harder.

Awesome, so you have the Three Ps to set you up for success. Now let me give you some general nutrition advice when preparing your meals and meal plans. Remember I mentioned how nurse Sarah would come home starving from work because she hadn't eaten? And how when she came home she would literally eat anything and everything? This is not uncommon, and I'm also guilty about accidentally skipping a meal because I was at my desk working in a complete trance. Instead of waiting for those bigger meals—breakfast, lunch, and dinner—eat a little snack in between. Just lightly grazing on a healthy snack will silence those stomach grumbles while giving your body enough energy to function optimally.

I break it down like this: breakfast, mid-morning snack, lunch, mid-afternoon snack, then dinner. Think about snacks that are higher in protein (so you stay fuller longer) or that have some quality natural sugars in them to keep your blood sugar afloat (i.e., fruit). Sometimes those two p.m. crashes are not from lack of sleep, they're because your stomach, which I refer to as your gas tank, is on "E." Something as easy as cut-up berries or even pretzels with hummus can be the fix. It's okay to snack, and they will actually help you to not overindulge or binge on your next meal because you've starved yourself throughout the day.

Another tip about nutritious eating is to eat more quality foods. Rule of thumb: less packaging equals more nutrients. At the grocery store, try shopping mostly on the perimeters of the store because that is where the whole foods are located—the fresh fruits and veggies, the meats, and the unpackaged foods. These whole foods contain the *quality* macronutrients such as proteins, fats, and carbohydrates that when eaten are properly digested and used for quality fuel for the body. Skip the meal replacement shakes and fill your stomach with quality foods. Since they don't come in packages, they don't have the high sodium, simple carbs, and highly processed chemicals.

Remember, these are very general nutrition guidelines and I've made them this way purposely. Notice I haven't gone into some rant about how one diet is better than another. I want you to understand that nutrition needs to be viewed from its very natural, very simplistic roots. Every woman is different and requires different nutrition guidance, so please reach out to a professional when creating a specific meal plan and make sure they hold your best interest.

STEP FIVE: CREATING YOUR SELF-CARE PLAN

While putting a fitness and nutrition plan together is a giant leap into the realm of self-care, mental health also needs to be properly nurtured and fueled. Self-care isn't just about taking bubble baths, the occasional girls night out, or winding down with a nice glass of pinot and Netflix after a long day. It's about checking in with the brains of the operation, the one who is in charge of taking on every little task and putting those mental chores into your daily reality. My God, she's in charge of *a lot*, so let's show her all the love we can and make sure she knows she's appreciated and well taken care of.

Self-care means different things for each individual. There's no right or wrong way to give yourself the care you need. But I want you to practice self-care at least once a day every day, including the weekends. That's the only part of this actionable plan that doesn't allow for wiggle room. This part of the plan should be done day in, day out to keep those feelings of stress, anxiety, and depression at a minimum. And yes, I completely understand that for some, like my father, depression due to the chemical imbalance in the brain must be strictly monitored with medication and clinical assistance. What I am saying is that even though you may be diagnosed with depression, there are still wonderful ways to cope with those crippling symptoms through self-care and simply showing yourself the kindness you deserve.

Because you, my friend, are one beautiful boss babe who should be showered like the amazing queen you are.

So let's go through some self-care techniques you can start as soon as *today*. Just like your fitness and nutrition weekly plans, write down these techniques in your journal, your phone, and/or your calendar. Block off times of self-care throughout the week like you would any other appointment. For a busy woman, nothing is more important to honor than appointments with yourself. They make everything else possible.

This first one is not super exciting to do, but I promise as soon as you do it, you're going to feel like the biggest weight has been lifted off your shoulders. Remember when I mentioned surrounding yourself with women and people who will equally empower you and not make you feel guilty for being in charge of your optimal health and wealth? Well, the ones who *don't*, have simply got to go. I'm not saying you have to call them up right now and give them the laundry list of ways that they belittled you or made you feel like total crap. I'm talking about "trimming the fat" and perhaps not taking your valuable time to go to any events with them that you're already dreading. You *know* you're going to feel absolutely drained and exhausted after being around them, so why the hell put yourself in that situation in the first place? Your time and energy is too valuable. Pull the plug on these "energy suckers" and give yourself the permission you need to protect your energy and to protect your mental health.

I know this one might be easier said than done, but try it for yourself. Give yourself permission to say no. Wouldn't you rather do something nice with yourself or your family than go to another girls night where all Karen wants to do is talk crap about her boss, her boyfriend, and your mutual friend that you adore. Do it, get it over with, and don't look back. Your brain will thank you for the extra space to think about things other than if Karen will finally dump the idiot she keeps complaining about. Every. Single. Day.

Don't be scared of letting old, toxic friends go, as they may have served you well in the past, but it's overdue to let go. It's time to build your tribe of fellow empowered females. Look around your new gym classes, your networking events, and even at your kid's after-school programs. That's where you'll find them. The universe (or God, or source—however you view the one in charge of this whole thing called "life") is going to be doing all the work in the background to bring you the women you must surround yourself with in order to be your healthiest, happiest, and vibrant self, I promise.

All right, now that that's out of the way, it's time for the good stuff we can all get behind. Ever wonder why those yoga girls down the street always come out farting unicorns and rainbows? I mean, there has to be some kind of logic behind it. Besides the crazy positions they can get themselves into, there's got to be a reason why they believe they are so "zen" if you will. Perhaps it's because of the breathing techniques, the slowing of the heart rate, the calming of the everyday thoughts? I know yoga is not for everyone, and I'm not telling you to go off and join one of those month-long yoga retreats in India, but hey . . . if it serves you, then go.

Here are some other mindful actions you can start doing today without having to go off and join a goat farm.

INTENTION SETTING

Before you roll over to look at your phone in the morning, before you even open your eyes to start thinking about the eight million things you have to do, take the time to set your intentions. Ask yourself, *What do I want to get out of today?* You were put on this Earth to enjoy your happiest, healthiest life, so how are you going to change your mindset to manifest those intentions to reality? Even if it's just at your desk, close your eyes for thirty seconds, one minute, three minutes, so you can plan your intentions and what you want to do *this* day that serves you and plants a beautiful little seed in your mind. Just as I mentioned earlier, it can be as easy as: "I want to take care of my body today." That's it, you did it! Your brain will thank you for taking the time for yourself and your day will look a little brighter, a little more focused on all things about YOU.

JOURNALING

Relax, it's none of that "Dear Diary" nonsense—unless it serves you. What about writing down three things you're grateful for today? This will take you a grand total of zero minutes as you quickly jot down what comes to mind. Oh, you're grateful that you got to go to the bathroom in peace today without the kids banging at the door? Great! It's still something you're grateful for and can write down. I like to do this one first thing in the morning so I set an awesome tone for the day of positivity. It's amazing how once you start journaling just three things you're grateful for, more and more positive events and opportunities begin falling right into your lap! Train your brain to see the beauty in your life and you will find the universe delivering so many goodies right in front of your face. We've all heard the term "like attracts like." Well, girl, this is most definitely one of them. Try it now for yourself. Write down those three things you're grateful for. Maybe it's even taking the time to read this book and nourish your soul.

MINDFUL BREATHING

Take note of your breath, the way you're breathing right this very second. Are you a shallow breather? Meaning your core is tight and you are only breathing from your lungs? Or are you breathing from your lungs and stomach, which is deep breathing. You might have just noticed that you're breathing with your stomach muscles tightened, which you didn't even do on purpose. This shallow breathing does not allow for proper oxygen delivery throughout the body and, most importantly, to the brain.

Why not take three to five minutes while you're at the desk, before you go to bed, or when you're standing in the shower, to close your eyes and just breathe fully. Better yet, why don't you practice right now? Sit up tall and place one hand on your stomach. Take a deep breath that fills to your belly, which you can physically feel your hand pushing out. Hold that breath for five seconds and slowly release. Do this about five times through and feel as your heart rate slows down. Taking this short time to breathe mindfully will deliver the oxygen to your brain in order to help with brain synapse communication, which leads to lower stress levels and anxiety. If needed, set a reminder alarm in your phone, just as in reference to working out. This small mindful breathing technique will allow for a quick boost of relaxation while giving loving care to the brains of the operation.

MEDITATION AND/OR PRAYER

Call it what you want—energy, the universe, God—but there's got to be someone or something out there running this circus we call life. This is my secret weapon and most powerful tool I recommend for myself and clients when beginning to get into an effective mental health routine. It can even tie back into mindful breathing, as you can do both of these synergistically. Sit in silence, and quiet the mind. What do you need today? What are you looking to achieve in this life? Just seeing it in your mind's eye is enough to plant the seed of positive intention in order to manifest those intentions into reality. Whatever you need, the universe will deliver.

Think of source energy like your own personal butler, who will wait on you hand and foot to make you the most comfortable, most happy woman on this planet. I mean, that's their job, right? Make sure you're connecting yourself with this amazing flow of energy, as it will only boost you into the happiest version of yourself you ever dreamed. If you're still a bit confused on where to start with this, I usually recommend searching a quick three-to-five-minute guided meditation online. It may seem a little awkward at first but the more you do it, the more comfortable you will be with it, and the more aligned with the universe you will be. If you're a gal who just cannot sit still, that's okay too. This prayer and/or meditation can most definitely be done in nature. Outdoors is such a wonderful place to clear your mind, ground yourself, and get aligned with that source of energy. You can speak out loud, envision your needs in your mind, or just use your senses to breathe, smell, and watch the beauties of nature in front of you.

TREAT YOURSELF TO A MASSAGE, FACIAL, OR MANI-PEDI

I know, this one is the best one. Enjoy yourself and enjoy the luxuries provided to us. These small little upgrades will not only boost your happiness, but also boost your confidence on your journey to stepping into this ultimate, empowered life. Keep putting yourself first, and understand, wholeheartedly, that you are deserving and worthy of this royal life you are creating before your eyes. (If you need a little help with justifying your manicure splurge, refer back to Amanda's actionable plan and see how you can fit these small luxuries into your life and budget.)

So there you have it, sisters. If you can just take one of these self-care techniques with you throughout your journey to optimal well-being, you're on the right track. I'll repeat this again and again—put these techniques in your calendar the way you would make an unbreakable appointment for anything else in your life. The more you prioritize self-care and giving back to your mental health, the more you will truly encompass the full circle of true optimal health and happiness. And if you truly, from the bottom of your heart, know and feel you deserve this life, the universe will serve it.

Now it's your turn to put all these tangible actions into place to start showing up for yourself, shining your bright light for the entire world to see, and bringing your A game to both your personal and professional life as a modern woman in charge of her health. If you haven't already, use your journal or your phone to record these daily workouts, meal plan, and self-care actions to set your course in motion. This Actionable Health Plan was created for anyone to feel good and to begin with confidence!

Let's quickly recap its five steps so you don't miss any aspects of how to create this empowered life of health:

Step One: Understanding Your Why (Determine your values as to why you want to create and achieve this optimally healthy life.)

Step Two: Goal Setting (Both long-term goals and short-term goals used as benchmarks.)

Step Three: Creating Your Fitness Plan (Remember, just thirty minutes a day, four to five times a week, combining both strength and cardio.)

Step Four: Creating Your Nutrition Plan (Keep the Three Ps in mind: Prepare, Plan, and Prep your way to optimal fuel for your mind and body.)

And finally, **Step Five: Creating Your Self-Care Plan** (Start with even just one of the techniques to let the brains of the operation know she is getting taken care of and that you love her and want what's best for her and her mental health.)

This is truly the 360° approach to optimal health. Again, please outsource when needed and know that this is a huge investment in yourself that your future self will thank you for.

All because you came to the conclusion that your beautiful self is both deserving and worthy of this amazing life.

CHAPTER FIFTEEN

HEALTH EMPOWERMENT

Now that you are armed and ready with your Actionable Health Plan, it's time to light the fire that starts in your soul. It won't always be easy and there will be numerous speed bumps along the way, but there's nothing you cannot overcome with your tenacious heart to make health and happiness your ultimate priority. We've worked through your past narratives of guilt and how you can overcome the voice in your head. I've shown you how to walk before you learn to run by going over baby steps in creating a healthy initiative that works for your unique life.

Now how are you going to start showing up for yourself today so your future self with thank you? How are you going to be a role model for ultimate health and happiness so you can impact yourself and the woman sitting next to you? How are you going to pave the future of women's health and empowerment by showing the little women around you what it means to be a woman in charge of her mind and body? These little women are our future, our legacy.

According to the Department of Labor, 47 percent of women in the U.S. are in the workforce. That's almost half the population. We literally cannot afford to diminish the need to be healthy in order to provide an income for ourselves and our families. The Department of Labor also states that mothers are the primary or sole earners for 40 percent of households with children under eighteen today, compared with 11 percent in 1960. Wow, just wow. Those facts alone make me want to yell off a rooftop, preaching the absolute need of promoting women's health. The statistics also challenge the quality of life us women are living. If 47 percent of women are in the workforce, and you'll recall *one-third of these women will die from heart disease*, what does this say about not only our physical, but our mental health and stability? Perhaps we are putting too much stress on the importance of running the eternal rat race of income success that we have neglected our health entirely, putting too much stress on the powerhouse of the body, our heart.

If these sets of facts don't perpetuate the desire to put your Actionable Health Plan into place, then this will. According to WHO (World Health Organization), women suffer from mental disorders such as depression, anxiety, and stress at a higher rate than men.[8] I truly believe it's because we haven't shifted our mindset flow from the past narrative of guilt—those hideous voices in our heads telling us we're not enough and we're not doing enough. That, coupled with society's views on women who now need to be *both* the caretaker and breadwinner of the household.

Understanding these facts, are you truly shocked that these mental disorders are more prominent in women than men? I'm going to have to say, "No, not really." We are under an incredible amount of stress here as females, yet no one is talking about it.

We can no longer afford to be a part of the statistics. We must be part of the change and the change needs to happen now. But in order to change these statistics we need to fight for our health and well-being. We must protect our vital life force, and together we can change the narrative of what being a healthy woman really means.

As an empowered female, let's recognize that the energy, the narrative, and the mindset of ourselves and others need to continue to shift, to combine the awareness of mental and physical health equally, especially in women who are suffering the most. We truly cannot have one without the other. How can you be mentally healthy if you are not physically healthy and vice versa? Rather than comparing ourselves to one another, we must recognize that our journeys are all different, all unique, and all beautiful. Instead of shaming and judging our neighbor, how can we use this shift to be a role model for the woman we want to be and the women we want to see in our tribe of empowered females? Ask yourself: How can I be of service to my own health while being there to help another in their time of need?

As we put our Actionable Health Plan into play, it's important to acknowledge that it won't always be easy and there will always be speed bumps along the way. Let me help you by shining a light on the most common speed bumps I encounter with my own clients, so you can have some defense against these barriers if they creep in between you and your healthiest self yet.

MOTIVATION

Let's start with the big one, and probably the most important: sustained motivation. This is my number one most common speed bump that sits between my clients' goals and their ultimate health. Let's say you've been doing great for about two months and you can see and feel the difference in your body, your mind, and your confidence. It's great hearing all the compliments you receive from family, coworkers, and friends. You are feeling your best. This is actually a very vulnerable time to start turning back to old habits. Why? Because for so long we have been fooled into thinking that a healthy routine is solely for the purpose of losing a few pounds, perhaps fitting into an old pair of jeans, or looking a certain way for a vacation. As wonderful as it is achieving these small benchmark goals, we must think long term. Just as I mentioned in your Actionable Health Plan, it's about achieving short-term goals that extend to your long-term goals that ultimately become second nature in your daily habits.

Commonly, after achieving our first short-term goal, we might celebrate with an indulgent meal. But that one indulgent meal can turn into another, which turns into another, which turns into your old eating habits of improper fueling for the body. Or perhaps you start to slack on your thirty minutes of physical activity a day because you have already achieved your goal weight for summer vacation in Jamaica. Again, we must completely shift our mindset, which is something as a female population we are not used to doing in the complex world of health. We are sometimes so focused on a number that we forget why we've started this journey in the first place.

I understand that the feeling of motivation is always strongest in the beginning, but I challenge you to self-reflect at times of low motivation. Get back to your *why*. Why did you start this journey and why is your physical and mental health so important to you? If you're not sure what your "why" is, then refer to the previously listed statistics. Use them as fuel to change the curve and help the female population thrive, as a whole. Use those deep-rooted "whys" as motivation to move past this speed bump.

I know that with my own clientele, if I see less check-ins for workouts and/or less mindful eating, we hop on the phone as soon as possible. It's important to acknowledge this feeling of losing motivation and "nip it in the butt" before it completely derails all the healthy initiatives you've been putting together. It's important to know when to outsource for help. Seek a professional trainer, coach, and/or health consultant that holds your best interest while also holding you accountable for the life of health you want to achieve. Understand that this lifestyle change is for the long haul and that you're going to do everything in your power to make this part of your everyday life. Make it so that all three of you women in the room have a fighting chance to beat the odds of heart disease.

THE SCALE

The first speed bump leads me perfectly to the dreaded scale of doom. As a trainer, I see firsthand how a silly ol' number on a scale can turn a perfectly healthy woman into a number worrier and act as if they are the biggest failure to themselves and humanity. I am so tired of watching diet fads "guarantee" ten pounds off your first month or your money back. Why are we continuing to drive the false myth that our health is directly correlated to the number on the scale. This absolutely needs to stop, as we are only continuing to put ourselves down as a female population if the number on the scale doesn't reflect the thin, stick figure, bathing suit model facade that we have been ingrained into our minds to be "healthy."

If this book is about all things female empowerment, than this chapter is the means to change what beauty, health, confidence, and vibrant energy really looks like on a modern woman. A number cannot and will not accurately describe your new outlook on health or the healthy initiatives you've worked so hard to put in place. The number will not give you insight into how much you've been acknowledging your mental health and how you've been coming home from work a little earlier to have more quality time with your family. The number will not show you the dedication you've promoted in putting in your quality thirty minutes of fitness a day to not only work your muscles but to stimulate the release of endorphins through your body.

More scientifically, this irrelevant at-home scale encompasses your entire body's mass. It does not break down the fat mass, the muscle mass, the water mass, and the bone mass. In fact, 75 percent of your body is made up of water. What does that tell you of the deception of the scale right there? If you are dehydrated, you will weigh less. If you are fully hydrated, you will weigh more according to the scale. If you are looking to the scale day to day, trying to watch the weight come off, you're setting yourself up for failure. Furthermore, as females our weight naturally fluctuates day to day due to our natural menstrual cycles in order to balance hormones. How are we ever going to get an accurate weight when our body weight as a whole fluctuates so often? We must ditch the scale once and for all and not become a slave to this false perspective on health.

You may be asking yourself, "Okay, well then how the heck do I track my progression?" Ah, I'm glad you asked. The most accurate way to track your progression and transformation is to check in with yourself. You can do this by taking monthly pictures of yourself and keeping a journal to evaluate how you're feeling by means of your energy, your overall happiness, your ability to walk up the stairs without being winded. None of these internal evaluations can be measured by one simple number on a scale.

I will tell you this one story, and it is in no way to shame my previous client, as she was able to finally take a step back and understand that the number she viewed on the scale was completely irrelevant. Anne (not her real name) came to me at the age of thirty, asking me to help her get back to her weight when she was in her early twenties. She told me that she was currently ten pounds over what she used to weigh and, although wasn't unhealthy by any means, said she preferred being her former weight. I first began by addressing the fact that with this ten-year gap comes regular female hormone and body composition changes and that while yes, that goal is achievable, it will not happen (or at least be sustainable) in a healthy manner without restrictive diet and limitations. Anne was firm on this pre-set number she wanted to achieve and the stubbornness of this conclusion to her "happiness" intrigued me. It proposed the question in my mind as to why she thought *this* certain number would bring her happiness.

During our consultation I asked, "Anne, how will being ten pounds lighter make you happier?" That's when the outpouring of past experiences and events came spilling out of her like it had been pent up in her mind for years. In her early twenties she received a lot of attention from others and had so much confidence in how she looked. This really struck a nerve within me that I knew I had to challenge. "Anne, not once have you told me how you *felt* when you were this weight. You just keep saying you were happier but what does that mean?"

Here it came, the answer I had been looking for. Anne told me with a sadness in her voice that when she had weighed less in her early twenties, she was skipping meals, working out more than once a day, had chronic headaches, used prescription medication to curb her appetite, and would use her scale each morning to determine what she would, or would not, eat that day. She told me that although she had confidence when she wore a bathing suit, she was never quite happy in her mind.

As we sat on the phone, I discussed the importance of not only being happy in her skin, but being happy in her heart. After just one month of training and nutrition coaching with me, I was able to help her change her relationship with food and the way she looked at herself in the mirror. I'll admit it was a challenge to keep her off the scale for those first two weeks as she would say, "Michelle I've only lost one pound this week." I understood I had to tread lightly and be empathetic to her past experiences . . . so I told her verbatim: "TOSS THAT HUNK OF JUNK IN THE TRASH!" To my amazement, she did exactly that.

In just one month Anne happily reported, "I've never had these bumps on my arms before."

I laughed and said, "Oh, you mean your *biceps*?"

"Is that what they are?" she said. "I feel so strong, stronger than I ever have before!" Never once since then has she mentioned her weight to me again.

To this day Anne is my client and she continues to have a new perspective on what happy means to her body and her heart. She unashamedly posted pictures in her bathing suit from her vacation to the Caribbean two months ago with a radiating smile! She recently told me she went to the doctor for her annual checkup and she is but three pounds lighter than when she started training with me. Yet for the first time in her life, she is okay with that because her health and happiness mean more to her than the number on a deceptive scale.

As a female collective it's time to finally ditch the meaningless scale and not let that number get in the way of our healthiest, strongest, and happiest selves. After all, how can one physically weigh the happiness of the heart and mind? It's time we step off that dreaded scale and start celebrating our non-scale victories. Why not celebrate the fact that you got an A+ on your yearly physical, being cleared of any underlying heart disease problems? Maybe celebrate the fact that your therapist has been able to slowly decrease your depression medication because you've been able to holistically manage your own symptoms with your Actionable Health Plan? These are such amazing achievements that must be celebrated and rejoiced. And not one of these wins are depicted by one single number. How about that?

INJURY AND ILLNESS

This speed bump can really be a pain in the butt, quite literally sometimes—especially after an empowered female like yourself has already started and maintained a healthy routine. You're looking and feeling your absolute best practicing this new lifestyle, and then, *bam*—you break a bone, come down with the flu, have a sudden flare of arthritis inflammation, and so on. There are so many spontaneous injuries and illnesses that can arise when all you've been doing is trying your best to live a healthy and happy life. Believe me, after breaking my leg during gymnastics, I know how bad it truly stinks to be completely knocked off your routine. It feels so hopeless as you're lying there with a cast and a pair of crutches to limp from one side of the house to the other. All while looking down at your unused limb and seeing the atrophy of the muscle and loss of strength.

These times of injury and illness can take days, weeks, and sometimes even months off our fitness routine and make us feel as though we have failed yet again. I'm here to tell you that even during these times there are, and should be, actionable measures to put your immediate health first. Let's say you slipped a disc in your back and have been recommended by your doctor to stop resistance training activities due to overuse and overstrain to the spine. Instead of taking this recommendation as the doom of death, ask her or him what you *can* do. Are you able to do light walking, light stretching, and/or perhaps water activity? So many times in the past my clients call me in a panic saying their doctor has told them to stop their current physical routine after ailments such as arthritis flared up. They're in a panic because they think their doctor has sworn them off any kind of physical activity.

In actuality, I've worked closely with physical therapists who encourage the activities I listed above, including water aerobics, light walking, and light stretching such as yoga. Make sure you don't take your doctor's recommendation as some kind of death sentence. I'm here to tell you there's always a way to incorporate your Actionable Health Plan even during these exact times.

QUICK TIP: If you must be completely off your feet for extreme cases, I advocate you ask your doctor for a recommendation of a trusted physical therapist specializing in your specific injury or illness. Although it may take a few weeks or months to get you back to your baseline health, I promise it will be much easier for you to do if you are still keeping up some kind of physical health routine.

As for getting back to resistance training, I can tell you firsthand, as well as from my previous clients who suffered an injury, that muscle memory is on your side. Muscle memory is the adaptability of your muscles to regain their former strength due to previous muscle stimulation patterns such as strength training. So many times I hear "I'm never going to get this strength back" or "How am I going to make sure I don't put the weight back on?" First, if you've already been working out routinely prior to your injury, as soon as you are cleared and ready to get back to your former routine, you will find that your muscles will remember exactly what to do and you will get back to your previous strength faster than someone who is just starting a health routine from square one.

Secondly, if you are worried about weight gain, make sure you are doing all you can to continue eating mindfully in order to fuel the body and to heal faster. Just because your workout routine is on a hiatus does not, I repeat *does not*, mean that you shouldn't continue eating more healthily and mindfully throughout this time. Remember, an empowered female eats to fuel her mind and body daily, not just when she's working out. I will also add, when you eat these quality foods, you are providing your body with more quality nutrients to heal bones, decrease inflammation, increase white cells to fight off bacteria and viruses, and so, so, so much more. You cannot simply throw in the towel and give up on all healthy initiatives. Do what you can to keep your nutrition game strong, especially during these times. Not only will it help you heal faster, but if you're eating these quality nutrients you're preserving the muscle mass which helps balance fat stores. This means the more you fuel your body with adequate protein, carbohydrates, and fats, the more your body will feed the most important systems of the body including the muscular, lymphatic, cardiovascular systems and so on, rather than just being stored as excess fat.

No one likes feeling like the carpet has been ripped from under them, so instead of viewing your injury or illness as a time to fall back into old habits, use it as a proactive time to do what you can in order to heal as fast as you can. You'll be right back up and at 'em before you know it, and your mind and body will thank you for not falling back into old ways. You're a total badass, remember? You'll get through this with more motivation to continue your routine as an empowered boss babe.

We must stop the constant comparing, the judging, and the crappy self-talk. Enough is enough. This speedbump is just like that mean bully on the schoolyard who told you her book bag was prettier than yours, so you went home, threw a fit, cried, and felt horrible about your "not-so-pretty" book bag even though you thought it was so cool the way you decorated it by attaching dozens of fuzzy keychains to add some "pizazz." Don't let the hideous beast of a bully in disguise, known simply as "comparison," get in the way of you and your healthiest, most empowered life.

Comparison is the exact reason I absolutely loathe the fact that women, especially young women, look to social media for so-called fitness role models in string bikinis flaunting their Photoshopped bodies around with tag lines such as "Can't wait to reach my goals, still so much work to do." It hurts my soul to see women with such effective health regimens say "There's no point to this routine; I'm never going to look like that girl on Instagram." Hold up. You're telling me that you acknowledge the fact that you're putting in the *quality time* for yourself, for your daily workouts, and your mindful eating, yet you're comparing yourself to another woman who has a completely different bone, genetic, and/or hormone structure than yourself . . . not to mention her ability to use Photoshop like the editors of fitness magazines? This barrier poses a serious threat to the already proactive actionable plan you first set in place for yourself. I'm sorry but if somewhere in your Actionable Health Plan you wrote something like "I want to look like that fitness girl on Instagram," I'm begging, no I'm demanding you go back and change it right now. How are you going to compare your unique journey to ultimate health and happiness to someone else's? We're here because we want to be happy and empowered females. But how are we going to be those things if we keep setting ourselves up for failure with the comparison of another?

As I mentioned in the Actionable Health Plan, your health plan is completely different from the woman's sitting next to you. You've set up your health plan so it is uniquely designed for yourself, not anyone else. Therefore, *your* journey is so uniquely different that it simply cannot be compared to another.

Let's turn this monster of comparison into something proactive in itself. Instead of comparing, how about we celebrate and enjoy not only our own journey, but that of another uniquely vibrant and beautiful woman? In a time where female health is beginning to shift as to that of both mental and physical optimality, it's also the time to build each other up, celebrating all those small wins and benchmarks. As we continue shifting the narrative, we are becoming an unstoppable force of empowered females who celebrate in the skin we're in, in order to be a role model not only to ourselves, but the other women in our lives that need this kind of confidence. *So what* if your metabolism has changed and you can no longer eat what you want and have a flat stomach. *So what* if you've had a child and no matter how much weight you've lost you can't get rid of the stretch marks?

So what if you x, y, z? All these things are what make you, *you*. Let's use these life events as times to celebrate what your beautiful body is capable of and what it can do for you. How amazing is it that you can grow a whole baby in your abdomen, push him or her out of there, and get right back to life as if nothing happened? So amazing and so empowering. Instead of resulting in such shallow views of what the female body "should" look like, let's rewrite in terms of how to celebrate each female body.

I'm telling you, if it helps to unfollow certain "fitness models" on social media, do it. We need to be realistic and empathetic to our own unique journeys. It's not fair to yourself to diminish all your efforts in promoting this happy and healthy life just because you're not able to look like Sallyfit432 on social media. She's not you and you're not her. Be thankful you've created a healthy lifestyle that you can feel good about while sometimes mindfully indulging in all the goodies life has to offer.

You are better than comparison. You are so beautifully, uniquely perfect just the way you are right here, right now.

STRESS, ANXIETY, AND DEPRESSION

I truly, from the deepest part of my heart, understand. I understand that these mental health conditions pose their own crippling symptoms and deserve their own subcategory in the topic of speed bumps that can get between you and you living your healthiest and happiest life. I have saved this barrier for last, as I believe it deserves the most attention and the most awareness. Referring back to the staggering statistics, women predominate in having these serious mental disorders. It's just not fair that as a society we have yet to shed the empathetic light on these serious conditions for women and are continuing to turn a blind eye to the effects of these disorders on ourselves, our families, our communities, and more. As an empowered female who has seen the damaging effects of these conditions firsthand, it is my duty to stand and say, "NO MORE." No more will you be a slave to these crippling effects and no more will you be sent off with a simple prescription to a local pharmacy for medication with no resources for immediate health.

I am not a therapist, but as a healthcare professional I work closely with therapists who encourage that, in addition to prescribed medication, a holistic approach to overall well-being must be encouraged and promoted more within our female-driven communities. This holistic approach includes promoting your Actionable Health Plan—encompassing fitness, nutrition, and self-care—in order to become more in tune with your body. The more in tune you become with your energy, your mind, and your body, the more you will feel and acknowledge the beginnings of downward spirals toward stress, anxiety, and depression before they completely take over your day-to-day life. If you suffer from these conditions, then I'm sure you can begin to "feel" the storm brewing in your body ready to take over like the monster it is. I encourage my clients and you to first acknowledge these feelings arising, then take preventative measures to ensure these painful barriers do not get in the way of you living out your empowered health plan.

Remember, this chapter is all about being empowered, so do just that. Find yourself empowered not by your mental illness symptoms, but by knowing that you are armed with the tools and knowledge to fight back. Fight with all your mind, body, and soul, and outsource when needed. I completely understand that the term "fighting" is easier said than done, but you have to throw everything at it. You are the powerful creator of your own empowered life and you get to choose how you will fight. You were not meant to live a life of pain alone, nor in any pain at all. Use this Actionable Health Plan, your friends, your family, and/or your therapist as tools to combat these symptoms and to always stay one step ahead.

It's our time as a community of empowered females to end the stigma on mental illness, especially in women. It is our time to rise and join one another in promoting holistic care for mental health conditions. I will note, I am an advocate for medication and I do not recommend that females with mental health disease stop taking prescribed medication. I will say, I am a strong believer in the power of both western and eastern medicine, and that by combining the two, you are giving yourself the fighting chance you deserve to live your healthiest and happiest life. In the famous words of Jim Carrey, "I believe depression is legitimate. But I also believe that if you don't exercise, eat nutritious food, get sunlight, consume positive material, surround yourself with support, then you aren't giving yourself a fighting chance." Don't be a slave to your symptoms. Make yourself the courageous being of light you are in order to stand in the face of these challenges and show the universe you're showing up for your gorgeous self with optimal health and happiness.

How do you feel now after going through those potential barriers that stand between you and your most healthy and empowered life? Do you feel a little more at ease with beginning your Actionable Health Plan? Do you feel like you're better suited for the speedbumps that will undoubtedly creep their way into your life? Rest assured, it's all about being prepared and armed with the knowledge you need to keep your head and your heart pointed in the right direction for your optimal health and happiness, no matter the challenges that may arise. I want you to really think about those earlier statistics, not to scare you or intimidate you, but in hopes that you can use these statistics as fire for your personal motivation and fulfillment of sticking with your Actionable Health Plan.

Could you imagine a world where all females took the selfless time they needed to put their physical and mental health first? No matter how busy that female may be, no matter how many others she needs to take care of, no matter how many emails await her in her inbox . . . we'd be unstoppable. We are living in a time where women are making more money, taking highly positioned careers, and taking on more responsibility. Yet, the gap between female and male wages is still an underlying problem.

Now let me ask you this, what would it look like in a world where women made their health their non-negotiable priority? How would this not only affect their personal lives, but professional lives? Would more women ask for what they're worth and what they deserve? Would their newfound confidence in their skin and their mindset assist them in closing this wage gap? Not to speak for anyone else, but I think: "YES, QUEEN, MOST DEFINITELY!" There's no doubt in my mind that if as a collective group of healthy and happy women, we could finally start pulling up those deeply rooted illegitimate words and ways of society, and start planting our own fruitful seeds of equality in health and wealth.

AFTERWORD

BECOMING THE
HEALTH AND WEALTH SISTERS

Even though we live states away, as sisters we are quite literally attached at the hip. We call each other at least once a day, sometimes more depending on what we need to talk about. We use these calls to catch up on the past twenty-four hours as well as be each other's life coaches in the ultimate end goal of females taking over the world. Okay, that might be a little dramatic, but we've always shared the same passion of empowering women through our gifts and talents.

We love sharing success stories of our female clients as well as sharing the successes in our own businesses. It just so happened that we both fell into the role of entrepreneurism with a strong focus on female empowerment as our niche and life's mission. Call it a coincidence, but if you're a believer like us, then you full-heartedly understand that there is no such thing.

Throughout these calls we would see such overlapping details, as we both interacted with vulnerable women who needed someone in their lives who believed in them and showed them how they, too, could be in charge of their own lives. Amanda would talk about women who were newly divorced and who for the first time were able to understand where their money was and how to grow it properly with her help. They would form a relationship in which the woman would sometimes admit to having sleepless nights, more frequent stress eating, and weight gain resulting from the stress of the divorce. In the same light, Michelle would tell of a client who was doing so well with her training, but she would be worried she wasn't spending her money correctly or always seemed to be living paycheck to paycheck even though she had a highly paid position at her company.

We are special in that we're able to form meaningful relationships with our clients that become part of our true sisterhood. We both take these clients under our wing and make sure we're doing the absolute best for them and their unique situations. We can't tell you how many clients' weddings we've attended, along with baby showers, and even family vacations. Our clients become family, as we become theirs. It's the most rewarding gift as our female tribes continue to grow with so much love and power. This close-knit relationship has helped during times when one of Michelle's clients would mention money concerns. "Well you know Amanda is a financial planner, right?" Right away Michelle's clients were relieved as she would give them Amanda's contact information, later to find out how much her sister was able to help. Then in the same light, Amanda would get on one of these calls and say, "Michelle, my client is reaching out to you tomorrow because she needs help getting her confidence back and wants you to help her with a fitness and nutrition routine." We were already working together and didn't even know it.

As sisters, we kept asking the universe how we could further work together and help women on their unique journeys through life. It came to us one day when Michelle was on the phone with a fellow holistic pregnancy coach who called to ask how Michelle was able to train women online and get results without being in person. She was curious to see if she could find a way to help more women online rather than just in her community. Michelle then went on a thirty-minute monologue as the pregnancy coach listened to her passionately ramble about what she does for busy women and how incredibly rewarding her career was. With excitement in her voice, the coach interrupted and said, "Wow Michelle, I can tell you're very passionate about what you do."

Michelle laughed and said, "Yeah, I kind of can't help it."

Then the other coach uttered a statement that blended our whole world together almost like an epiphany. "Michelle, you're the trainer for the modern woman!"

Michelle paused and literally felt her heart skip a beat as everything was finally so crystal clear. "Oh my God, that's exactly who I am!"

Michelle spent her whole life trying to help these busy women who were mothers, employees, business owners, caretakers, and so on, trying to fit in healthy routines that worked specifically for them and around their busy schedules. The modern woman is someone who has to fulfill millions of responsibilities while also being a provider to her family, while balancing her personal roles and professional roles. The modern woman is someone who needs to be financially stable while also being physically and mentally stable in order to complete these daily tasks while continuing to put herself first. And what was Amanda doing? The exact same thing in the light of their own wealth! This was the first time in our lives that we knew we were doing something so special, and part of something much bigger than ourselves.

Of course, as soon as Michelle got off the phone, she called her sister and said, "Amanda, I got it, I got it. I'm the personal trainer and nutrition coach for the modern woman and you're the financial advisor for the modern woman." Amanda really liked that one and replied, "That's exactly who I am and exactly who I want to continue to help. You're health and I'm wealth for the modern woman."

A smile lit up on Michelle's face ear to ear. "Amanda, *that's it* . . . health and wealth, the Health and Wealth Sisters." It was that day that our spoken words combined in the universe, which planted the very small seed to begin our journey as the Health and Wealth Sisters. Each day we would talk about how we were going to make this connection happen. We wanted women to understand that true female empowerment comes from a woman's optimal health and optimal wealth. You truly cannot have one without the other.

We speak for women who are in the same shoes as ourselves. We each share our unique journeys, stories, and roles in life. Yet we all share the same mission, including you, which is to be the best version of you for yourself. We were put on this Earth to enjoy life to the fullest and enjoy each moment, each luxury the world has to bring us. In order to lead this life filled with an abundance of joy and love we must acknowledge that each woman has the absolute right to be their healthiest and wealthiest selves.

We knew that until women understood that neither health nor wealth, on their own, make a whole woman, but instead that it is the complete and absolute entanglement of these two things that make a powerful, confident, beautiful, strong, and empowered woman who feels whole and complete.

And enough with putting others before yourself because quite frankly, there's no you without you.

In all our lives, we reach a tipping point in both of these areas of health and wealth—when we decide it's time to make a change and get things figured out once and for all so we can start living without worry. If you've reached your tipping point and you're ready to feel empowered by your health and your wealth in order to live your most fulfilled life, then now's the time to say, "I'm not going to go on this journey alone. I'm going to make sure I'm doing things the right way. I'm going to commit to a 360° action plan for both my health and my wealth, BECAUSE I DESERVE IT!"

And, ladies, that is why the Health and Wealth Sisters do what we do every day.

ACKNOWLEDGMENTS

This book, our journeys, and our lives wouldn't have happened without our mom. While she refuses the spotlight, she is always behind us Riley sisters as our biggest fan, and also the woman who will give it to us straight—no *azucar*. We love you and are so thankful that you raised us to be independent, strong, and brave women—just like you.

Thank you to our beautiful friends, family, and *framily* who have been with us throughout our journey. Our lives are made more amazing because you are in them.

And thank you to our editor, Patrick Price, who believed in two sisters on a mission and worked tirelessly to bring this book to life.

NOTES

Introduction
1. https://www.cdc.gov/heartdisease/facts.htm

Chapter Six: Your Wealth Empowerment Plan
2. 2019 U.S. Census Bureau.
3. U.S. Bureau of Labor Statistics. "Number of Jobs, Labor Market Experience, and Earnings Growth: Results from a National Longitudinal Survey."

Chapter Seven: Financial Empowerment
4. U.S. Bureau of Labor Statistic, 2013.
5. State Street Global Advisors' survey, "Assessing the Landscape: Female Investors and Financial Advice," 2015.
6. Harvard Business Review, Boston Consulting Group Survey, "The Female Economy," 2009.
7. Prudential's study – Financial Experiences & Behaviors Among Women, 2010.

Chapter Nine: Taking Charge
8. https://www.who.int/mental_health/prevention/ genderwomen/en/

https://www.heart.org/en/get-involved/advocate/federal-priorities/cdc-prevention-programs

https://www.who.int/gho/women_and_health/en/

ABOUT THE AUTHORS

As a Certified Financial Planner™ and a Certified Divorce Financial Analyst®, **Amanda Campbell** has made it her life's mission to ensure that every woman, in any walk of life, understands wealth in a real and meaningful way. She is an active member of the Financial Planning Association (FPA), where she serves as cochair of the Women in Finance committee for the Maryland chapter. Amanda is a graduate of McDaniel College with a bachelor of arts in business administration, economics, and accounting economics with a minor in accounting. She enjoys spending any free time with her friends and family, and traveling. Amanda currently resides in Sykesville, Maryland, with her husband, two daughters, two Labs, and cat.

Instagram: @amandacampbellwealth

Michelle Riley is the owner of Fierce & Fit women's online training and nutrition coaching services. She understands the need and urgency to empower women through their physical, mental, and spiritual well-being for a happier, longer, and healthier life. After graduating from University of Maryland, Michelle received her certifications for Personal Training (AFAA), Nutrition Coaching (NASM), and Group Fitness (AFAA).

Originating from Sykesville, Maryland, Michelle and her husband, Stephen, move frequently but happily due to his military career, with their Australian shepherd fur babies, Mildred and Mabel.

www.fierceandfit.com
Instagram: @michellerileyfit

CPSIA information can be obtained
at www.ICGtesting.com
Printed in the USA
FSHW010800180221
78690FS